Modi's South Asian Foreign Policy: Recent Perspective

Modi's South Asian Foreign Policy
Recent Perspective

Dr. Ajay Parmar

PRASHANT PUBLISHING HOUSE
DELHI-110094

Published by :
Prashant Publishing House
C-34, 28 Foota Road, Gali-3,
West Karwal Nagar, Delhi-110094
Phone : 011-22963970, Mob. : 9810396373
e-mail.: prashantpublishinghouse@gmail.com

Modi's South Asian Foreign Policy: Recent Perspective

First Published 2017

ISBN 978-93-80565-9-03

PRINTED IN INDIA
Published by Mr. R.K. Jha M/s Prashant Publishing House and Published at H.S. Offset House Press, Delhi.

Contents

Preface

India's foreign policy opportunities and challenges in mid-2014 under the leadership of India's new Prime Minister Narendra Modi will expectedly acquire bold and audacious contours dispelling the earlier ten years of appeasement and timidity.

The most significant initiative made by the Narendra Modi government is the focus on neighbouring countries and major Asian powers coupled with emphasizing on the two decades old Look East policy. Asia being the major focus area of his foreign policy, Modi and his foreign minister chose several Asian countries for their initial bilateral visits. He has made state visits to Bhutan and Nepal and Japan within the first 100 days of his government and also hosted Asian leaders like Prime Minister Tony Abbott of Australia, President Xi Jinping of China and Prime Minister Nguyen Tan Dung of Vietnam, apart from inviting SAARC leaders in his inauguration ceremony. External Affairs Minister Swaraj has also made official visits to several Asian capitals like Dhaka, Bangladesh, Kathmandu, Nepal, Naypidaw, Myanmar, Singapore, Hanoi, Vietnam, Manama, Bahrain, Kabul, Afghanistan, Dushanbe, Tajikistan, Male, Maldives, Abu Dhabi, United Arab Emirates, Seoul, South Korea and Beijing China.

Even before becoming the Prime Minister Narendra Modi hinted that his foreign policy will actively focus on improving ties with India's immediate neighbours which is being termed as neighbourhood first policy in the media and he started well by inviting all heads of state/heads of government of South Asian countries in his inauguration and on the second day on office he held bilateral talks with all of them individually which was dubbed as a mini SAARC summit by the media. Later during a launch event at ISRO he has asked Indian scientists to take the endeavour to develop a dedicated SAARC satellite to share the fruits of the technology like tele-medicine, e-learning etc. with the people across South Asia to complement the currently operating Indian Technical and Economic Cooperation Programme program in the region.

Time and again Modi emphasized his belief in the 21st century being the Asian century and also asked whether it would be the Indian Century. China, Japan and India being the first, second and third largest Asian economy respectively are among the most likely candidate to lead the strategically important Asia in the later part of this century. But China's increasingly assertive postures in the region recent years have raised concerns in the respective quarters. It seems Modi's foreign policy is focused on improving bilateral relations to higher levels with strategically located Asian countries like Japan, Vietnam, Australia without forging any formal security alliance in the Indo-Pacific region to avoid direct confrontation with China. India, due to its good relation with both Russia and United States, is often considered to be the swing state in the race for strategic dominance in Asia between the democratic alliance of Japan and US and China-Russia club on the other hand. All the matter that has been given in public domain and we have just compiled it.

This book contains the fundamental and basic information of the subject and useful for teachers, students and researchers.

—*Editor*

1

Introduction

SOUTH ASIA POLICY

Even before becoming the Prime Minister Narendra Modi hinted that his foreign policy will actively focus on improving ties with India's immediate neighbours which is being termed as neighbourhood first policy in the media and he started well by inviting all heads of state/heads of government of South Asian countries in his inauguration and on the second day on office he held bilateral talks with all of them individually which was dubbed as a mini SAARC summit by the media. Later during a launch event at ISRO he has asked Indian scientists to take the endeavour to develop a dedicated *SAARC satellite* to share the fruits of the technology like tele-medicine, e-learning etc. with the people across South Asia to complement the currently operating Indian Technical and Economic Cooperation Programme program in the region.

West Asia policy

Indian External Affairs Ministry refers the region of 'Middle east' as West Asia and not as Middle East which is a more popular attribution, particularly in the western countries. The region plays a vital role in India's economy as it supplies nearly two third of India's total oil import, bilateral trade is also flourishing in recent years particularly with UAE and other gulf states. Over the years millions of Indian mostly working class have migrated to the gulf looking for jobs and they account for a sizeable share in the total remittances received from abroad.

Link West policy

In an attempt to strengthen ties with India's western neighbours specially the gulf countries Modi proposed this policy to complement his Act East policy concerning East Asia. Although it is called 'Link West' (west of India) which gives it a bigger geographical connotation, it is most likely to focus on the middle-east and some of the India's strategic thinkers are calling it as Modi's middle-east policy. The West Asia Approach of India is working successfully and its relations with Middle East are improving since Modi came in power. The West Asia Approach" of India is now its key strategy to win Middle East. Indian foreign policy makers say that India's interests in the GCC countries are intimately linked with its energy security, trade, employment for Indians and remittances while Middle Eastern foreign policy experts believe that India has showcased itself as "Security Partner" during Modi's visit to UAE. Given the economic and human security interests, the stability and security of the GCC countries is crucial for India because huge flow of remittances that comes from GCC to Indian economy.

Stand against ISIS

On 16 December 2014, Home Minister Rajnath Singh announced in the Parliament that ISIS is banned as a terrorist organization under the United Nations schedule. Following the arrest of few Indian individuals with ISIS connections, on 26 February 2015 India put fresh bans on 'The Islamic States/ Islamic States of Iraq and Syria/Islamic States of Iraq and Levant' with all its manifestation and all its affiliates under the Unlawful Activities (Prevention) Act. There were also unverified claims that India may send its Air Force to fight against the group in Iraq.

2014 Israel-Hamas conflict

At the height of the tension between Israel and Hamas in July India offered a rhetorical condemnation holding both sides responsible for erupting violence and asked Israel to stop "disproportionate use of force" in Gaza which was read by many as departure from tradition of more vocal supports for the Palestinian cause. External Affairs Minister Swaraj insisted that "there is absolutely no change in India's policy towards Palestine, which is that we fully support the Palestinian cause while maintaining good relations with Israel. " clarifying India's current position on the issue. That might sound like fence-sitting, but it is a policy shared by all Indian governments of the past 20 years following the establishment of formal diplomatic relation in 1992.

Sushma Swaraj, a seasoned parliamentarian, had herself blocked the opposition demand in Rajya Sabha for passing a resolution condemning Israel for 2014 Israel-Gaza conflict by saying that "India has friendly relation with both Israel and Palestine and therefore any such move may impact its friendship negatively".

Although later in a symbolic gesture India joined others BRICS nations in voting at the United Nations Human Rights Council for a probe into the alleged human rights violation in Gaza. Which generated mixed response among media and analysts in India.

Overseas Indian crisis

Iraq

With the rise of ISIL in northern Iraq, where hundreds of thousands of Indian migrant workers live, the security of those overseas Indian came under threat. On 16 June, the Ministry of External Affairs (MEA) set up a 24-hour helpline at the Indian embassy in Baghdad for assistance of Indian nationals stranded in the conflict cities. It has been reported that 46 Indian nurses were abducted from the Iraqi town of Mosul who were later freed and flown back to India. Moreover, 39 Indian workers from mainly from Punjab were taken hostages and the fate of those workers still not known. There were wide spread speculations about their lives and on 27 November 2014 *ABP*

News reported, citing Bangladeshi migrant co-workers, death of all the 39 men. Although the following day External Affairs Minister (EAM) Swaraj made a statement to theparliament neither rejecting nor confirming such possibility and re-assured the nation about MEA's commitment for continuing search for the Indians in Iraq.

Libya

A similar situation occurred in Libya where many Indian nationals are stranded because of the armed conflict that broke inBenghazi and other parts of the country. Swaraj informed parliament that her ministry was evaluating all possibilities to secure the safe evacuation of all Indians stranded in both Iraq and Libya. A chartered flight from Djerba, Tunisia brought over 200 nationals back to India. A further 216 national left on 8 August, with a total of another 1,500 nationals having been evacauted. About 3,000 more nationals registered with the embassy in Tripoli in order to return.

On 5 August 44 nurses returned to India on a special Air India flight; they were predominantly from Kerala with some from Andhra Pradesh and Tamil Nadu. A further three Goans were reported to be safe in Libya with full employment and had not requested repatriation. Goa's Director of NRI Affairs U. D. Kamat said that it was ascertaining whether there were Goan workers in the country.

Yemen

After the outbreak of areal attacks by the Saudi led coalition following the coup by the Houthi rebels in Yemen, Govt of India launched a massive rescue operation called *Operation Raahat* (meaning: Relief) to save hundreds of non-residential Indians located there. Minister of State for External Affairs Gen. V K Singh himself overview the entire rescue operation right from the battle ground town of Sana'a and Aden in Yemen and the Indian base of operation in Djibouti. In the process the Indian Navy deployed its front line ships such as INS Mumbai, INS Sumitra and others while the Indian Air Force too deployed its

C-17 Globemaster tactical airlifter to airlift the stranded Indians there, in this process the national carrier Air India also took active part by ferrying passengers. The operation was highly successful and received huge acclamation from across the globe as it rescued not only Indians but thousands of foreigners stranded in the war torn country too.

ASIAN FOREIGN POLICY OF NARENDRA MODI GOVERNMENT

The most significant initiative made by the Narendra Modi government is the focus on neighbouring countries and major Asian powers coupled with emphasizing on the two decades old Look East Policy. Asia being the major focus area of his foreign policy, Modi and his foreign minister chose several Asian countries for their initial bilateral visits. He has made state visits to Bhutan and Nepal and Japan within the first 100 days of his government and also hosted Asian leaders like Prime Minister Tony Abbott of Australia, President Xi Jinping of China and Prime Minister NguyÅn T¥n Ding of Vietnam, apart from inviting SAARC leaders in his inauguration ceremony. External Affairs Minister Swaraj has also made official visits to several Asian capitals like Dhaka, Bangladesh, Kathmandu, Nepal,Naypidaw, Myanmar, Singapore, Hanoi, Vietnam, Manama, Bahrain, Kabul, Afghanistan, Dushanbe, Tajikistan, Male, Maldives, Abu Dhabi, United Arab Emirates, Seoul, South Korea and Beijing China.

Asian Century

Time and again Modi emphasized his believe on 21st century being the Asian century and also asked whether it would be the Indian Century. China, Japan and India being the first, second and third largest Asian economy respectively are among the most likely candidate to lead the strategically important Asia in the later part of this century. But China's increasingly assertive postures in the region recent years have raised concerns in the respective quarters. It seems Modi's foreign policy is focused on improving bilateral relations to higher levels with strategically located Asian countries like Japan, Vietnam, Australia without forging any formal security alliance in the Indo-Pacific region to avoid direct confrontation with China. India, due to its good relation with both Russia and United States, is often considered to be the swing state in the race for strategic dominance in Asia between the democratic alliance of Japan and US and China-Russia club on the other hand.

China

Prior to election Modi had expressed reservation over alleged Chinese 'expansionism' into India's frontiers as India and China locked into bitter territorial disputes over last fifty years. During his Japan trip, Modi has said eighteenth century mind-set of vistaar-vad or expansionism won't work and vikaash-vad or peaceful development is needed for sustainable peace and tranquility in the world which was read by a portion of media as a subtle jibe on China. But he is also in favour of enhanced economic partnership with China.

Economic activity defines relation with China as it is India's biggest trading partner in goods. Soon after taking office commerce Minister Nirmala Sitharaman has already made two visits to China. The two countries have forged a mechanism called 'strategic and economic dialogue' (SED) to discuss the trade and other economic issues. Modi has publicly expressed his willingness to enhance trade and economic cooperation with China. Describing the newly found activism in bilateral relation Modi said India China relation moving "INCH (India-China) towards MILES(Millennium of Enhanced Synergy)".

India sent National Security Adviser Ajit Doval as a special envoy of Prime Minister Modi to Beijing to negotiate the agenda and the schedule of the presidential visit to India which is appreciated by the top Chinese leadership who are known to be fond of diplomatic decorum. President Xi Jinping, only thirdChinese President to visit India, arrived in Ahmedabad, Modi's hometown, on 17 September which coincides with Modi's birthday. China is expected to commit investment over US$100 billion in India's infrastructure projects including in high speed trains and dedicated Chinese industrial parks to balance the huge trade deficit exists in China's favour. The two leaders had earlier met in Brazil this year on the sidelines of BRICS summit.

Japan

Japan occupies a very important place in Modi's Asian strategy, as India is looking toward Japan, at a time when it is becoming 'normal state' amending decades old pacifist constitution, to forge a security alliance to balance an increasingly assertive China in the Indo-Pacific region. Maritime cooperation is most likely and bilateral naval exercises are on the cards. Significantly in 2014 Japan participated in the Malabar, a primarily bilateral naval exercise between India and US, held in Sea of Japan. Negotiations progressed recently for selling of US 2 amphibious aircraft to Indian Navy and the long pending civil nuclear agreements which would eventually help strengthen the strategic partnership.

Modi visited Japan on a five-day official trip from 30 August to 3 September which was labelled as his fist bilateral state visit outside the subcontinent also by the media. His 2014 visit further strengthened the ties between the two countries and resulted in several key agreements, including the elevating the already established strategic partnership to the "Special Strategic Global Partnership". Business ties are stronger than ever with a commitment of US$33.5 billion Japanese investment in India in the next five year. India is in the process of importing Shinkansen technology form Japan as part of Modi's Diamond Quadrilateral project for introducing high-speed rail in India.

His visit to Kyoto supervised the signing of a cooperation agreement between Varanasi and Kyoto both regarded as heritage city and cultural centre in their respective country.

Myanmar

Despite sharing a long border with India Myanmar (erstwhile Burma) often left out of India's neighbourhood policy, but lately Myanmar was identified as India's gateway to the

Southeast Asia and therefore the focus is on rebuilding the historic relations between the two counties. Modi visited the eastern neighbour to attend a couple of multilateral meetings including the East Asia Summit. He met President Thein Sein for the first time on 11 November 2014 and they identified three 'C's to strengthen their bilateral relations, those are connectivity, cultural links and people to people contacts.

Among which connectivity is all set to get a big boost with projects like upcoming Imphal-Mandalaya Bus service, India-Myanmar-Thailand trilateral highway, Kaladan Multi-modal Transit Transport Project and the two sides also focused on the need of direct air links. The two sides also discussed the possibility of Indian investment in Myanmars's special economic zones and ways to enhance bilateral trade which stands at US$2 billion, well below the potential.

He also met the Nobel laureate and Myanmar's opposition leader Aung San Suu Kyi and referred her as "symbol of democracy" for her untiring efforts for the restoration of democracy in her country and he presented her with a special copy of Mahatma Gandhi's commentary on Bhagwad Gita. Suu Kyi also reciprocated by calling India, her "second home" recalling her early days spent in India. The two leaders have discussed the importance of democracy for the stability of the region as a whole.

Singapore

Singapore is amongst the top source countries of foreign direct INVESTMENT (FDI) coming to India. Economic cooperation dominates the India Singapore relations given Singapore's strategic importance in India's 'Look East' policy. External Affairs Minister Swaraj visited Singapore on 16 August where she held talks with her counterpart Shanmugam and Prime Minister Lee Hsien Loong regarding Singapore's INVESTMENT in India and their potential role in Modi's pet smart city project.

Earlier Modi played host to Singaporean Minister for Foreign and Law K. Shanmugam where he recalled his policies as Gujarat chief minister to expand cooperation between the two countries in, amongst others, public housing for the middle and lower classes based on Singapore's expertise.

The former Singaporean prime minister, Goh Chok Tong, visited India on 10 September and held several high-level meetings with the Indian prime minister and other ministers; later in conversation with a selected members from the media he referred to the former Indian prime minister, Vajpeyee, as a scholar, but Modi is a "Man of Action", while reassuring once again his country's full cooperation on the smart city project.

Vietnam

Vietnam, strategically located in the South China Sea, plays an pivotal role in India's Southeast Asian policy and it is often referred as the important pillars of its 'Look East Policy' by the Indian diplomats. Defence and security cooperation in recent years define the strategic partnership along with fast growing bilateral trade which stands at US$8 billion in FY 2013.

Visiting Indian President Pranab Mukherjee called Vietnam, "a trusted friend and an important pillar of India's Look East Policy" which emphasized the depth of their strategic partnership. The leaders reiterated their desire and determination to work together to maintain peace, stability, growth and prosperity in Asia. And the two side vouched for 'freedom of navigation' in the South China Sea, which China claims as its exclusive economic zone, and called the parties concerned to exercise restraint, avoid threat or use of force and resolve disputes through peaceful means in accordance with universally recognised principles of international law, including the United Nations Convention on the Law of the Sea-1982.

India-Vietnamese defence cooperation has multiplied in recent years with emphasize on maritime security which includes training of Vietnamese naval personnel with Indian naval ships making frequent port-call in Vietnam in past few years. Recently it extended a US$100 m Line of Credit for purchase of Fast attack craft for Vietnamese navy from India.

Vietnam is also interested in acquiring Brahmos supersonic missiles, an Indo-Russian joint venture project, Vietnam has friendly relation with both Russia and India a precondition for exporting the missile system and talks regarding the deal is believed to be in the advanced level.

Agreements signed in oil exploration cooperation between India and Vietnam as it earlier offered India to explore strategically located oil blocks in South China Sea, which is disputed by Chinese claims. On the following day Chinese Foreign Ministry through an official media statement expressed its objection to India's activity in what it refers its exclusive economic zone.

External Affairs Minister earlier during her Hanoi trip said the state-owned ONGC Videsh will exploit the opportunity provided in Vietnam, a development China sees as an aggression into its backyard. Economic ties are fast growing with US$8 billion bilateral trade and the two sides emphasized the need of increasing people to people contact which is set to get a boost with upcoming launch of direct flight between Delhi and Ho Chi Minh City and using Bollywood to promote Vietnam to Indian audience.

Security Cooperation

In his address to the Australian parliament Modi made his apprehension public about maritime disputes and freedom of navigation in the oceans with a veiled reference of growing Chinese hegemony in the region.

This has led to speculations among policy makers that Australia is re-joining the Malabar naval exercise amid Beijing's displeasure. Australia could join the India-US-Japan grouping, which is certain to set off alarm bells in Beijing. The issue of Australia joining the quadrilateral security dialogue was believed to be discussed at the highest level during Modi's Canberra visit on 17 November 2014. Earlier the two sides also agreed to enhance Maritime security cooperation in the Indo-pacific region and future joint naval exercise in the Indian Ocean.

Taiwan

As Modi has identified economic cooperation as a major thrust area in his foreign policy and introduced policies like Make in India to invite foreign direct INVESTMENT (FDI) in manufacturing sector, Taiwan was one of the first to respond to his call. India Electronics and Semiconductor Association (IESA) and Taipei Computer Association signed memorandum of understanding for local manufacturing of semiconductors and electronics, even there are plans to set up 'Taiwanese hardware park' in about 200-300 acres of land. Although India was among the first few countries to recognize PRC therefore jeopardizing relation with the island but later developed an official relation with ROC which it maintains through India-Taipei Association ITA a De facto embassy in Taipei.

A NEW POWER STRUCTURE IN ASIA: INDIA, CHINA AND JAPAN ANALYSIS

India under the leadership of Narendra Modi may be able to ease the symbolic tension between China and Japan, and also rise quickly to join them to co-lead a new age of politico-economic vicissitude in East-to-South Asia in the wake of the diminishing influence from the United States.

Geo-economics is the foundation of this emerging India+China+Japan (I+C+J) power structure. India is at the mid-way of the southern Silk Road — the Bangladesh-China-India-Myanmar (BCIM) corridor, one of China's ambitious mega Silk Road projects to upgrade its Eurasia logistics. The Indian Ocean is also at the middle of the maritime Silk Route which has the potential to stretch from Dalian in northeastern China to Cape of Good Hope in South Africa, about half of the globe diameter. For a state with 1.26 billion population (which will outnumber China's 1.35 billion very soon) to thrive, Modi who has hands-on co-operation experience with China for steering economic growth in Gujarat knows that India must reach out to foster export, including the valuable human resources such as the expertise in software programming. If and only if he has brought home plenteous growths can he overpower the sectarian and regional challenges at home so as to launch all sorts of socio-political reforms. Modi will make the best use of this geo advantage to facilitate India's international trades within and outside Asia.

Equipped with 120 nuclear heads and three aircraft carriers to safeguard the security of the Indian Ocean, India is a heavy weight power in South Asia. Despite its military might, however, in East Asia, India is not threatening in any way and appears to be impartial between China and Japan. India's neutrality and presence could play a positive role to mediate any possible tension between the two leading giants, thus bringing forward a triple-win situation. If China's export-led and infrastructure-backed economic growth model is going to be duplicated in India successfully in the coming two decades, India as a huge market for cranes, electricity grids, infrastructure knowhow and finally all sorts of consumer goods will transform itself into an influential player in East-to-South Asia on all fronts.

India's proactive engagement into East Asia has been salient. In as early as 2007, a study group was agreed among the states to establish an ASEAN + 6 Free Trade Area (10 ASEAN members plus India, China, Japan, South Korea, Australia and New Zealand). The economic ministers of these 16 states met in Brunei August 2013 to confirm their serious intention in finalizing this Regional Comprehensive Economic Partnership (RCEP) by 2015, a concept of free trade zone from Indian Ocean to the West Pacific covering 3.35 billion people and 27% of global GDP. Whether this RCEP can be cemented will partly depend on New Delhi's ability (and also Modi's charisma) to turn the East Asian nations into a phalanx to cope with economic ups and downs. Another I+C+J co-operation can be noted from the establishment of the Recommended Transit Corridor (IRTC) in 2012 among China, India, Japan and South Korea to co-ordinate navy escort for deterring pirates' attacks on commercial vessels,. In the private sector, Tata Group is one of the pioneers to promote business synergy for these three countries by manufacturing Land Rover cars with Chery in

China and providing 3G telecommunication services in hand with Docomo.

In less than three weeks after Modi's inauguration, Chinese Foreign Minister Wang Yi rushed to New Delhi to tell him: "Through years of negotiation, we have come to an agreement on the basics of a boundary agreement, and we are prepared to reach a final settlement". Nowadays, it is simple common sense that what government leaders seek for is eminence while entry into war can be enormity. By the time Modi has finally hammered a deal to end the decades-long India border row with China, it will become an unprecedented show case for all other nations to realize that immense common commercial interests can really solve territorial disputes.

Despite continual provocations by bellicose politicians and jingoistic analysts since Shinzo Abe came back to power in 2012, the two competing East Asian nations have actually never stopped holding bilateral semi-official talks. From the 2013 meeting between Japanese business leaders led by Fujio Cho of Toyota and the Chinese Commerce Minister, to Beijing's warm welcome for the incumbent Tokyo governor Yoichi Masuzoe in April 2014, and then the friendly discussion in May between Masahiko Komura (vice-president of Japan's ruling Liberal Democratic Party) and Zhang Dejiang (the third ranking member of the Politburo Standing Committee and the chairman of the National People's Congress), low profile but pragmatic communication between China and Japan has been carried on persistently.

Knowing that it will never be easy for the White House to garner sufficient support from the general public to send American soldiers to die for several uninhabited islands in Asia, indicating that a superpower shift is inevitable, both China and Japan are sagaciously making use of the islands in dispute as the excuse to compete for the new game setter status of the region. With reference to the "India-China agreement", if could be historically achieved, Tokyo and Beijing would eventually work out a compromise diplomatically to set the new "rules of Asian game" for the distribution of political powers and financial interests, and then an agreement for settling the spat over the islands. If making concession is necessary, to better serve Japan's national interests, Tokyo would probably do it for securing a deal with Beijing and New Delhi rather than with Washington.

All these developments have laid down a solid framework for the rise of the new I+C+J power structure. Without the relatively complicated relation between the Christians and Muslims, the atheist Chinese and Japanese who are culturally compatible with the Hindu Indians will not hesitate to seize the opportunity to collaborate so as to set their own rules of a new multi-polar politico-economic game in Asia.

INDIA'S FOREIGN POLICY OPPORTUNITIES AND CHALLENGES IN MID-2014

India's foreign policy opportunities and challenges in mid-2014 under the leadership of India's new Prime Minister Narendra Modi will expectedly acquire bold and audacious contours dispelling the earlier ten years of appeasement and timidity. India's foreign policies in the 2004-2014 periods failed to exploit the strategic leverages that were being bestowed on India, internationally and regionally, in recognition of India's emerging major power potential in the process of crystallising till mid-2004.

Perceptionaly, what is evident in mid-2014 is the debris of collateral damages of obsessive Pakistan-centric and China-centric Indian foreign policy with no gains visible for indulging in appeasement of these two prominent India's military adversaries. Perceptionaly again, India during the preceding ten years seemed to have outsourced and mortgaged its foreign policy directions to Washington which was more sensitive to Pakistan's and China's sensitivities than Indian national security interests.

Prime Minister Modi's opening move even before oath-taking as PM was South Asia-centric and not Pakistan-centric as was being made out by the Indian media. PM Modi made a significant and imaginative political outreach to the SAARC

Nations when he invited their leaders for his oath-taking ceremony. That all of them came was a measure of the Indian Prime Minister's personal leadership waiting to unfold and his underlying objective of attaching first priority to India's SAARC neighbours. They all came despite the very negative propaganda and demonization of Mr Modi indulged in by India's then ruling Congress Party from 2002-2014. PM Modi's opening foreign policy act was therefore well conceived by him as in light of the above negative campaign it gave an opportunity to SAARC leaders to personally size-up PM Modi and vice versa.

In a further act of reinforcing his India's neighbourhood-priorities policy it has been announced today that PM Modi's first foreign visit would be to Bhutan, a nation strategically important for India because looming large over it is China. Nepal having been lost to China by the flawed policies of the previous Government, India cannot afford to let Bhutan slip under China's influence likewise because of Indian insensitivities. Now moving to the larger canvas of India's opening moves under the new leadership of PM Modi, one would like to advocate that India's foreign policy initiatives to be classified in two major categories.

Category I nations would be those nations which present promising "Opportunities" to India in terms of evolution of more robust and substantial partnerships and in which their past record does not carry any baggage of discord or tensions with India. Such nations would also be those nations which in the contemporary global security environment enjoy strategic convergences with India and can hopefully be strategic assets in India's ascendant power trajectory.

Category II Nations would be those nations which are not likely to shape or emerge as "Opportunities" for India but would always be "Challenges" for India's foreign policy decision makers. Such countries have a record of discord, strategic distrust of India and many irritants exist in their relationships with India. They cannot be wished away but nor can India afford to allocate disproportionate time and effort to win them over.

In Category I Nations for Indian foreign policy attention I would like to include Japan, Vietnam, Indonesia, Israel and France and possibly Germany. In Category II Nations I would primarily classify and include USA, Russia, China, and Pakistan. These nations do not present opportunities for India to ascend the power-trajectory and more often than not would impede that process.

So as PM Modi starts planning his diplomatic calendar of foreign visits, it is the Category I Nations that should figure first. Japan should be PM Modi's' first foreign visit as both countries enjoy significant strategic convergences on Asian and Indo Pacific security and stability. A strong Strategic Partnership exists between the two nations and these need to be reinforced significantly, by Japan being PM Modi's first port of call. Needless to state that in Asia there are only three major powers, namely, China, Japan and India. China is not willing to cede or share strategic space in Asia neither to Japan nor India. Further China is in a conflictual relationship with both Japan and India.

Vietnam has long and historic ties with India and also a Strategic Partnership with India. Geostrategically located, it is also a significant geopolitical player in South East Asia and ASEAN region. Combining his visit to Japan with a visit to Vietnam on the return leg would be a significant step for India and Asian security.

France also has been a good friend of India and has been a reliable and trusted supplier of arms and armaments to India, besides a substantial Strategic Partnership. The Indian Ministry of Defence has for far too long sat on and impeded the126 MRCA Rafael Fighter aircraft. This has seriously affected India's cutting edge defensive and offensive aerial combat capabilities. PM Modi with his dynamic style should prod the Indian Defence Ministry to finalise the deal within three months as it stood finalised a number of years back but for some nit-picking by the previous Government. The United States has been placed in Category II because its intentions' and approaches to India have always been ambiguous and at times contentious.

Its National Security Strategy in the past has included references to prevention of rise of hegemonic nations in Asia including India. Except for the short span of 2-3 years in the md-2000s the record is not of substantive support to Indians national security interests despite a much-touted Strategic Partnership. United States has still not forsaken playing balance- of- power games in the Indian Sub-Continent by balancing Pakistan against India. Too many trade irritants also exist. India would be well advised to go-slow in rushing head-long into a resuscitation of the Strategic Partnership and let it be reinforced by the pressure of the unfolding international power-dynamics.

Russia too has been placed in Category II because Russia in terms of Asian security still persists in giving weightage to China strategically over India. Gone are the days when Russia stood as a bulwark in India's favour as a countervailing power. India can afford to wait till geopolitically the Russia-China strategic nexus wears thin. Lastly one comes to India's military adversaries namely China and Pakistan. No Nobel Peace Prizes await any Indian Prime Minister for a breakthrough in their adversarial relationships and postures against India. Without wasting disproportionate time on both of them, India should follow the policy of "Congagement" with Pakistan and China. 'Strategic Distrust' would continue to predominate for a long time to come until their domestic political dynamics bring about radical transformations in their political cultures.

PM Modi can be expected to bring about a radical transformation in India's military capabilities and higher defence structure endowing an inclusive role to India's military hierarchy in national security affairs.

This would make India's defence capabilities that much stronger and enable India to withstand any military coercion or destabilisation by China or Pakistan besides making Indian foreign policy that much more robust.

Concluding, one can only refer to the pointers that are coming where China is making the first moves to establish contacts and dialogues with the new Modi Government in India and Pakistan would follow suit. Pakistan is not India's long term threat. It is China that is India's long term and potent threat and this strategic reality should not be wished away in our foreign policy making. In terms of systemic changes in India's foreign policy structures, PM Modi should dispense with the system of Special Envoys system (a slot for retired IFS diplomats), Track II initiatives and so many other Tracks which foul up the foreign policy making structures.

Let institutionalised foreign policy be the rule and if dramatic results are to be achieved it should be the prerogative and be coming from the dynamism of PM Modi himself. With so much on the plate to be handled in terms f India's foreign policy by Prime Minister Modi as he sets out to map India's foreign policies, it is incumbent that India's foreign policy objectives be prioritised and be categorised into "Opportunities" and "Challenges" in relation to India's national security interests. In the field of foreign policy formulation "Opportunities" are always fleeting and need to be grasped instantly. "Challenges" will always abound and must wait till geopolitical dynamics offer leverages to convert challenges into opportunities.

INDIA'S NEW GOVERNMENT AND ITS FOREIGN POLICY OPTIONS

The major determinants of the foreign policy of any nation are its national security interests and its economic interests. Logically, it is these two national interests around which should revolve the various formulations of the country's foreign policy. Foreign policies of nations do not function in a vacuum insulated by delusional moral and ideological obsessions. Foreign policies perforce, have to take into account the prevailing regional and international strategic realities with which a nation has to strike workable equations based on one's own existing power attributes and strategic utility to the key global powers.

India's foreign policies in the last eight years under the previous Bharatiya Janata Party (BJP) led Government can be assessed as successful when measured against the above indicators. The BJP Government's foreign policies did make

India "shine" in the international arena, not by delusional rhetoric but by an initial display of power potential by carrying out the nuclear weaponisation in 1998. It was a defining moment. Initial opposition by the United States and others were soon converted into opportunities for strategic partnerships/strategic cooperation with United States, Israel, France, UK, Vietnam and Myanmar. For the first time, even joint naval exercises were held with China. India's then foreign policies were also successful in bringing significant international pressure on Pakistan to change tack.

Foreign policies of any nation need bi-partisan support, as the country's national interests do not change with a change of political power. While the economic determinant could change in terms of nuances with a change of Government, the national security determinant cannot and should not, as the strategic perspectives that go into its formulation have to be long range.

Regrettably, the new Indian Government, led by the Congress Party and through its flip-flop and ill-considered statements has given indications, that it is all set to undo the foreign policy gains of India in the last eight years. The Congress Party's election manifesto, formulated by its present Foreign Minister reflected the Congress Party's traditional dislike of the United States and it also reflected this Party's resentment with the gains made by the BJP Government in terms of evolving a strategic partnership with the United States. In generic terms, India's new Government has three options open in relation to giving shape to its foreign policies, and these are:

1. Non-alignment Foreign Policy.
2. Independent Foreign Policy.
3. India's Inter-dependent Foreign Policy with United States Option.

The ramifications of each are discussed in the succeeding paragraphs.

Non-Alignment as Foreign Policy Precept

Non-Alignment was Nehru's brainchild and the Congress Party's foreign policy fetish thereafter. Non-Alignment also seems to be the obsessive mind-set of the Congress Party's present Foreign Minister and many of his genre in the Indian Foreign Service.

However, even in the heyday of Non-Alignment India was never genuinely non-aligned. It had a marked tilt towards the former Soviet Union, Communist China and the countries of the Communist/Socialist bloc. The key components of India's non-alignment policies were opposition to United States policies in all the strategic sub-systems of the world.

The danger today is that a combination of the Congress Party's attachment of non-alignment combined and seconded by the Communist Parties as leading members of the Congress Coalition Government, and furthered by a Foreign Minister with an obsessive-mindset of non-alignment could veer away India's foreign policies in this direction. The chief manifestations of this option in terms of India's foreign policy would be:

- United States policies in Greater Middle East, South East Asia and East Asia to be opposed, based more on inclination than substance.
- Enhancement of India's relations with Russia.
- Enhancement of India's relations with China in the pursuance of the "Panch Sheel" Concept-a concept much abused by China against India.
- Devaluation of United States-India evolving strategic partnership.
- Military-to-Military contacts with United States to be downplayed.

Proponents of this foreign policy option, fail to take into account the following ramifications of the above manifestations:

- Non-Alignment, even in the most genuine form was applicable only in a bi-polar world.
- Non-Alignment today exists as " fossilized remains" of Indian's delusional foreign policies.
- India cannot afford politically, strategically or economically to remain at odds with the United States as the "unipolar power".

India's non-alignment years in terms of her foreign policy formulations and attitudes were a national waste both strategically and economically. India's new Congress Government, in the interests of India's national security and economic development should not "inflict" this option on India.

INDIA'S INDEPENDENT FOREIGN POLICY OPTION

The Congress Party keep freely mixing up and using the word "independent" with "non-alignment". The two, in the option of the author are entirely different. "Non-Alignment" was a policy precept of the Third World countries, as relatively powerless countries against the Big Powers. An "independent foreign policy" precept connotes that a nation has such highly developed national power attributes, that it is not susceptible to political and economic coercion by stronger powers and also that its national power attributes endow on it the strength to chart-out an independent foreign policy without fear of restraint from any quarter. India today has not reached the 'independent foreign policy' stage as yet due to the following reasons:

- India's half-a-century of mis-governance has thwarted the materalisation of its power potential.
- Nearly half-a-century of non-alignment foreign policies has left India with no genuine friends in the international arena.
- Decades of ineffective national security management has left India with not even regional power capabilities in the Indian sub-continent.

An "independent foreign policy" option in its most genuine and purist form is presently not available as an option to India. Taking "independent stands" on international issues without the "muscle to back-up it up" does not constitute an "independent foreign policy" It is only rhetoric.

India's Inter-Dependent Foreign Policy With United States Option

In a globalised world, inter-dependence transcends national barriers not only in the economic field, but also extends to the strategic and political fields. It has also extended itself to the fields of terrorism and crime-syndicates. The United States is the world's predominant power.

Its predominance extends in all fields from economics, politics, strategic and control of global financial and energy resources. Its likes and dislikes shape the international strategic realities. No amount of efforts to create a " multi-polar world" by China or France, for over a decade now, has borne fruit. Why, in fact, China itself rose to 'super-stardom' by weaving foreign policies inter-dependent with those of USA in the late 1970's and 1980's.

India has no option today but to follow foreign policies of interdependence with the United States, for the following reasons:

- India's economic advancement and consequent rise to regional power status and key global player can only come about with United States strategic and political concurrence.
- India's economic modernisation and strategic mobility upwards can only be ensured by United States military presence in Pakistan and Greater Middle East. The same would constrain India's long range threat from China.
- India's aspirations to become an "Indian Ocean Power" cannot materialise without convergence with United States national security interests.
- India's vast outlay of financial resources for infrastructure and economic development cannot come about without United States direct involvement and goading of international financial institutions.

India for all practical reasons needs the United States, in terms of materialisation of her national aspirations and protection of her national security interests.

Concluding Observations

India's foreign policies cannot be made captive to the delusional non-alignment gladiators or India's Communist

Parties who have never been known for their objectivity or to India's minority Indian Muslims vote banks where every issue is viewed in a pan-Islamic context.

In today's global security environment and the international strategic realities likely to persist for the next 50 years, India neither has the luxury nor the time to find new anchors for her foreign policies from the fossilised remains of Nehruvian Non-Alignment or her "presumed power potential" not concretised so far.

In the last eight years the centre-piece of India's foreign policy has been the evolution of a strong political and strategic partnership with the United States. United States and India recognized the mutual convergences and imperatives and have been engaged in establishing a substantive bi-lateral relationship.

India's national security and economic interests dictate that this is India's only foreign policy option available. India's national aspirations can best be met by formulating India's foreign policy inter-dependent with United States national interests and not in opposition to it.

NEIGHBOURS FIRST: MODI'S FOREIGN POLICY MANTRA

India's neighbourhood, comprising countries crucially strategic for India's national security, stood grossly neglected in foreign policy formulations of the previous political dispensation for the last 10 years. In the decade, it was internationally being held against India that if India could not re-order its own neighbourhood in the Indian sub-continent, how could she aspire to surge forward as an emerging Asian power and a global player? What this implied was that Indian foreign policy processes stood atrophied by lack of dynamism and proactive approaches to win over confidence, and influence its neighbours.

The Pakistan-centric policy formulations of the last government, under pressure from the US, led to the foreign policy neglect of the rest of the all-important Indian sub-continental neighbourhood. It was being commonly said that during the last 10 years, India's foreign policy stood outsourced to Washington.

Had India diverted equal effort and time to focus on its foreign relations with Nepal, Bhutan, Bangladesh, Myanmar and Sri Lanka, it would not only have gained significant strategic successes, but would also have erased the international criticism that India was found wanting in spreading its influence in its own immediate neighbourhood. This Indian neglect created a strategic vacuum in which China gleefully entered much to India's discomfiture. The situation was further complicated by inadequate government responses that permitted Indian states like West Bengal and Tamil Nadu to dictate foreign policy responses on the plea that 'political coalition compulsions' fettered India's foreign policy.

Long Overdue Priority

'Neighbours First' was the foreign policy mantra propelled by Prime Minister Modi even before he took oath as India's new prime minister. This was a long overdue foreign policy priority dictated by the previous political dispensation's gross neglect of India's neighbourhood.

Prime Minister Modi's political outreach to the neighbourhood emerged in the form of an invitation to leaders of all SAARC countries to attend his swearing-in ceremony. This was willingly accepted by all leaders, except Pakistan, which took time to accept the invite due to compulsions of the Pakistan Army.

With his political outreach, Prime Minister Modi facilitated a splendid opportunity for first hand interaction with SAARC leaders even before he embarked on a proactive foreign policy. Valuable political discussions with SAARC leaders fostered mutual understanding of both the visiting leaders and Prime Minister Modi.

It also helped the Indian Prime Minister to tailor his initial foreign policy blueprint for the neighbourhood based on his personal perceptions of each SAARC leader. Significantly, Prime Minister Modi selected Bhutan and Nepal for his first visits as part of his 'Neighbours First' foreign policy initiative. He virtually synchronised the visits of Indian Foreign Minister Sushma Swaraj to Bangladesh and Myanmar as part of the political outreach to all neighbours.

Strategic Significance

Prime Minister Modi's priority in selecting Bhutan and Nepal as his first ports of call in India's neighbourhood was systematically missed in Indian media analyses. Strategic determinants, so far absent in Indian foreign policy planning, came into play.

Nepal and Bhutan are strategically crucial for India's national security as they not only share borders with India, but also crucially with an overbearing China in the north. Nepal and Bhutan, therefore, are 'strategic buffer states' which impede China's direct access to Indian boundaries along a wide stretch of our Himalayan borders.

Nepal was virtually gifted away to China's influence by the unimaginative and flawed policies of the previous government. India handed over Nepal to the Nepalese Maoists and facilitated their political legitimacy, something which they could not win in a decade of violent insurgency. Regrettably, no Indian prime minister visited Nepal for the last 17 years.

Bhutan, India's long-standing, steadfast friend, has lately been under Chinese pressure, both diplomatically and militarily. China has indulged in intrusions into Bhutanese territory to enlarge the Chumbi Valley salient pointing at India's Siliguri Corridor.

Prime Minister Modi's visit to Bhutan, therefore, carried rich symbolism both in terms of strategic reassurance and political support appreciative of its India friendship. The visit of the Indian prime minister was well received by Bhutan at all levels and promises to have overcome any minor irritants that may have existed. Prime Minister Modi's 'Mission Nepal' was more challenging and called for adroit statesmanship.

India had to virtually reclaim Nepal to India-friendly postures after decades of anti-India hysteria propagated by both Nepalese domestic politics and Chinese moves. Prime Minister Modi's visit to the only Hindu nation in the world, including paying obeisance at the historic Pashupatinath Temple in Kathmandu, was particularly welcomed in Nepal. Modi's gesture symbolised the rich common civilisational heritage of both countries.

Imaginative and Visionary Step

Significantly, the 'Modi Magic' seemed to have worked in making his Nepal visit successful. Even top Maoist political leaders were fulsome in praise of Prime Minister Modi and his offerings to Nepal. Significant was his declaration in Nepal that India would never interfere in the country's domestic political dynamics as an overbearing neighbour.

It needs to be noted that Prime Minister Modi took an imaginative and visionary step in selecting Bhutan and Nepal as the first neighbours to be visited. Besides reasons outlined earlier, it was symbolic that even India's small neighbours would henceforth be accorded equitable respect in the Modi government's foreign policy.

Like Bhutan and Nepal, Myanmar also is a strategically located country with long borders with China contiguous to India's Arunachal Pradesh claimed by China as 'Southern Tibet'. In the 1990s, India's late Prime Minister P V Narasimha Rao, despite Western opposition, initiated the first significant Indian diplomatic outreach to an internationally isolated Myanmar.

The process has somewhat continued thereafter, but without the dynamism that should have been imparted. Prime Minister Modi's initiative in sending the foreign minister to Myanmar in the opening months of his government has injected the necessary dynamism to India's approach to Myanmar. Hopefully, prime minister himself would be able to visit this important neighbour in the near future. Bangladesh was accorded a similar priority by the visit of Sushma Swaraj. Bangladesh, under the continuing present political dispensation of Sheikh Hasina, has valued friendly and cordial relations with India. It is a pity that the previous Congress government could not come up with matching fast-track initiatives.

In a well-timed, friendly gesture in July 2014, India gracefully accepted the maritime boundaries award given by the Permanent Arbitration Commission of United Nations arbitrating on maritime boundaries disputes. This was a significant confidence building measure extended by the Modi government to Bangladesh. It is an assurance that under his leadership, the river water sharing agreement would also take some positive shape. Interestingly, with this generous gesture, India's international reputation soared even as China has obdurately refused to accept any arbitration on the South China Sea disputes.

With Prime Minister Modi at the helm, India's atrophied foreign policy formulations and processes would acquire imaginative and dynamic contours befitting an emerging Asian Power and a global player.

INDIAN FOREIGN POLICY ORIENTATION IN THE TWENTY-FIRST CENTURY

It is a truism that the foreign policy of any major state will be predicated upon and shaped by its perception of what constitutes the core national interest as leavened by the principles and value systems that the state in question adheres to. The related extrapolation is that the national interest, desegregated into its principal constituent elements, viz: political, military and economic determinants, would have to be protected, nurtured and advanced, as the case may be, in a complex and on occasion contradictory manner. State itself as an entity is located in a definitive spatio-temporal context and this provides the backdrop against which individual states evolve distinctive foreign policies. The regional and global strategic systemic consequently becomes a referent that defines the contours of domestic foreign policy and the latter evolves in a dynamic manner. The temporal determinant acquires greater salience when we note that both the state and the systemic have their own transmutative trajectories in the long cycle of history. This chapter seeks to examine the past evolution and current orientation of India's foreign policy (FP) and dwells in some detail on certain regions and countries. The chapter argues that there is an element of continuity and change that is discernible in India's FP and that this has been impelled by a combination of factors specific to the Indian experience. If FP is perceived as a 'strategy' to realize the larger national interest, a useful and succinct definition (for a word that has elicited a plethora of multi-disciplinary interpretations) is provided by John Lewis Gaddis who defines it as: "the process by which ends are related to means, intentions to capabilities, objectives to resources."

In relation to the process of evolving a FP, it may be added that the strategic culture of the state and its ruling/governing elite play a central role and this is very noticeable in the Indian case. India's strategic culture, as is the case of many other states, is a distillate of two ontological features-geography and history – filtered through the cultural impress of its ruling elite at any given point in time. As a civilizational-state (a characteristic it shares with China) there is an inherited, albeit burnished dominant narrative about the past even as it seeks to grapple with modernity in all its manifestations. To that extent, while independent India post 1947 sought to outline an appropriate FP, its genealogy goes back to the immediate and buried past – which in this case links the DNA of imperial British India with the tenets of the *Arthashastra* that goes back to circa 302 BC! Hence this chapter argues that there are certain elements of continuity by way of tangible objectives in India's FP that are inexorable and dictated by existential characteristics such as geographical location and size. These are further transmuted by contemporary politics and the constraints and opportunities exuded by the prevailing international strategic systemic.

This chapter is confined to the trends in the evolution of post- 1947 Indian FP and its current orientation and the first significant articulation about India's objectives, interestingly, precede 1947. India which was coming out of the colonial yoke through the Gandhian path of 'ahimsa' (non-violence) had a set of nationalist leaders led by Pandit Nehru and in September 1946, while providing an outline of the interim government's objectives on the cusp of Indian independence, Nehru stated: "It is because of this expectation of an early realization of full independence that we have entered this Government and we propose to function so as progressively to achieve independence in action both in our domestic affairs and our foreign relations...as a free nation with our own policy and not merely as a satellite of another nation."

There is further elaboration of the Nehruvian vision of Indian FP and a few months after he became Prime Minister of independent India, he observed: "Foreign policies...are not just empty struggles on a chess board. Behind them lie all manner of things. Ultimately, foreign policy is the outcome of economic policy, and until India has properly evolved her economic policy, her foreign policy will be rather vague, rather inchoate, and will be groping."

There is a sense of prescience in Nehru's later articulation for the effectiveness of India's FP in the early decades – the objectives it may have set for itself – were not backed by adequate and appropriate national resources and capabilities. Hence many of the lofty aspirations were not realized, thereby resulting in the chequered nature of India's foreign policy effectiveness in the period 1947-62. However this paper argues that there is a core consistency by way of the security and strategic concerns that under grid foreign policy and in the Indian case, the linkages and departures with the policy of imperial British India are instructive. 19th century European geo-strategic rivalry among the major powers became the 'Great Game' (a la Arthur Conolly and not Rudyard Kipling) and the central objective of then ascendant Britain was to keep the Russian Bear from accessing the Indian Ocean through the Central Asian region. Historians aver that even the Mughal emperors had much the same unease about any Russian foray to the subcontinent and this geo-strategic chess-game informed much of the foreign policy of the then major powers.

Theoreticians introduced the 'heartland versus rim land' theory and the dictates of the continental power and the salience of maritime power. Post World War II, when the mantle of the dominant power had passed to the USA, the 'game' continued but with a different packaging – namely the containment of communism.

The former Soviet Union was the new 'bear' whose advance was to be resisted and the global systemic evolved along the grid of bipolarity. Here one may introduce the co-relation between the foreign policy of individual states and the manner in which it is shaped by the compulsions of the global systemic. The proposition is that very few states barring the hegemon have the ability to conduct truly autonomous or independent foreign policies and the thumb-rule for all other states – to the extent they are relevant to the systemic – is that their manoeuvrability and space is shaped by the power compulsions of the systemic.

Bipolarity was the flavour of the Cold War decades and most of the world was divided along the East-West axis and their related military alliances. India, under Nehru, which had already anticipated this power block divisiveness had made its fundamental choice Non alignment. In his December 1946 speech, Nehru had already asserted: "We propose, as far as possible, to keep away from the power politics of groups, aligned against one another, which have led in the past to world wars and which may again lead to disasters on an even vaster scale."

Consequently the existential force of bipolarity and the postures of the two superpowers shaped the choices for the rest of the world – including the non-aligned group. India, as a nascent post-colonial state had its own internal consolidation to address as a first priority but its foreign policy, this chapter argues, flowed from an innate sense of how best to manage its more relevant strategic space. This was most succinctly summed up by the British High Commissioner to India at the time (1951) in a secret cable to London elucidating India's security-foreign policy orientation. Sir Archibald Nye opined that the Indian policy could be perceived as "operating in three concentric circles, the principles governing each of which bear little or no relation to the principles followed in the others."

This has been further interpreted as the innermost circle of contiguous states – viz: Afghanistan, Ceylon (now Sri Lanka), Nepal, Tibet and Burma – where it was perceived that India had 'vital' interests. The second circle included the rest of the world minus the four major powers at that time, namely the USA, USSR, UK and PRC. The second ring was prioritized as areas that were more relevant such as SE Asia to minimal relevance as say South America. Sir Nye added, even at that time, that Pakistan was a 'unique' case. The more detailed elucidation that followed suggested that the policies – security and foreign – followed by India were very different for each set of circles and that while the innermost elicited a kind of hard-nosed realpolitik approach *a la* Bismarck, while in the second circle, "Indian policy was characterized by anti-colonialism and support for nationalism, with perhaps a smattering of realism in Asian countries like Malaya and Iran, where India's interests were engaged." And with regard to the outermost circle, India's foreign and security policy posture was "to a great extent determined by her passionate desire to keep out of conflict and to stand aside from Great Power struggles."

This chapter argues that Indian FP was and is shaped by a set of three determinants – namely the external international systemic and the dominant strategic discourse and practice; the Indian perception about what constitutes the core national interest and the national resources and capabilities it can bring to bear to protect or advance this interest; and finally the cognitive perception of the ruling/governing elite at the time. Within this matrix, there is both continuity and change by way of specific trend lines and initiatives taken by India over a 60 year period – from 1946 to 2006. I would further aver that this entire policy response trajectory is to be located within the domain of India's distinctive strategic culture – which has also been evolving over this period.

Broadly desegregated, the trends in Indian FP may be divided in the temporal periods 1947-1962; 1962-1991; 1991-

1998; and 1998-mid 2006 and refereed along the three elements identified earlier. The early phase from 1947-1962 was a period when nascent India was seeking to consolidate its identity as a free and independent state with the attendant mix of aspirations and anxieties and to that extent the immediate priority was internal and domestic. The aftermath of partition and the grapple with participative democracy when economic and fiscal resources were modest, consumed greater part of national funds and energy – but it would be fair to state that on the foreign policy front – the Nehruvian approach was followed. A degree of realism where India's vital interests were affected was one component, while issues such as de-colonization and support for freedom struggles comprised the other. On larger global issues such as nuclear weapons, a normative, humanistic approach was preferred and vis-à-vis the superpowers, nonalignment was the preferred stance. If the domestic ambiance and the persona of a leader like Nehru were two of the drivers, the ambiance of the external global strategic systemic as manifest in the early phase of the Cold war (post Cuban missile crisis in 1962, the author would argue, the Cold War entered a different techno-strategic phase) was the more significant determinant in shaping Indian FP.

The rationale for the creation of an independent Pakistan is beyond the scope of this chapter but suffice it to note that the reality of a Pakistan in August 1947 brought the Great Game DNA through the Cold War filter into the calculus of Indian FP. Pakistan's willingness to join the US-led military alliances such as the CENTO and SEATO during the 1950's and 1960's made it the problematic 'other' for India and a number of Indian FP initiatives including those relating to Kashmir were directly affected by this Cold War undercurrent. One may hypothetically aver that an undivided British India would have perhaps adopted a different kind of FP orientation for there were no fundamental divergences with the US led Western alliance. Nehru himself had no special love for the ideology of communism so much so that India would have crossed over into the red camp in retrospect appear misplaced. On the international canvas, India acquired a certain profile that belied its nascent political pedigree and underdeveloped economic profile. This was evident in the Indian support to Japan immediately after Hiroshima, the Indonesian freedom struggle, the Korean and Indo-China wars, the mantle of Asian leadership et al. The brief 1962 Sino-India war punctured this self-image and is a major punctuation in the evolution of India's strategic culture, security perceptions and foreign policy orientation.

Disillusionment and a rude awakening were the leit motifs of the trauma and humiliation of 1962 and this experience scarred Nehru personally and the Indian polity collectively. Bitter recrimination followed about the great Chinese betrayal and the invalidity of Asian solidarity on one hand and a realization that India's inherent national resources and tangible capabilities – in this case military – were woefully inadequate to underwrite the foreign policy contours that had been earlier envisioned. To go back to Gaddis, there was a mismatch between the objectives and the availability of resources.

Post 1962 was a period of consolidation for India and Nehru died a broken man in 1964. His successors – Lal Bahadur Shastri briefly and later Indira Gandhi were wedded to the mantra of nonalignment on the global stage but introduced certain nuances in the practice of foreign policy. The external dynamic of the Cold War entered Asia through the Vietnam war and later the nettlesome issue of Cambodia.

Both these events had considerable negative impact on India's relations with the USA and SE Asian nations– the focus of this chapter. In the post Nehru decades – that is from 1964 till the tragic assassination of Mrs. Indira Gandhi in 1984 – India engaged in two wars with Pakistan – in 1965 and 1971 – the latter leading to the birth of Bangladesh – and the 1974 Peaceful Nuclear Explosion, and here one notes a certain caution and assertiveness in Indian FP. The Indian disillusionment with the US and other western powers – such as UK (which in any case was becoming more and more dependent on the trans-Atlantic alliance and the US) in the aftermath of the 1962 war and the subsequent Chinese nuclear test in 1964 led to a gradual tilt towards the former USSR and in about a decade – from the mid 1960's onwards, the USSR emerged as India's major supplier of military inventory and a trusted friend over issues such as Kashmir when they came up in the UNSC.

This tilt had its corrosive impact on India's relations with the USA and its allies – leading to what is often described as the 'estrangement' between the world's oldest and largest democracies – ironically when the values that were being contested in the Cold war were freedom and the threat to democracy.

Subsequently the Soviet occupation of Afghanistan in 1979 and the Iranian Revolution brought the Cold War closer to India on its western flank and the estrangement with the USA was further enhanced through India's muted response over Afghanistan and the call for the Indian Ocean as a Zone of Peace among other foreign policy responses.

The period 1984 till 1990 was one of further consolidation for India under the stewardship of Rajiv Gandhi (this was the period when India embarked upon its Peace Keeping Operation in Sri Lanka) and some significant regional FP initiatives were pursued including a thawing of relations with China (which had gone into the deep freeze after the 1962 war) and improved relations with the USA.

This was also a period when India's fiscal prudence was not as astute as it may have been and while on one hand there was a visible element of India's military capability being effectively enhanced – as perceived in the Indian Navy's expansion and the swift assistance to Maldives in November 1988 which was threatened by a renegade takeover – the macro economic and fiscal indicators were deteriorating. This was also a period of considerable internal turbulence for India and there was a quick succession of Prime Ministers and short-lived Central governments. Political instability was compounded by the terrorist assassination of Rajiv Gandhi and a very complex internal security environment. Apart from Jammu and Kashmir, the prosperous state of Punjab witnessed a rash of separatist violence that was finally quelled.

This was also the period when the Cold War was coming to an unintended end and Gorbachev's glasnost-perestroika and the rapprochement with the USA led to a dramatic turn of events. Overnight on December 8, 1991, the Soviet Union became 'former' and Russia emerged with a very different geography and political identity. Bipolarity was relegated to the pages of history and a very new global strategic systemic was born. Unipolarity – or so it seemed. The USA which had just led a very successful coalition in early 1999 for in Gulf War I – the War for Kuwait, was perceived as the sole hegemon with no challenger in sight – China was still recovering from the opprobrium of Tiananmen. It is the contention of this paper that while the end of the Cold War led to a complete review and re-orientation of the FP of most nations, for the global strategic grid was completely transformed, it was the equivalent of a double-whammy for India since the domestic situation was also undergoing considerable turbulence. PM Narasimha Rao assumed office in June 1991 succeeding two predecessors who had served for less than a year each. India's economic health was frail and the fiscal indicators were alarming with a balance of payment crisis looming. India's forex reserves were down to a few weeks. Thus the country was faced with an exigency wherein all three determinants that shape and influence FP were in a state of flux-namely the global systemic, national capabilities and resources, and a new leadership that was grappling with political, economic and social turbulence – the right-wing BJP party was gaining ground in India at the time.

India's major FP transformation came about in the Narashima Rao years (June 1991-May 1996) and much of it was impelled by the economic liberalization that Delhi was embarked upon. India's socialist command planning model and the license-raj permit economic and trade system gave way to a more liberalized approach and in many ways the Indian economy was freed from the politico-bureaucratic shackles imposed upon it for decades. The macro-results were very favourable. The inflexible Hindu rate of growth suddenly accelerated and this was also enabled to a great extent by deft financial planning led by then Finance Minister Dr. Manmohan

Singh and the global techno-commercial wave related to the computer and information revolution. As Baru has noted: "after recording virtually no growth in the first half of the 20th century, the (Indian) economy grew at an annual average rate of 3.5 percent in 1950-80 and 5.4 percent in 1980-90 and 6.2 percent in 1990-2000."

Thus the economic sinews were strengthened under the Rao-Singh stewardship and I would argue that to achieve this objective, necessary changes were brought about to India's FP orientation. Trade and investment were accorded a higher priority as opposed to ideological positions and much of this is reflected in India's relations with the USA, ASEAN and China – the later focus of this chapter.

2

Indian Foreign Policy under Prime Minister Modi

Bhartiya Janata Party's (BJP) chose to appoint Gujarat Chief Minister Narendra Modi to head its 2014 poll campaign committee. While by no means assured, the move is the clearest indication yet of Modi's 'first amongst equals' status in the race to emerge as the party's prime ministerial candidate ahead of next year's national elections.

If that were to happen and the BJP cobbles together a winning coalition under Modi's helm, the effect on India's foreign policy will be cataclysmic. After all, the Prime Minister's Office has consistently overshadowed the External Affairs Ministry in recent years in framing the contours of New Delhi's foreign policy as seen in the case of the nuclear deal with the United States or the peace process with Pakistan.

What would be the terms of engagement with a Prime Minister long given the cold shoulder by the West for his alleged role (albeit never proven in a court of law) in the bloody sectarian violence that engulfed Gujarat in 2002? In the aftermath of the riots, which left more than 1,000 people dead—mostly Muslims—the United States and the European Union declared Modi *persona non grata*, cutting off diplomatic engagement with the state. In 2005, Washington rejected Modi's visa application amid continuing concerns over the alleged subversion of justice in Gujarat.

In October 2012, in a development indicative of Modi's rising profile in Indian politics, Britain's high commissioner in New Delhi, James Bevan called on Modi in Gujarat's capital of Gandhinagar, in what seemed to be a decisive step towards the Gujarat chief minister's international rehabilitation.

The decision by the UK to end its isolationist policies towards Modi stemmed from fears of losing ground to countries like Japan, China and Israel, which had made large investments in the state in recent years. The conviction of Maya Kodnani, a former state minister in Modi's government, to 28 years in prison for her role in the 2002 riots provided the perfect alibi for London to begin engaging with Gujarat.

Leading up to the general elections in May 2014, one can expect Washington to replicate the UK's move—including granting Modi a visa—to avoid the deeply embarrassing prospect of having to engage with a prime minister it until recently viewed as a pariah.

However, expect India-US ties to cool significantly should Modi become the prime minister of the world's largest democracy, which the US has been eager to court. In addition to greater strategic understanding, ties between New Delhi and Washington have benefitted greatly from the personal chemistry between Indian and US leaders—notably Prime Minister Singh and President Obama.

In an interview with Fareed Zakaria in January 2012, Obama named Singh among five world leaders he considered to be among his closest friends. Others in the list included Turkish Prime Ministers Tayyip Erdoðan, German Chancellor Angela Merkel, British Prime Minister David Cameron and former South Korean President Lee Myung-bak.

With a liberal Democrat president occupying the White House until 2016, how would his dealings with a conservative Hindu-nationalist Indian leader affect Indo-US ties? For starters, do not expect a second visit from Obama to India or anything similar to Obama's feting of Singh as his first state guest at the beginning of his presidency in 2009.

Interactions between Prime Minister Modi and President Obama would likely be strictly business and would probably take place on the sidelines of multilateral events like the annual United Nations General Assembly conclave or the G-20 meets. In any case, Modi is unlikely to forget Washington's slight over the past decade, ensuring that potential parleys between US and Indian leaders would remain cool if he becomes prime minister.

On the other hand, if Modi were to become PM, expect ties with Israel—already a key defence partner—to expand dramatically. While it was a Congress government that established diplomatic ties with Israel in 1992, it was under a BJP-led government from 1999 to 2004 that Indian ties with the Jewish State blossomed. This period lead critics to believe that this was not just a security partnership but also a relationship with strong religious and ideological moorings.

In 2003, while addressing a gathering of the American Jewish Community in Washington, India's then National Security Advisor in the BJP coalition, Brajesh Mishra, called for a trilateral alliance between the US, India and Israel to "jointly face the same ugly face of modern-day terrorism" while contending that "such an alliance would have the political will and moral authority to take bold decisions in extreme cases of terrorist provocation".

Coming in the aftermath of the September 11 attacks, the proposed alliance acquired ideological trappings fuelling fears of a Samuel Huntington-style clash of civilizations. The pinnacle of the Indo-Israeli engagement was the visit of then Prime Minister Ariel Sharon to India in September 2003. Sharon was the first Israeli premier to make the trip.

Traditionally, Indian politicians—wary of alienating Muslim voters—have resisted being seen as close to Tel Aviv and have avoided visiting Israel or even hosting Israeli leaders. However, Modi is one of the handful of Indian political figures to have visited Israel, suggesting that he would not be averse to undertaking what would potentially be the first Indian prime ministerial visit to the Jewish State. Lastly, on India's all-important ties with Pakistan, Modi as Prime Minister could either setback the fledgling peace process or it could result in a diplomatic consensus on several issues. During the previous period of BJP rule, India fought a brief war with Islamabad in 1999 after Pakistani troops entered Indian-held Kashmir.

The Kargil conflict was followed two years later by a massive troop build-up on the border after New Delhi blamed Pakistani militants for an attack on its parliament in December 2001. The build-up also happened against the backdrop of nuclear tests by both countries in 1998. If Vajpayee's tenure is anything to go by, Modi's hawkish credentials are likely to lead to an aggressive and muscular foreign policy stance vis-à-vis Pakistan.

However, the same government, under then Prime Minister Atal Bihari Vajpayee, mounted a diplomatic effort to improve ties with Pakistan. This policy has continued under the current Congress-led government.

The emphatic return of Nawaz Sharif as Pakistan's new Prime Minister and the potential election of Modi as Prime Minister in India could present a window of opportunity for the two countries to negotiate a lasting agreement on less controversial territorial disputes such as Sir Creek and the Siachen Glacier. Such a step could be a prelude to a broader peace deal that would also involve Kashmir.

NARENDRA MODI'S IMPRINT ON FOREIGN POLICY

Narendra Modi has surprised many by investing considerable political capital in high-powered diplomacy in his first 100 days in office, even though he had little foreign policy experience when he became Prime Minister. His hosting of leaders from India's neighbourhood when he was sworn in, his highly effective visits to two of India's neighbours, Nepal and Bhutan, his diplomatic dexterity at the Brics (Brazil, Russia, India, China, and South Africa) summit in Brazil, and his watershed trip to Japan are coming to define his nimble foreign policy approach. Since his thumping electoral mandate, foreign dignitaries have made a beeline to call on him.

Instead of bumptiously enunciating a Modi doctrine in foreign policy, the Prime Minister is allowing his actions, including diplomatic successes and breaks, to define his approach. From the big bear hug with Japanese Prime Minister Shinzo Abe that symbolized the dawn of an India-Japan alliance to his scrapping of scheduled foreign secretary level talks with Pakistan after its high commissioner defiantly met Kashmiri secessionists, Modi has managed to put his stamp on foreign policy faster than any predecessor, other than Jawaharlal Nehru. Indeed, as India's veto at the World Trade Organization talks in Geneva exemplified, Modi will even stand up to a powerful, rich nations' cabal when national interest is at stake.

Signalling his intent to boost India's economic and security interests through multidirectional collaboration with like-minded powers, Modi has embarked on building a democratic axis with Japan — an alliance that can help reshape Asian geopolitics and accelerate India's development. Modi deliberately made Japan his first foreign port of call beyond the Indian subcontinent to highlight that country's centrality to Indian interests. In fact, not only is Abe the most India-friendly of any world leader today, but also Japan is ready more than any other power to assist in India's economic rise through aid, investment and technology transfer. Proof of that is its $35 billion pledge this week.

To be sure, India's relationship with Japan began blossoming before Modi assumed office. The real architect of this axis is Abe, whose push for closer ties with India dates back to his first stint as Prime Minister in 2006-07, when Japan and India unveiled their strategic and global partnership. However, Modi — recognizing Japan's importance to his own goal to boost economic growth and restore national pride — has been quick to seize the opportunity to build an entente with Tokyo.

This mission has not dissuaded him from reaching out to archrival China, despite increasing Himalayan border transgressions by its military. In a tricky act, he has sought to tame China's belligerence through economic courtship designed to rope in that country — with its $4 trillion foreign-exchange reserves — as an important partner in India's development, like Japan.

Indeed, Modi has gone out of his way to befriend China, negating early assumptions that he would be less accommodating toward Beijing than his predecessor. He even delayed his Japan tour by several weeks so as to first meet Chinese President Xi Jinping on the sidelines of the Brics summit. Their body language at that summit indicated the two had formed an easy personal equation. But getting Xi to make progress on the issues that divide India and China won't be easy. China represents Modi's diplomatic gamble. He has invited Chinese investment in his plan to modernize India's infrastructure, especially railroads, power stations and industrial parks. China's foreign direct investment in India, however, remains trifling, with Chinese companies preferring to import primary commodities from India while exporting an avalanche of finished products. China, by strategically expanding such lopsided trade with India, has raked in mounting profits, carving out a $30-billion trade surplus in its favour last year. By dumping its products, it is undercutting Indian manufacturing. How long will Modi be able to walk the tightrope on a country that poses the most difficult challenge for India?

Make no mistake: The extraordinary warmth and harmony that characterized Modi's Japan tour is unlikely to be replicated in a summit with any other country. In fact, the Prime Minister's diplomatic skills are about to face a stiffer test in upcoming bilateral summits with Xi — a former military reservist who symbolizes China's new militarism — and US President Barack Obama, a lame duck increasingly under political siege.

Still, Modi's actions thus far suggest he has a clear vision of how to proactively recoup India's regional losses and to boost its global standing. Even his decision to call off talks with Pakistan has made more sense with each passing day, given the political mayhem there. Can any meaningful talks be held at a time the Pakistani military is busy neutering the elected PM and stepping up border provocations against India? Pakistan's cocky high commissioner is lucky he was not expelled or put in the doghouse for brazenly going against the Indian Foreign Office's counsel. But he won't be lucky twice. One trademark of Modi's foreign policy is that it is shorn of ideology, with pragmatism being the hallmark. The policy's overriding objective appears to be to enhance the country's economic and military security as rapidly as possible. Of course, it is too early to judge the consistency, strength or effectiveness of the Modi diplomacy. But after a long era of ad hoc, reactive, weak-kneed diplomacy, the new clarity and vision represent a welcome change for India.

RISE OF A MULTI-POLAR ASIA: A VIEW FROM INDIA

Continuing tensions over Ukraine notwithstanding, including a US-led boycott of the Victory Day Parade commemorating the 70th anniversary of Germany's surrender in World War II, Russia under President Vladimir Putin has retrieved much of its eminence as a great power and even managed a handsome recovery of its sanction-hit rouble. By tweaking its West-centric gaze towards Siberia and the Arctic (which Putin likely visited during a mysterious absence some weeks ago); towards Asia, the Middle East, South America and Africa, Moscow straddles a multipolar world and a multipolar Asia. Given that the bulk of its vast territories embrace the Asian landmass, it would be a mistake not to think of Russia as an Asian power.

The reality that it is already a multipolar Asia would not have escaped Beijing, which in recent years is expanding its global footprint while seeking a commanding presence in its Asian neighbourhood. Given its deep economic and strategic ties with Moscow, Beijing obviously recognises that Russia will pursue its interests in Central Asia, Europe, Iran and the Islamic world, with India, and elsewhere.

The People's Republic will have to accept that there is no escape from sharing eminence with rising powers like India and Iran, which, like Russia and China, share strategic and economic interests in the same regions. Nor will it be possible to exclude countries like Japan, Vietnam, Australia, Indonesia and Malaysia, to name a few, from pursuing their interests in the Asia-Pacific. The Chinese leadership will therefore have to come to terms with the fact that Beijing is unlikely to enjoy the 'sole superpower' status that the United States briefly enjoyed after the collapse of the Soviet Union in 1991.

Currently, Beijing resents India's assertiveness in Asia and even more in the Indian Ocean where India has a commanding presence by virtue of its geographical location. More importantly, many countries feel less threatened by the rise of India and favour New Delhi assuming greater responsibilities in protecting the sea-lanes from the African coast to the Indonesian islands. India is accordingly prioritising modernisation of its navy and air force. By scaling down the strength of the new mountain strike force from a proposed 90,000 to around 30,000 troops, the Modi government has defanged the hardliners who were upping the ante on the border dispute with China, both before and during his visit to that country.

The Indo-China border dispute, a legacy of the British Raj, has been made intractable by China's annexation of Tibet and acquisition of Indian territory (Aksai Chin, to consolidate its hold on Tibet) from Pakistan, which the latter has illegally occupied in contravention of UN Resolutions. This unresolved dispute has been aggravated by Beijing nibbling at Indian territory in Ladakh (Jammu & Kashmir) in recent years.

In April 2015, Beijing announced an ambitious China-Pakistan Economic Corridor from its Xinjiang province to the Gwadar port in Baluchistan (Pakistan), via Gilgit-Baltistan which legally belongs to India, being part of the erstwhile princely State of Jammu & Kashmir. The plan is to link its New Silk Road and Maritime Silk Road ('One Belt, One Road') initiatives with Central Asia and later the Middle East, Europe, and Africa. While professional Cassandras loudly declaimed that China was challenging India in her maritime backyard (Arabian Sea), they omitted to mention that New Delhi is investing $100 million to develop the Chabahar Port in Iran, which will grant it access to Afghanistan and Central Asia, bypassing Pakistan. China's proposed corridor has, however, sparked deep resentment in Gilgit-Baltistan and may not be easy to implement. New Delhi summoned the Chinese envoy to protest against this project. However, the earthquake that that struck Nepal on April 26, with strong aftershocks hitting the region even after three weeks, could affect the viability of projects in this mountainous region.

There is also real danger from jihadist outfits that Pakistan has nurtured in pursuit of its strategic objectives in Afghanistan and India. Central Asia is the new frontier of radical Islam; Chechnya, Fergana, and Xinjiang are the new recruiting ground for the Islamic State in Iraq and Syria (ISIS), which recently established a base in the Afghanistan badlands. Hence, Russia, China, Iran, and India will have to cooperate in fighting the jihadi menace.

Chinese claims on the Indian State of Arunachal Pradesh – first articulated in 2006 when it was called South Tibet – are a baseless tactic to pressurise India. The claims were rebutted by the 14th Dalai Lama, who asserted that Arunachal Pradesh was historically never a part of Tibet. The claim seems to be a ruse to avert a situation in which Tibetans claim that the next incarnation of the aged Dalai Lama is born in territory outside Chinese control (the sixth Dalai Lama, Tsangyang Gyatso, was born near the Tawang monastery in Arunachal Pradesh). As an aside, one may mention that India's Kushan empire included Kashgar (Kashi), Khotan and Yarkant in the Tarim Basin, and Kushan control over the road from China to Gandhara (Afghanistan) facilitated trade and travel across the Khunjerab Pass and enabled the spread of Mahayana Buddhism to China.

While Beijing's hostility to Prime Minister Narendra Modi's visit to Arunachal Pradesh in February this year was unwarranted, it suggested that there would be no forward movement on the border issue, notwithstanding the high optics accompanying Modi's visit (May 14-16), which began with a trip to President Xi Jinping's hometown of Xi'an, from where Xuanzang set off for a pilgrimage of important Buddhist sites in India in the seventh century, and even arrived at a monastery in Modi's hometown, Vadnagar, Gujarat. But Xi'an is also the new axis of power in China, with three of the seven top leaders of the politburo standing committee, eight of 25 politburo members and four out of 11 members of the central military commission belonging to the 'Shaanxi group'.

Shrewd and pragmatic, Modi refused to allow establishment hawks to dictate the terms of engagement and accorded priority to civilisational, commercial, and civilian ties.

At the Tsinghua University on the last day of his tour, he articulated the Indian position on all issues firmly while moving to improve bilateral trade and investment opportunities. India, he said, currently enjoys a growth rate of 7.5 per cent and is working to create next generation infrastructure – roads, ports, railways, airports, telecom, digital networks and clean energy. Yet, he said, it is imperative to bridge the doubts and distrust in the relationship, to settle the boundary quickly, and to first settle the ambiguity regarding the Line of Actual Control.

Modi specifically mentioned the tensions over trans-border rivers (from the Himalayas) and unilaterally extended electronic tourist visas to Chinese citizens, even as critics bemoaned the stapled visas for Indians from Jammu & Kashmir and Arunachal Pradesh. He refused to let Pakistan's growing strategic relationship with Beijing derail his engagement with China and remained focused on his larger perspectives: he inked fresh deals worth $22 billion (in addition to previously pledged investments of $20 billion), and sought China's support for India's permanent membership of a reformed UN Security Council and the Nuclear Suppliers Group.

A signature theme of India's security establishment for over a decade has been China's 'string of pearls' strategy to encircle India, a reference to China's growing ties with Sri Lanka, Myanmar, Bangladesh and Pakistan. The decibels rose sharply when China began building the Hambantota port in Sri Lanka (a project declined by India) and again when, in 2014, then President Rajapaksa twice permitted a Chinese nuclear submarine to dock at the island nation. Modi intervened, quietly but decisively, and after Maithripala Sirisena came to power, the Colombo port project with China was deferred and the Mattala Rajapaksa International Airport, opened in 2013 with a Chinese investment of $200 million, rendered defunct.

Actually, an undue pessimism pervades India's security establishment because it continues to harbour a Nehruvian worldview, and has not been able to overcome the trauma of defeat in 1962. Yet, when the then Prime Minister Atal Bihari Vajpayee visited China in June 2003, he secured Chinese recognition of Indian sovereignty over Sikkim (which it once disputed), and for the first time since 1960, both sides appointed special representatives (SR) to negotiate the boundary dispute. In 2013 and 2014, China agreed to pull back its soldiers from eastern Ladakh.

In recent times, India's engagement with Russia has appeared rather muted. But the day before the Prime Minister left for China, President Putin telephoned him and Modi confirmed his participation in the forthcoming BRICS summit and Shanghai Cooperation Organisation summit, both in Ufa, in July. New Delhi's quest for full membership of the SCO may be approved at this meeting. The two leaders also discussed a range of issues concerning expansion of the Russia-India privileged strategic partnership.

Indeed, Russia, China and India and even Iran have converging interests in stabilising Afghanistan and curbing its multi-billion dollar drug trade, as well as containing terrorism in Central Asia and the neighbourhood. India does not endorse the Western line on Iran, Syria or Ukraine; at Fortaleza, Brazil (August 2014), Modi reportedly assured Putin that he would not support the US/EU (not UN) sanctions against Russia.

Fortaleza was Modi's first global engagement after coming to power, and it was here that the members decided to launch the New Development Bank with a $100 billion fund and currency reserve pool of $100 billion, to help third world countries access loans without 'unfair' conditions imposed by West-dominated multilateral financial institutions such as the World Bank, International Monetary Fund and Asian Development Bank. India has appointed KV Kamath as the first chief of the Shanghai-based bank. China's ambitious Asian Infrastructure Investment Bank (AIIB), mooted in 2013 to support infrastructural projects in the region, has acquired over 40 members, including America's western allies who are keen for Chinese investments and trade.

Modi was quick to understand that the coming era belongs to the non-West and is keen to receive the fruits of the Russia-India-China (RIC) grouping. Russia is reportedly keen on an India-China rapprochement, so that the RIC can emerge as an economic and strategic axis that can challenge the dominant West, especially the United States. To be stable and viable, such an alliance needs Iran (RICI), which is a force to be reckoned with in the Gulf region. The interests of all four nations converge in many areas.

In fact, China's One Belt One Road, India's Cotton Route and Project Mausam, and the Russian-led Eurasian Economic Union (EEU), are all complementary projects based on the old land and sea-based trade routes of the ancient world. Even in the centuries BC, the land and sea commerce between India, Persia, Egypt, up to the African coast, was protected by different dynasties; China joined this trade only under the Han dynasty, but expanded it exponentially.

Currently, the Sino-Russian alliance is the fastest growing. Trade between the two countries stands at $100 billion annually, and some long-term energy deals – driven by Moscow's need to counter a Western attempt to throttle its pipelines – have cemented the relationship. In May 2014, the two signed a 30-year $400 billion gas deal and another $325 billion gas deal in November 2014, sharply reducing Russian reliance on Europe. In fact, cash-strapped Russia has agreed to sell its most advanced air defence system, the S-400 missile, and 100 Sukhoi Superjet airplanes, to China. Beijing will invest $5.8 billion to extend the Moscow-Kazan high speed railway into China. In all, the two nations have signed 32 infrastructure related agreements during President Xi's visit to Moscow in May.

Russia is also moving ahead with Turkish Stream, a trans-Black Sea pipeline that will deliver natural gas to Turkey by

December 2016; Putin has offered Greece to fund an extension of the pipeline to the heart of Europe. So far, Serbia, Macedonia, Hungary and Greece have expressed a desire to be part of the project. The Turkish Stream is a Russian counter-offensive to the West's attempt to checkmate its South Stream pipeline at Bulgaria.

President Xi was the principal guest of honour at Moscow's Victory Day celebrations (an estimated 25 million Russians sacrificed their lives during the War), but leaders of around 30 nations attended despite Washington's boycott call. Nations who participated in the parade at Red Square included India, China, Mongolia, Serbia, Azerbaijan, Armenia, Belarus, Kazakhstan, Kyrgyzstan and Tajikistan.

Beijing is now planning its own end-of-World War II military parade in September to highlight its contribution to the War (in which an estimated 15 lakh Chinese soldiers died) and challenge the West-centric narrative that has hitherto dominated the history books. This is yet another symbol of the rise of Asia.

DECONSTRUCTING THE MODI FOREIGN POLICY

India — home to more than a sixth of the human race — punches far below its weight. Internationally, it is a rule-taker, not a rule-maker. A 2013 essay in the journal *Foreign Affairs*, titled "India's Feeble Foreign Policy," focussed on how India is resisting its own rise, as if political drift had turned the country into its own worst enemy.

Since the Berlin Wall fell 25 years ago, the world has witnessed the most profound technological, economic and geopolitical change in the most compressed time frame in history. Unfortunately for India, despite its impressive economic growth overall, much of its last 25 years has been characterised by political weakness and drift. For example, between 1989 and 1998, India had a succession of weak governments. It is not an exaggeration to call Prime Minister Manmohan Singh's two terms "the lost decade" for India strategically.

Waning regional influence

The result of the prolonged leadership crisis has been a sharp erosion in India's regional and extra-regional clout. The gap in power and stature between China and India has widened significantly. After all, this was the quarter-century in which China took off.

More troubling has been India's shrinking space in its own strategic backyard. Even tiny Maldives had the gall to kick India in the chin and get away with it. It kicked out its Indian airport operator from the capital Male and publicly dressed down the Indian Ambassador without fear of consequences. In Nepal, India found itself competing with China. And in Sri Lanka, India became content to play second fiddle to China.

The paradox is that India's economy continued to grow even as India's regional influence waned. This shows that GDP growth by itself cannot translate into stronger foreign policy in the absence of a dynamic, forward-looking leadership and cogent, strategic goals. In fact, when India was economically weak under Indira Gandhi, it had a fairly robust foreign policy, with no neighbour daring to mess with it.

"Mr. Modi faces major regional challenges, exemplified by the arc of failing states around India. This tyranny of geography demands that India evolve more dynamic and innovative approaches to diplomacy and national defence."

Against this background, the political rise of Narendra Modi — known for his decisiveness — could be a potential game-changer. It is too early to define, let alone judge, his foreign policy, given that Mr. Modi has been in office for just six months. Yet, as he focusses on revitalising the country's economic and military security, five things stand out.

First, Mr. Modi continues to invest considerable political capital in high-powered diplomacy so early in his term. Critics may contend that his exceptionally busy foreign-policy schedule, coupled with campaign meetings in serial State elections, leaves him restricted time to focus on his most critical responsibility — domestic issues, which will define his legacy.

Powered by ideas

No previous Indian Prime Minister participated in so many high-powered multilateral and bilateral summits in his or her first months in office as Mr. Modi. U.S. President Barack Obama's high-profile visit in January will keep national attention on diplomacy. To be sure, Mr. Modi's focus on the grand chessboard of geopolitics to underpin national interests suggests a strategic bent of mind that only one previous Prime Minister credibly demonstrated — Indira Gandhi.

Second, the Modi foreign policy is powered by ideas, not by any ideology. Indeed, Mr. Modi has demonstrated a knack to skilfully employ level-headed ideas to shape a non-doctrinaire vision and galvanise public opinion. On domestic policy, too, he is using the power of ideas, such as "Swachh Bharat" (or Clean India). In the strategic domain, he is taking his "Make in India" mission to the heavily-import-dependent defence sector. The real test ultimately will be Mr. Modi's ability to translate his ideas into transformative accomplishments.

Third, he has projected a nimble foreign policy with pragmatism as its hallmark. Nothing better illustrates this than the priority he has accorded — by shaking off U.S. visa-denial humiliation heaped on him over nine years — to restoring momentum to the relationship with America. Mr. Obama's scheduled visit as chief guest at Republic Day represents both a thank you to Mr. Modi for rising above personal umbrage and an effort to lift the India-U.S. relationship to a higher level of engagement through the major new opportunities being opened up for American businesses by Mr. Modi's commitment to pro-market economic policies and defence modernisation.

The U.S. already conducts more military exercises with India than with any other country. And in recent years, it has quietly overtaken Russia as the largest arms supplier to India.

Food security issue

Fourth, Mr. Modi has put his stamp on foreign policy faster than any predecessor, other than Jawaharlal Nehru. Yet, he appears to have no intent to enunciate a Modi doctrine in foreign policy. In contrast to the meretricious "Gujral Doctrine," which delivered little more than words, Mr. Modi wants his actions to define his policy trademarks.

In fact, his actions have started speaking for themselves — from his moves to engineer stronger partnerships with Japan and Israel (countries critical to Indian interests but which also courted him even as the U.S. targeted him) to his mortars-for-bullet response to Pakistani ceasefire violations. His firm stand at the World Trade Organization (WTO) on the food-stockpiling issue, central to India's food security, stood out.

After vetoing the WTO's Trade Facilitation Agreement in Geneva, Mr. Modi made the U.S. climbdown on the food-stockpiling issue, yet earned praise from Mr. Obama for helping to break the impasse. Even the head of the U.N.'s International Fund for Agricultural Development backed the veto, saying the real choice for India in Geneva was between "feeding" its citizens and "creating jobs" for wealthy economies. After all, the main providers of agricultural subsidies are the rich countries plus China.

For monsoon-dependent, drought-prone India, stockpiling food through a minimum support price to farmers serves as an insurance policy against a 1960s-style mortifying situation that saw New Delhi beseeching foreign food aid, including under U.S.'s PL-480 programme. At Bali, however, the Dr. Singh government meekly delinked the Trade Facilitation Agreement from a deal on food stockpiling. By agreeing to kick the can on the stockpiling issue to 2017, it put India's food security at risk in case no deal was reached by that deadline — a probable scenario. Mr. Modi has succeeded in undoing Dr. Singh's egregious concession by clinching a deal under which the developing counties' food-stockholding programmes will face no WTO challenge until a permanent solution is found, thus shielding them from pressures indefinitely.

Looking East

Fifth, Mr. Modi — unlike the leaders who preceded him — attaches major significance to diplomatic symbolism. For example, with the opening of the South Asian Association for Regional Cooperation (SAARC) Summit coinciding with the sombre anniversary of the Mumbai terror attacks, he gave the cold shoulder to his Pakistani counterpart, Nawaz Sharif, for refusing to prosecute the masterminds of that Pakistani scripted and executed operation. Mr. Modi shook hands with Mr. Sharif only the following day at the Dhulikhel retreat. In fact, to concentrate on his broader regional and global agenda, Mr. Modi has done well to sideline Pakistan, a noxious issue that weighed down Mr. Atal Bihari Vajpayee's foreign policy. Mr. Modi, in any event, faces an important dilemma on Pakistan: With whom to engage there? After being politically cut to size by the military establishment, Mr. Sharif is like a parrot perched on the generals' shoulders, trying to echo their lines on India, even if stutteringly.

To be sure, Mr. Modi faces major regional challenges, exemplified by the arc of failing, revanchist or scofflaw states around India. This tyranny of geography demands that India evolve more dynamic and innovative approaches to diplomacy and national defence. India must actively involve itself regionally to help influence developments, which is what Mr. Modi is seeking to do. Indeed, his priority — apparent from the time he invited regional leaders to his inauguration — is to retrieve India's lost ground in its backyard. As Pakistan's obstructionism at Kathmandu to greater intra-regional cooperation highlighted, SAARC is likely to remain a stunted organisation. India, while building stronger bilateral linkages with other neighbours, must strengthen its "Look East" policy. India indeed has little choice but to look east because when it looks west, it sees only trouble. The entire belt to India's west from Pakistan to Syria is a contiguous arc of instability and extremism. Looking east allows India to join the economic dynamism that characterises the region to its east.

For a politician who came to office with virtually no foreign-policy experience, Mr. Modi has demonstrated impressive diplomatic acumen, including in taking bold new directions, charting a vision to reclaim India's lost strategic clout, holding his ground in talks with world leaders, and responding to provocations by regional foes. Mr. Modi has shaken India's foreign policy establishment with his proactive approach and readiness to break with conventional methods and shibboleths.

All in all, the Modi foreign policy appears geared to reinvent India as a more competitive, confident and secure country claiming its rightful place in the world. A robust foreign policy, however, can sustain itself only on the foundation of a strong domestic policy, a realm where Mr. Modi must prove he can help transform India.

NARENDRA MODI: WHAT DOES HIS VICTORY MEAN FOR AMERICA, CHINA AND PAKISTAN?

When Narendra Modi, 63, formally assumes the highest executive office in this simultaneously troubled, joyous, chaotic democracy of 1.25bn people, he will have to reconcile the ideological and the pragmatic.

His campaign has already achieved this. Throughout India's protracted five-week election, his Bharatiya Janata party (BJP) carefully blended promises of economic development – reforms, better services, more jobs and security for all – with references that were both religious and cultural.

These ideas were rarely explicitly articulated, but were nonetheless clear in Modi's choice of Varanasi, the holy city on the Ganges, as a seat to contest and the occasional deity that appeared, in contravention of electoral codes, behind the stage at meetings. There were a series of statements by local BJP officials that appeared deliberately aimed at exploiting tensions between specific communities. There were also more assertive statements directed at neighbours Pakistan – with which India has fought four wars – and China – with which India has had one conflict – and a promise that Modi in power would create an Indiathat no one could talk down to on the international stage. There was even an apparent threat to revise India's "no first strike" nuclear weapons policy.

All came together in the slogan "India First", which apparently resonated with 180 million people tired of an uninspiring and apparently uncertain Congress party-led coalition government and its dynastic leaders. It got Modi to power, with the first majority seen in the Indian parliament for 30 years. But no one is quite sure what it means in terms of this huge and often fabulously insular country's relations with the region, and the rest of the world.

Modi is a polarising figure. He has emerged from, and is supported by, the Rashtriya Swayamsevak Sangh (RSS), the hardline Hindu nationalist organisation. The BJP is intimately linked to the RSS, which has been banned three times by Indian authorities. The RSS is deeply distrusting (and worse) of other religious minorities in India, suspicious of former colonial powers and the US, and committed to economic self-sufficiency for India.

And while his supporters see a man with an established record of honest, efficient and effective government, critics accuse Modi of harbouring deep sectarian prejudices and of allowing, or even encouraging, violence in which 1,000 people, largely Muslims, died while he was in power in Gujarat state in 2002. Though a supreme court investigation has found insufficient evidence to support the charges – which Modi has always denied – concerns remain.

His foreign affairs in-tray is overflowing. There are major multilateral issues such as climate change to get to grips with. An election is underway in Afghanistan, with 2014 a critical year for Indian interests there. To the east, political strife in Bangladesh is subsiding but few believe any calm will last long. India has proved unable to protect its businesses even in the tiny Maldives and in Burma. Further afield, the whole aftermath of the Arab Spring presents huge difficulties. India needs lots of fossil fuels, and huge quantities of imported oil. Iran is a long-term ally but demanding. The history of the Gujarat riots and the RSS connection is not going to simplify diplomacy anywhere in the Islamic world. The relationship with Europeans is underperforming, with negotiations on a trade agreement taking so long they have become a stock joke of ambassador's receptions in Delhi. British ministers keep turning up, keen to stress how much they admire all things Indian, especially large contracts. With all his interactions internationally, there is one obvious questions: which will triumph? The job-creating, wealth-building pragmatist or the ideologue? The three big tests, experts agree, will be relations with Pakistan, the US and China. Sitting in the back room of the BJP headquarters as the scale of Modi's win became clear, is Ravi Shankar Prasad, an ebullient lawyer turned politician whose vociferous style of argument is well-suited to the noisy shouting matches that pass as debates on Indian television. Prasad, deputy leader of the BJP in India's upper house and a key campaign strategist, is in a very good mood. India will be an "assertive power", he says, but one "with dignity, with responsibility and constitutional integrity".

However, Prasad explains, though India wants to dismantle the "wall of terrorism" that has separated Pakistan and India since partition, "the Pakistanis" need to be aware that "terrorism promoted from their soil" would no longer be tolerated.

The outgoing Congress government has struggled with the question of Pakistan. Manmohan Singh, the technocrat prime minister, was born in the neighbouring country before partition. But the attacks on Mumbai in 2008, when militants from the Pakistan-based Lashkar-e-Taiba group killed 166 people in India's commercial capital, sent a relationship that was already cool into deep freeze.

Some now say Modi, who has no need to prove his conservative credentials, could bring about a breakthrough. Pakistan, also a nuclear power, is currently run by a conservative, pro-business government under veteran politician and industrialist Nawaz Sharif. His brother, Shahbaz, in a recent interview with the Guardian, blamed his nation's powerful military for the failure to generate greater commerce between the two nations. Modi's commitment to economic development could see him push hard to broaden these commercial links – or even attempt a more radical gesture.

"It could be that Modi is Nixon in China for India and Pakistan," says Professor Ashutosh Varshney, of Brown University in the US. "Hindu nationalist visionaries have typically been better in dealing with Pakistan." Varshney's hopes are echoed by some Pakistani diplomats too. The precedent is the previous BJP administration of Atal Bihari Vajpayee, who travelled to Pakistan in 1999 to sign a peace deal, a year after ordering nuclear tests that brought about international sanctions.

The other sticking point for Pakistan is the disputed territory of Kashmir, where a low-level separatist insurgency continues. The BJP is committed to withdrawing the special constitutional provisions that guarantee Kashmir a degree of autonomy within India.

Concessions on this would be tough for Modi to envisage, let alone enact, experts say. On top of that, the region is evolving rapidly as the US and other remaining international combat troops are withdrawn from Afghanistan by the end of this year. Indian security officials fear this could result in a small army of unemployed militants who will head, or be directed, towards Kashmir or India itself, with the support of some elements of Pakistan's security establishment.

Even optimists such as Varshney admit that a major terrorist incident traced back to, or blamed on, Pakistan, could derail even the most committed effort to make peace. "Another Mumbai [attack] – which is unlikely but not impossible – would create serious pressure," he says.

Rivalling the relationship with Pakistan for complexity and potential for misunderstanding is that with the US.

As protocol demands, Barack Obama called the Indian prime minister elect over the weekend to express his hope that his win would help "fulfil the extraordinary promise of the US-India strategic partnership". Crucially, and here no one would have missed the significance, "the president invited Narendra Modi to visit Washington at a mutually agreeable time to further strengthen our bilateral relationship," said a government spokesperson.

This could occur as soon as the UN General Assembly in New York in September, when Modi could also visit Washington.

The visit is likely to be an extraordinary event with Modi – a teetotal, celibate, ascetic outsider who has shunned the sophisticated salons of India's power elite – suddenly pushed on to the world stage, and into a gruelling round of diplomatic engagements.

The public boilerplate, as it so often does, hides a difficult and often acrimonious relationship. If he has been happy to welcome US investors to Gujarat over the 13 years he has governed the state, there has been little love lost between Modi and Washington.

The administration of President George W Bush denied Modi a visa in 2005 under a 1998 US law barring entry to foreigners who have committed "particularly severe violations of religious freedom".

A boycott by senior US officials was only lifted earlier this year, when the US ambassador to India finally travelled to Gandhinagar, the state capital of Gujarat, to meet its chief minister. This, witnesses say, was a frosty occasion.

"I spoke to [Modi] a few years back about the boycott and whether he wanted me to push for it to be lifted," said one Modi aide, with international connections, last week. "He said: 'No, let them come to me. They will,' and he was right. They did."

Though Rajnath Singh, the powerful BJP president who is also close to the RSS, told the Guardian as the campaign opened, of the party's wish for better relations with the US, there is much repair work to be done.

Trade is still significant. Last month, Nisha Biswal, the top US diplomat for South Asia, said that the US wants bilateral trade of $500bn a year, up from about $100bn currently.

But, after an improvement a decade ago, and a controversial nuclear deal,relations between Delhi and Washington hit a new low five months ago when Devyani Khobragade, the Indian deputy consul general was arrested for visa fraud in New York, strip-searched and held in police custody. She was eventually released and flew back to India but the affair prompted a vitriolic reaction to what Indians saw as disrespectful bullying by the "Ugly American". This in turn prompted US commentators to accuse India of oversensitivity and behaviour unbecoming of an aspirant future power.

Still, some experts are optimistic. Michael Kugelman, at the Woodrow Wilson International Centre in Washington says Modi may get a warmer welcome than some predict. He points out that the only US government agency to be critical of Modi for some time is the US Commission on International Religious Freedom, which warned of the impact a Modi-led government might have on minorities in India.

"Washington doesn't know him very well and I think that's the major concern. There was never any real hostility," Kugelman says. Indeed, Modi's backstory, the former tea seller who "pulled himself up by his bootstraps and then embraced capitalism and the free market and became seen as a decisive and confident leader", has much appeal in the US.

"There are a lot of tensions in the relationship but they tend to revolve around economics and I could see him as a pro-investor and pro-trade leader saying: 'Let's try and make some progress'," Kugelman adds.

Perhaps the biggest challenge for Modi on the world stage will be China. Few in India, where annual economic growth has dropped to less than 5% in recent years, now talk of catching up their neighbour.

Indeed, for Modi, China may appear to be less a rival than an opportunity. He has been there four times on official visits – more than any other country – and, aides say, admires what has been achieved in the country. On his last five-day tour, Modi carried red business cards printed in Chinese.

Modi is also said to feel more at home among the technocrats of Beijing than in the west. Critics frequently accuse him of authoritarian instincts in his career so far, of muzzling the press, of creating a "climate of fear" and of sidelining those who disagree with him. If Washington sees a Horatio Alger, Beijing may see a figure who represents less an American dream and more an East Asian one.

But Modi will still come up against the fundamental tension between his nationalism and his desire to accelerate economic development.

He may want to see Chinese investment in India's insufficient infrastructure – in trains, roads, power stations – but China has already proclaimed its ownership of the 21st century and Modi's victory speech pronouncement that the coming decades would constitute "India's century" is unlikely to have been well received in Beijing. Nor his attack, while on the campaign trail, on the Chinese "expansionist mindset".

The two countries frequently dispute their Himalayan border. "There is a [border] transgression every two days and some [such incidents] are critical," says Professor Srikanth Kondapalli, a China expert at Delhi's Jawaharlal Nehru University. "A BJP prime minister will have a hard job to explain to the people why border transgressions are happening and he cannot do anything about it. As a nationalist leader, this sovereignty dispute will really test Indo-Chinese relations."

Kondapalli's prediction is that, for at least the first years of his term in power, Modi will put development before ideology but warns, as others warn of Pakistan, that the big test will come when India is seen to be provoked.

This week, Modi will form his government and pick his foreign ministers. His choice will be a key early indication of which way the man, who until two years ago was boycotted by the US and most of Europe, is leaning.

Will it be ideology or pragmatism? Nationalist pride and sovereignty first, or jobs and growth? Or perhaps a clever blending of both, like his campaign rhetoric?

Varshney believes Modi's landslide win will give him both a "long honeymoon" with voters and the legitimacy to hold the hardline nationalists at bay. He says: "So long as it is Modi's ambition to rise – not only on an Indian stage, but on a world stage – that drives him, he will discipline and restrain the extreme wing of the party. And as long as his driving force is the desire to reshape India and be remembered as the greatest prime minister since [independence leader] Jawaharlal Nehru, you will see a more pragmatic Modi."

But no one can be sure: either of Modi, or of his environment. In an unstable region, and in a vast country that is undergoing rapid social, political and cultural change, there are too many possibilities for anyone to be overly optimistic. The consensus among analysts is that it is not Modi's policy-making that could give cause for concern, but his potential response to a crisis – particularly if that crisis prompted a wave of nationalist indignation or anger.

After all, there are many in India who see Modi's victory as a sign of greater changes to come. One is Anuraj Dikshit, 40, a marketing executive who splits his time between Mumbai and Gurgaon. He talks of not of India but Bharat, a Sanskrit-origin word describing a Hindu civilisation.

"This is not about warmongering but about this country's culture," he says. "India has been there since 1947. Bharat has been there since time immemorial. Now Bharat has come back, validated and endorsed by the voters of this country."

UNTANGLING THE WEB OF INDIA, CHINA AND PAKISTAN DIPLOMACY

On the eve of Prime Minister Narendra Modi's visit to China, Xinhua published a rare opinion piece by his Pakistani counterpart Nawaz Sharif. The obvious choreography of the visit and article shows the delicate balance in relations between China, India and Pakistan.

For Beijing, both powers are important if it is to realize its ambitious strategy of trade and economic corridors emanating from the Middle Kingdom under the rubric of the Silk Road Economic Belt. For current governments in Islamabad and New Delhi, Beijing's economic miracle offers a way of helping develop their economies. Yet we are some way off before this trilateral relationship will be able to live up to its potential as the economic powerhouse at the centre of Asia. Islamabad reaped substantial benefits from President Xi Jinping's delayed visit to Pakistan. The formalization of the China-Pakistan Economic Corridor (CPEC) to the tune of $46 billion signalled a major investment by China into Pakistan's future (even if one takes a skeptical view that the money was repackaged old deals and multiple-year contracts conflated for a public announcement).

The current outline for the CPEC is a multistage strategy starting with the development of Pakistan's parlous energy infrastructure and the redevelopment of its road, rail and pipeline network. A series of economic zones will be established along the CPEC route in Pakistan to attract industry that is finding itself increasingly priced out of Chinese markets. As envisaged, the corridor will not only open up China's western regions to the seas through Gwadar Port, but also create a latticework of prosperity across Pakistan.

India has traditionally seen a close China-Pakistan relationship as a source of concern. Seeing it as a relationship that is built on the foundations of anti-Indian sentiment, hawks in New Delhi are concerned by this proximity. But the new government of Narendra Modi has appeared willing to open up a new conversation with Beijing, one that tries to look beyond these historical tensions to build stronger economic ties, resolve long-standing border disputes and helps reshape the global order to the advantage of the two Asian giants. China has also offered a direct link to India in one of the numerous trade corridors it is pushing out from Beijing — in the form of the Bangladesh-China-India-Myanmar (BCIM) Corridor.

But underlying these optimistic perspectives are a number of fundamental problems, the most central of which is regional security. In the context of CPEC, security in Pakistan (in the form of growing sectarianism, terrorism, as well as separatists in Baluchistan) and in neighbouring Afghanistan pose major threats to the route. And while India may be interested in the BCIM as a potential concept, it remains concerned about encirclement by China through the Maritime Silk Road and the network of relationships China is building in the Indian Ocean as well as the ongoing border tensions in Ladakh. India has continued to keep China out of SAARC and Modi's Project Mausam is a direct pushback to China's maritime strategy, in contrast to the country's willingness to engage on the BRICS Bank, AIIB and to work on joint projects in Iran.

And bringing the trilateral complexity of these relationships into focus are incidents like theattack on the Park Palace Hotel in Kabul. While it remains unclear what the ultimate target was, the potential presence of the Indian Ambassador and Indian casualties immediately painted the incident as part of the shadow war between Pakistani intelligence and the Taliban on the one side, and Afghan intelligence and their Indian supporters on the other. Such incidents stoke paranoia on all sides and complicate efforts to try to forge a regional peace and stability. The China-India-Pakistan trilateral relationship is a complicated one. All three need each other to succeed, but do not believe this to be the case, remaining fiercely independent in their outlooks and jealous when the other two appear to be moving closer together. On the one hand, China has the potential to act as an honest broker, offering economic investment to all while trying to help offer a platform for discussions. But in reality, China wants no part of a situation where it ends being responsible for brokering peace in such a fractious part of the world, and it continues to take advantage of opportunities to assert its dominance over its Asian neighbours. For India and Pakistan, history continues to be stuck in the legacies of partition.

Yet this is a trio of countries that together account for about a third of the world's population and where future prosperity is likely to come from. The danger at the moment is the assumption that economic development and prosperity will resolve everything and is the goal that needs to be achieved for regional stability. In reality, all three powers need to shed their historical legacies, and find ways of ending the paranoid tensions that underlie their global outlooks. Until this has been achieved, the CPEC, BCIM and any other regional economic framework will be undermined and no long-term stability will be found in the heart of South Asia.

PM TO PAK: READY FOR TALKS BUT VIOLENCE WILL BE MET WITH FORCE

A year into Narendra Modi's prime ministership, relations between India and Pakistan are in many ways unchanged. The role Pakistan plays in India's broader foreign policy, however, has been evolving and is increasingly complex. The initiatives taken by Modi, and his capacity to surprise outsiders' expectations, have gained him political space, both internally and externally. But India's position vis-à-vis Pakistan and more broadly in the Indian Subcontinent is increasingly constrained by China's growing clout in South Asian affairs.

Over the past 12 months, relations between the two countries have experienced everything short of open conflict. The invitation of Pakistan's Prime Minister Nawaz Sharif to Modi's inauguration prompted a cautious optimism. However, positive developments were soon soured by the unsettled question of Pakistan granting most favoured nation status to India and India's cancellation of the bilateral foreign secretaries' talks in July. By the end of summer, the two countries were exchanging artillery fire. However, foreign secretary S Jaishankar's visit to Pakistan in March marked the resumption of the dialogue between Islamabad and New Delhi. The meeting between the two foreign secretaries ended with no major announcement.

Substantially, the new policy has not borne any fruit and Modi has obtained nothing more than any of his predecessors and was probably not expecting to. New Delhi is still unable to coerce Islamabad into any agreement of its liking. Its strategic options remain limited to either punishing Pakistan or prompting dialogue, although both options can be avoided. Pakistan — more specifically the evolution of civil-military relations in Islamabad, rather than Indian politics — remains the key to eventual normalisation between the two countries.

It would be a mistake, however, to conclude that Modi's first year in office has brought no new developments in the bilateral relationship. By retaliating systematically to every Pakistani provocation in the early stages of his mandate he has strengthened his image as a strongman and gained domestic political support at no or limited cost and risk.

Externally, Modi has also managed to increase his ability to ignore Pakistan while avoiding international pressures. The message sent to Pakistan over the past 12 months has been consistent and simple: India is ready for dialogue, but will respond to any Pakistan recourse to violence with disproportionate force.

Islamabad has been cornered into a defensive position, forced to continuously demonstrate the seriousness of its willingness to talk to India while simultaneously exposing its own internal contradictions over the relationship. The result has been the Pakistani military and some like-minded civilians resorting to new provocations every time the government attempts to improve its relationship with India. However, it is no coincidence that these provocations have become increasingly less violent. The release of Zaki-ur-Rehman Lakhvi, a top leader of the Lashkar-e-Taiba and the mastermind of the 26/11 Mumbai terrorist attacks, may be enough to thwart any real dialogue between India and Pakistan, but it is much less lethal than the infiltration of terrorists across the LoC and potential terrorist attacks in Jammu & Kashmir or elsewhere.

The picture changes slightly in a broader perspective. India's relations with Pakistan are both facilitated and increasingly constrained by China's growing influence in the region. Modi's diplomacy vis-à-vis Pakistan has been aided by the rapprochement with Beijing and Washington initiated by his predecessor and reinvigorated since he took office. China's desire to benefit from India's economic growth and to prevent New Delhi from growing too close to Washington has prompted Beijing to pursue a more nuanced India policy. While Beijing remains Islamabad's strongest regional ally and will likely ensure that it remains a potential threat for India, the Chinese leadership also seems determined to not let its Pakistan policy stand in the way of better relations with India.

On the other side, the new Chinese attitude is not without risks for India. While Islamabad's policy vis-à-vis New Delhi is becoming increasingly contingent upon Beijing's own interests in South Asia, it comes with the growing influence of China across South Asia. China's dynamic economic diplomacy, which India is currently unable to match, makes Beijing's presence felt in every corner of the subcontinent. China may have a moderating influence on Pakistan, but it is now also a facilitator of Pakistan's policy in Afghanistan.

Even the United States' role in the region has become increasingly uncertain for India. Washington may be willing to cooperate with New Delhi on counter-terrorism, but its determination to extricate itself from the Afghan conflict by de facto delegating the management of the conflict to China and Pakistan only reinforces India's problem.

Modi cannot be held responsible for this situation. He inherited the structural and growing capacity problem he is facing vis-à-vis China in Pakistan and elsewhere. Pakistan is using its own weakness as an argument for requesting support as much with China as it does with the United States, even though the extent to which China is willing to play along remains unclear. A close examination of the actual investments announced by Xi Jinping during his recent visit to Pakistan shows more promise than actual commitment. For the time being, however, the Pakistani security establishment seems to take comfort in the idea that, at least economically, China will come to Pakistan's rescue should the need arise. This has allowed them to resist every attempt to normalise economic relations with India. In such conditions, Modi can at best be a skilful manager of the India-Pakistan relationship, but a skilful manager of the status quo.

3

Modi's Unexpected Successes in Foreign Policy

Exactly two years ago, Prime Minister Narendra Modi surprised both Indian and foreign observers by inviting the South Asian heads of government to his swearing-in. For a leader who had barely uttered a word about foreign policy during his election campaign, this dramatic and welcome gesture presaged the first of many foreign policy surprises that Modi would unveil.

His emphasis on strengthening ties with India's immediate neighbours, his redoubled investment in protecting Indian interests in the larger Indian Ocean region, his remarkable outreach to the United States despite past personal irritants, his intensification of the emerging partnership with Japan, his success in preserving balanced ties with both China and Russia, and his nurturing of important partners in Western Europe, Central and Southeast Asia, and in the Persian Gulf (where he demonstrated a geopolitical adroitness unusual in Indian foreign policy) have all been complemented by an unanticipated investment in building personal ties with Pakistan's Prime Minister Nawaz Sharif and in energising a diaspora that stretches from Canada to Fiji. Because these efforts have involved much globetrotting, they have often become objects of controversy within India. His critics have charged that his peripateticism betrays an addiction to the glamour of world travel to the neglect of his domestic responsibilities. Such criticism, however, is churlish: Modi's engagements abroad are in fact anchored in the astute recognition that India's domestic success is inextricably linked to how it can shape its external environment to national advantage. All Indian leaders since Jawaharlal Nehru have understood this fully, though their ability to play a winning hand was often hampered by political and economic weaknesses at home.

Thankfully today, Modi is less constrained on both these counts: He enjoys a lofty standing within the country, while the economy steadily recovers despite an unfavourable international environment. For all these assets, however, Modi recognises that, in an era of deepening globalisation, what happens abroad impacts India's strategic and developmental goals. His efforts at shaping international developments long before they actually affect India are thus completely warranted.

It is not surprising, therefore, that of the 40-odd trips Modi has undertaken since June 2014, the vast majority have arguably been focused on moulding the global environment to India's benefit. Whether this has involved shoring up ties with key neighbours such as Afghanistan, Bhutan or Bangladesh, or reaching out to states historically neglected by India, such as Mongolia, or strengthening links with nations that are critical for Indian economic success, such as Germany, or renewing ties with those Asian countries important for India's strategic interests, such as Australia, Japan or Singapore, and the "-stans," or further transforming relations with the United States, Modi has invested time and attention not merely in building personal ties with their leaders but also in persuading them to engage with India in ways that redound to its gain.

Beyond these geostrategic aims, Modi has focused at least a third of his foreign travels on advancing Indian economic aims. For the most part, these have concentrated on attracting foreign investment to India. By addressing complaints about the ease of doing business and by removing obstacles to investments, Modi has attempted to woo investors in countries as disparate as China, Japan, the United Arab Emirates, the United Kingdom, Ireland, Canada, and the US — not to mention the myriad middle powers in continental Europe. Pursuing closer foreign economic relations is no longer optional for New Delhi, as Modi fully realises: India simply does not save enough domestically to generate high single-digit growth rates consistently over a long horizon. This constraint, which affects everything from employment to investment, can be mitigated by external investment.

Finally, Modi has attempted to use a small but growing proportion of his time abroad to highlight India's desire to contribute to the production of global public goods as well as to spotlight the contributions of peoples of Indian origin.

Benefiting from India's new ascendency as one of the world's fastest growing major economies and consistent with his own vision of India as a "leading power", Modi has sought to burnish India's reputation as a good international citizen by increasing its contributions to everything from mitigating climate change to supporting nation- and State-building activities (especially in its neighbourhood) to promoting nuclear security to enhancing peace and stability in the Indian Ocean.

While these benefactions remain modest relative to India's potential, Modi's emphasis on them as a means of realising the Upanishadic ideal of Vasudhaiva Kutumbakam (the entire world is one family) bodes well for their persistence, as both idealism and realism promise to take India in the same direction.

The fact that individuals of Indian origin have widely succeeded in their adopted countries further incarnates this promise.

Viewed at the two-year mark of his term in office, Modi's foreign policy achievements have been outstanding. Some of his initiatives have admittedly fallen short, the attempted rapprochement with Pakistan being a conspicuous example. But even this exception does not besmirch the larger record. More than anything else, it signals India's return to a sensible activism in fashioning the world about it and, just as importantly, is driven boldly by the imperative of securing India's interests first.

GLOBAL POWER STATUS ON THE BASIS OF MORAL STANDING

India's foreign policy evolved as a "dual" pattern, encompassing a global as well as a regional role. The two roles were run on a very different basis, as relations with India's neighbours were conducted on a much more realistic policy course as opposed to the moralistic international policy. The regional dimension was based on the fact that India was the hegemon in the region and would do everything to remain so.

The Non Aligned Movement (NAM) was created out of the desire to orient India's foreign policy towards the group of newly decolonized states, hoping to create a larger area of peace by fighting common dangers of imperialism and racialism together.1 Nehru wanted India to be the leader of the developing world, in this way carving out a global role for the country. The principle of India's leadership was to be based on moral rather than economic power.

India's relations with the superpowers during the cold war were difficult as its non aligned status was never really accepted by the US who saw India as being in the Soviet camp. India's desire for economic self sufficiency also went against the grain of the concept of free market economy, which was being pushed by the western powers. On the other hand relations with the Soviet Union were cordial with substantial trade and barter trade underlying the relationship. However India never subscribed to the communist world's ideology, trying to combine a socialist economy with a democratic system at home. India refused to be apart of any defence pact or to take sides against either the western powers or the communist bloc.

Nehru believed that these idealistic broad concepts used in global policy formulation could also be used at the "micro-level", subject to some minor adjustments. Later, after Nehru's death this was dropped, making place for a more regional, realistic and forceful policy first under Indira Gandhi and later under Rajiv Gandhi, especially with regard to the South Asian region.

The main incident, which established India as a regional power, was the creation of Bangladesh. 1971 was crucial for India's position in the region. The flood of refugees that poured into India had severe effects on the economy and on India's social structure. Out of economic and strategic necessity India trained, armed and then gave combat support to the Bangladeshi refugees.2

India's regional priority has been to disallow the destabilisation of any neighbouring states by any internal or external forces. This includes the monitoring of ethnic conflicts on the borders in the North East, Bhutan or Sri Lanka, and the promotion of regional co-operation.

There are of course many obstacles to regional co-operation, paramount India's size and position as a hegemon, but it is also understood to be the only possibility for political and economic stability in the region. Nevertheless the regional part of the policy formulation was always rather ill defined and generally "reactive" in nature. The main emphasis was on establishing a security zone against possible threats from China.

The Chinese factor has been a sore point in India's foreign relations. Although China is a neighbour, it cannot be counted as part of the South Asian region, geographically set apart by the Himalayan mountain range. India and China are natural rivals and the relationship has been problematic over the years including border issues in Kashmir, India's North East, the status of Tibet and Sikkim.

Nehru's political understanding involved advocating a policy of friendship, avoiding the isolation of newly communist China. In this way he hoped to establish a "normal" world order where Indo-Chinese co-operation would lead the newly independent countries of the third world. Throughout this time India upheld China's issues at the UN and recognised Taiwan as part of China. When in 1950 China asserted its authority in Tibet, Nehru exercised restraint. In 1954 the two countries signed an agreement on Tibet which proclaimed the "Panchsheel" doctrine, the five principles of peaceful coexistence.

The Indian humiliation of Oct./Nov. 1962 at the hand of the Chinese armed forces, made the nation realise that its relatively unarmed foreign policy towards China had failed to provide the necessary security and that idealism was no substitute for realism. India felt it was threatened by both its immediate neighbours, Pakistan and China, neither of which subscribed to non-alignment, and therefore a modern defence force had become necessary. This section serves as a reminder how India's global and regional foreign policies were formulated prior to the economic reforms and to underline how until the early 1990s India's international foreign policy was idealistically oriented. India's national interest was seen both regionally and globally in solely in political and ideological terms with hardly any economic component.

The changes after the economic reforms

The 1991 economic reforms saw the birth for a new role for international economic and trade relations. India suddenly had to engage with the post cold war world and reassess its foreign policy priorities. The opening up the economy to international players also meant that foreign relations had an economic dimension and trade became a foreign policy tool. Leaving *swadeshi*, economic self-sufficiency behind and engaging in international trade was India's new way forward. The Congress government under Narasimha Rao initiated economic reforms, however worried that the economic pain of free trade and privatisation would hit the poorer section of India's society and increase the already large disparities.

After the Congress lost power, the United Front governments under Deve Gowda and I.K. Gujaral started to focus more on foreign policy and foreign relations. In part this was due to India coming to term with its first coalition government where consensus on domestic affairs was not always forthcoming. The I.K. Gujaral peace moves towards Pakistan were a direct result of this - as were Deve Gowda's economic interest in South East Asia and the *'Look East'* policy with a clear vision for India's North Eastern states.

The 'look East' policy was a part of India's re-assessment of its role in the wider region, for the first time looking at Southeast Asia as a neighbour which mattered politically and economically. As India was looking for new markets and relations with the US still had not warmed up, a strategic decision to focus on Southeast Asia was taken. Closer cooperation with ASEAN was seen as a new priority, as it became increasingly clear that due to frosty relations with the neighbouring countries, SAARC was not going to be a huge success in terms of multi-lateral trade.

The BJP's vision was one of a multi-polar world7 in which economic relations were going to be crucial. Regional policy became of prime importance, especially with regard to improving trade and improving the situation in India's border states. In part the BJP's moves towards Pakistan have to be seen in this light, but more so its' increase interest in the North East8, which included starting a peace process with various insurgency groups as well as improving relations with Myanmar. There seems to have been an inherent understanding that the region could not be developed without international cooperation across the border. The BJP's foreign policy priorities have not been that different to that of Congress – i.e. to be and remain the regional hegemon with global power aspirations. However the BJP realised that the post cold war world needed a different approach based on trade and not on Nehruvian morality and righteousness. The BJP, unlike previous Congress governments also saw that there are direct links between foreign policy formulation and domestic policy, especially in the economic realm.

Despite the fact that the BJP had campaigned on an anti economic reforms ticket, they continued and intensified the reforms after forming their coalition government called the National Democratic Alliance (NDA). India's opening up saw the rise of multi-national corporations, which resulted high growth with limited infrastructural development. The businesses – mainly multinationals, but also some large Indian firms gained better access to the Indian government in the 90s. Their agenda was focused on increased open markets and more trade, internationally as well as regionally. Indian businesses have always been aware that Indo-Pakistani and Indo-Chinese trade could be huge. As a result trade lobbies formed and have become more powerful in the political realm in Delhi in order to influence the decision making process. During the Kargil war, there were reports that businesses in India and outside were lobbying for a quick solution so as to not loose the multinationals and so that trade would not be lost either. Consequently since the economic reforms, businesses have become a new type of political actors or are at the very least influencing political decisions.

As a part of this new strategy, relations with the US, Israel and Myanmar were all revived. These were countries India aspired to keep away from for various reasons: the US for its imperialistic global bullying strategy, Israel for its war against the Palestinians and Myanmar for its undemocratic government in light of the 1990 elections. The 9/11 war on terror changed relations with the US for good. India saw in this an opportunity to ally itself with the US and portray the Kashmir problem as a part of the war on terror. The US was seen as a powerful economic ally holding the purse strings of various international funds. An agreement with Israel on the same basis meant that India could buy arms it would never had access to before. Peace or a dialogue about peace with Pakistan was seen as essential. Peace meant that India would finally be seen as an economically safe region for international investment. It also meant that the BJP would then be able to focus on internal changes. The government finally decided to tackle the China factor for the first time. India has for decades seen itself threatened militarily and economically by China. Disputed border issues have not been tackled as successive governments feared opening up 'Pandora's box'. However with China's increasing economic might in the region, India needed to improve relations and increase trade quickly. Finally the recognition of Tibet was exchanged against the recognition of Sikkim, a significant step in the move away from moralistic foreign policy vis-à-vis a neighbour.

These changes have '[...]to be understood as a larger re-orientation that has taken place since the end of the Cold War'9 where the US has come to dominate international politics. The Nuclear threshold was crossed by the BJP with the tests in May 1998 and showed the world that India would take on a more realist and pragmatic orientation. It was defended to Parliament with the statement: 'it is India's due, the right of one sixth of human kind'.10 The gamble paid off as it brought a closer engagement with the US.11

What this section wants to emphasize is that the aims of all governments, including that of the BJP12, have been the same as Nehru's – to make India a major world power. India has always been suspicious of US neo-imperialist designs, however engagement with the US was seen as a key element in defining India's future. The NDA was able to make the link between improved economic growth, willingness to reform and improved international standing.

Consequently since the 1991 reforms, but especially under the NDA government India's foreign policy formulation has been conducted on the basis of trade and power priorities as a mechanism to hegemony. At a larger level, this move fits in with globalisation and the increasing power of business in government policy formulation, not only in Asia but in the world at large.

INDIA TRIES TO FORGE A NEW RELATIONSHIP WITH CHINA

The visit by Indian Prime Minister Narendra Modi to China last week (May 14-16) was never going to be easy. Modi was hard-pressed to juggle his agenda of economic reinvigoration at home ("development agenda") with his firmer assertion of India's security interests. The balance-sheet of his visit underscores the policy dilemma.

Modi has reason to feel relieved that he is not returning to India quite empty-handed. His travels abroad and wanderlust (visiting 18 countries in the past one year) is being criticised in India as wasteful, extravagant and bombastic, and largely unproductive from the country's point of view, while his theatrical performances during visits abroad look jaded already to the Indian audience. Yet, this is one foreign visit where he could claim some business outcome.

After all, deals worth $ 22 billion were initialled, including substantial quantum of Chinese bank loans for Indian companies. This will be touted as a feather on Modi's cap. But then, on closer examination, many of these documents are in the nature of MOUs (memoranda of understanding) that are non-binding in character. They are good for the optics, but may not get implemented.

Indeed, there has been no tangible progress on the ground on the proposals regarding two "industrial parks" to be set up in India by China, which were mentioned during Chinese President Xi Jinping's visit to India last September. Nor is there any sign of Chinese involvement in India's railway sector other than by way of technical cooperation. There is no sign of China embracing Modi's "Make in India" plans, either. Clearly, issues relating to trade imbalance and India's investment climate are impeding progress.

Having pledged $ 46 billion for the China-Pakistan Economic Corridor recently, and another $ 40 billion in the South-East Asian economies for infrastructure projects, Beijing may not be in a tearing hurry to make investments in India. There were no focused discussions on China's "Belt and Road Initiatives" during Modi's visit. The Indian officials disclosed that China never so far broached the "Belt and Road" with Delhi.

No substantial progress on the negotiations for a border settlement could be discerned, although the topic figured, as usual, for a "fair amount" of discussion. The Chinese side didn't relent on the resumption of talks on the clarification of the Line of Actual Control (LAC), presumably reflecting its apprehension that an agreed LAC might morph into a de facto boundary. The fact of the matter is that China is playing the long game on its territorial issues and is not in a mood to compromise with anyone. In India's case, China will also wait and watch how India handles the election of the Dalai Lama's successor; that is going to be a defining moment in the overall relationship. So, for the present we have to make do with the small steps that the boundary negotiations offer and preserve the peace and tranquillity on the disputed border. A few more confidence-building measures have been put in place during Modi's visit, and there will be additional military-to-military exchanges. Period.

Equally, there has been no shift in China's ambivalent stance on India's bid to become a permanent member of the United Nations Security Council. Of course, China refrains from endorsing India's membership of the Nuclear Suppliers Group, too.

The overall impression becomes unavoidable that as regards the core issues, India-China relationship is set to maintain its incremental advancement of the recent years ("stable development", as the Chinese side puts it). In retrospect, the high hopes raised by Modi when he came to power were somewhat misplaced, although the rhetoric is still there — on Modi's part, at least.

In the media briefings, the Indian side claimed that "there was an overall sense that we needed to move on the outstanding issues, but we also needed to develop a more positive narrative of our relationship and to build higher levels of trust... today the relationship is poised at a very important juncture where there are possibilities of moving forward." It does sound like so being near, and, yet, so far away. Clearly, the strategic distrust cannot be wished away.

Modi himself framed it this way: "I stressed the need for China to reconsider its approach on some of the issues that hold us back from realising the full potential of our partnership. I suggested that China should take a strategic and long term view of our relations. I found the Chinese leadership responsive." The surprising thing is that he spoke up at all on these lines. Why did he have to?

But the Chinese side went out of the way to reciprocate Modi's personal enthusiasm for the Sino-Indian ties. President

Xi Jinping himself received Modi in his hometown of Xian in a first-ever departure from the established Chinese practice of receiving foreign dignitaries.

They clocked something like four hours together in Xian, talking politics or simply chatting up and enjoying themselves with the sights and sounds of the ancient city. It was almost an accurate replay of the cordial reception that Modi accorded to Xi in his home State of Gujarat last September — native vegetarian cuisine, colourful pageantry, pleasant informality and so on. The Chinese wouldn't quarrel with Modi's pet thesis that close personal equations at the leadership level can make a qualitative difference to the normalisation process.

But it is difficult to guage how far the Chinese really bet on Modi's capacity to bring about a big transformation in the bilateral relationship, which is ridden with complexities. During the past one-year period in power, Modi hasn't exactly lived up to his carefully cultivated image of being a "visionary".

Arguably, a window of opportunity would have been there in the early months of the Modi Government—and Beijing probably expected a breakthrough too, given the overtures it manife-stly made to the new government in Delhi—but that window slams shut with the Opposition regrouping in Indian politics and a combative edge reappearing lately. The main Opposition, the Congress Party, has alleged that Modi is compromising on India's national interests in his dealings with China.

If the ruling party continues to face electoral reverses in the provincial elections, especially in the forthcoming election in the second biggest State of Bihar in autumn, Modi's political standing could get seriously affected—and, indeed, his capacity to push through contro-versial decisions such as the border settlement with China will be in serious doubt.

Of course, Modi has no magic wand to disperse the huge backlog of strategic distrust that has accumulated in the relationship. On top of it, the Right-wing Hindu nationalist groups in India, which happen to be the mentors of the Modi

Government, deeply distrust China's intentions—notwithstanding Beijing's assiduous efforts to "cultivate" the Rashtriya Swayam-sevak Sangh in the recent years.

Modi has to contend with a formidable phalanx of institutional opposition to advance any transformative diplomacy vis-à-vis China. But, having said that, a degree of ambiguity always existed as to how far Modi himself would exert to marginalise these powerful forces arrayed against any flexible or pragmatic approach to China—or, to put it differently, whether he might not even be making use of them for his own purposes to create leverage and to impress the Chinese that India is not a pushover.

To be sure, India's need for friendship and cooperation with China today outweighs China's need to be seen holding India's hand. Yet, the nationalist lobby is convinced that India should be in no great hurry to woo China and should instead settle for the "Long March". Influential voices within the nationalist lobby even recomm-end an autarchic path for India's development that would altogether dispense with the need of getting Chinese investment and expertise by India simply getting its own act together in terms of the improvement of the domestic business climate and managing on its own resources.

The unspoken factor here is the massive upgrade of China's relations with Pakistan that is taking place, which not only upsets India's strategic calculus but is also a matter of great sensitivity to the Hindu nationalist groups mentoring the Modi Government, who are re-defining India's secular identity.

Quite obviously, China-Pakistan relationship is no longer India-centric and is fast assuming a trans-regional and global character, with the proposed Economic Corridor promising to be one of China's main gateways to the world market in a near-term, which in turn boosts the strategic partnership between the two "all-weather" friends. The development of the Gwadar Port and the strong likelihood of the Chinese Navy making its presence there and the expanding military ties between China and Pakistan lethally undercut India's aspirations as the pre-eminent power in the Indian Ocean region.

However, it is highly improbable that China will give up its leap of faith toward Pakistan, which is crucial to Beijing's global strategies, by way of accommodating the Indian wishes. (India has protested against the proposed Economic Corridor that passes through the disputed Kashmir region.) The spectre of a US-India alliance also doesn't seem to unduly worry China anymore, given the new level of self-confidence in the Chinese world-view and foreign policies.

This found reflected in the official Indian briefing on Modi's talks in China, which kept harping on the "two major powers dealing with each other, two major powers in the region and in the world... who will be dealing with each other with mutual respect and sensitivity, and who will be taking into account each other's concerns, interests and aspirations... (in) a constructive model of relationship... (of) strategic communication and strategic coordi-nation".

The briefing marked a noticeable shift in the narrative pursued by the previous government in Delhi. A keen sense of competition bordering on rivalry vis-à-vis China is apparent in the Indian policies in recent months. If China has a Silk Route, India shall have a Cotton Route; if Xi linked his visit to India with visits to Colombo, India would respond likewise by getting Modi into Ulanbator (where he headed, in fact, from China to experience "true friend-ship" from the Mongols, as he put it sardonically). India has at no time before edged this close as it is today with the US' Asia-Pacific strategies.

But what is the point? India lags behind China in development by half-a-century and its capacity to leverage a "new type of relationship" remains seriously in doubt. The complex relationship could have done without the injection of such heavy strategic baggage at this juncture and instead could have focused on building mutually beneficial content—in sum, a China policy that optimally tapped into that country's growth for catalysing the development of the Indian economy.

Modi's gambit is to keep Beijing off-balance, and a little worried, perhaps, by wooing other nations as a counterbalance to China, while at the same time on a parallel track attract investments and money from that country for galvanising his "development agenda". In essence, Modi is following in some ways the example of Japan, which too has plenty of political differences and strategic issues and an intractable territorial dispute to sort out with China, but maintains close economic relationship.

It's a gambit because India is not Japan, but Modi thinks he can pull it off.

INDIA-ISRAEL TIES UNDER NARENDRA MODI

India and Israel are now making their private affair public. Is this stark departure one of style or substance? Relations between India and Israel are experiencing a diplomatic renaissance. Indian Prime Minister Narendra Modi's landslidevictory in India's elections last year has ushered in a new, conspicuously more visible phase of bilateral ties.

Cooperation with Israel—conducted secretly throughout most of India's history—has now become a public affair. Modi has openly and enthusiastically embraced the Jewish state. Although some wonder whether the change is merely one of style rather than substance, there is no question that India's recent public displays of affection toward Israel are a stark departure from the past. If current trends continue, the Modi government could become the most pro-Israel government New Delhi has ever seen.

Throughout most of its post-independence history, India benefitted privately from Israel while refusing to publicly acknowledge it. New Delhi voted to recognize Israel in 1950, but Cold War alignments, fear of alienating its large Muslim population, and its need to maintain strong ties to the Arab world over the Kashmir issue resulted in New Delhi adopting an unsympathetic, if not outright hostile, posture toward Israel.

India reflexively supported the Palestinian position, viewing the conflict in zero-sum terms. But this did not stop New Delhi from covertly acceptingcritical intelligence and military assistance from the Jewish state during its wars with China in 1962 and with Pakistan in 1965 and 1971. The collapse of the Soviet Union brought with it the end of the ideological and geopolitical foundations of India's longstanding Israel policy. New Delhi sought a more pragmatic and balanced approach to the region. With some help from Washington, India finally established full diplomatic relations with Israel in 1992, the last major non-Arab country to do so. Both countries quickly moved to make up for lost time, pursuing cooperation in a wide array of arenas ranging from security and defense to education and agriculture.

Although it was India's left-leaning Congress Party that normalized relations with Israel, ties flourished under the country's Hindu nationalist Bharatiya Janata Party (BJP). Leaders in both countries expressly emphasized the ideological affinity their two nations shared as democracies and longstanding victims of terrorism. The two states embarked on a strategic partnership, with Israel emerging as one of India's most important military suppliers. Following the Congress Party's return to power in 2004, however, New Delhi appeared to revert back to past tendencies, preferring cooperation with Israel behind closed doors. Ties were shoved firmly back in the closet.

Ten years later, the outlook appeared very different. Modi had forged a personal connection with Israel long before becoming prime minister. In 2006, he visited Tel Aviv as chief minister of his home state of Gujarat and spoke glowingly about what India could learn from Israel. Modi actively courted Israeli investment and expertise, harnessing them to help achieve Gujarat's storied economic growth. Notably, Israel extended the invitation to Modi at a time when he was unwelcome in many countries, including the United States, for his purported role in failing to stem communal riots in Gujarat in 2002. Proponents of stronger Indian-Israeli ties hoped that a Modi-led BJP victory would lead to a more public relationship and even-handed approach to the region.

The optimism proved justified. Less than two months after Modi's election, signs emerged that New Delhi was again recalibrating its posture toward Israel and the Palestinian conflict. Just days after Israel launched its controversial Operation Protective Edge in the Gaza Strip last summer, India's Foreign Ministry released a statement signaling its alarm over the civilian loss of life, but at the same time also expressed its concern over "cross-border provocations resulting from rocket attacks" targeting Israel. The balanced statement represented a change from past official declarations that had instinctively denounced Israeli actions.

Days later, the Indian government rejected a parliamentary resolution seeking to condemn Israel over the conflict in Gaza. Sponsored by India's opposition Congress and Communist parties, the proposed resolution sought to denounce Israel over its use of "brute force" in Gaza. The government, led by External Affairs Minister Sushma Swaraj, refused to adopt the measure.

The personal chemistry between Prime Ministers Modi and Benjamin Netanyahu has also given India-Israel ties a powerful boost. Netanyahu was amongst the first world leaders to congratulate Modi last year following his landslide victory at the polls. In September, the two premiers met on the sidelines of the UN General Assembly where Netanyahu declared that the "sky is the limit" with India. Later that year, Modi sent Hanukah greetings over Twitter in Hebrew, delighting members of the Jewish community around the world. In March, Modi again tweeted in Hebrew to congratulate his "friend Bibi" on his re-election.

High-level exchanges between Indian and Israeli leaders quickly resumed. The outreach went beyond official meetings. Last September, Modi met with the American Jewish Committee just hours before his celebrated address to the Indian-American diaspora at Madison Square Garden. In less than a year, Modi had rekindled the romance between India and Israel.

But does India's unprecedented public embrace of the Jewish state represent a shift in policy or just in optics? India-Israel ties have undoubtedly assumed a more public dimension since Modi's election, but a question persists whether there has been a more significant change in India's foreign policy toward Israel.

Although conducted outside the public eye under the previous government, cooperation continued unabated. In 2008, for example, India launched an Israeli spy satellite, capable of surveilling Iran's nuclear sites. Even after rejecting the proposed parliamentary resolution condemning Israel last June, Swaraj emphasized that the BJP's Israel policy was unchanged.

Ultimately, it remains to be seen whether the new government has begun to fundamentally alter the trajectory of its Israel policy or whether the change is more cosmetic. At a minimum, it is clear that Modi is keen on expanding the political relationship. Many are hoping he will become the first Indian prime minister to travel to Israel. The visit would represent an unprecedented milestone and propel the relationship to even greater heights.

By bringing India-Israel ties out of the closet, Modi has brought focus, direction, and substance to the relationship. How long ties will remain in the public spotlight will largely depend on the results of the next Indian election still four years away. But regardless of the outcome, it is safe to conclude no government in New Delhi has ever been as enthusiastic about its affection for Israel as the one in power now.

India and Israel's Secret Love Affair

The Indo-Israeli defense relationship is once again in focus following Benjamin Netanyahu's "sky is the limit" comment after meeting Narendra Modi in New York back in September—and especially after the signing of the long-delayed $144 million deal on Barak I missiles in October. Another milestone was crossed in November when New Delhi and Tel Avivsuccessfully tested the Barak 8 anti-missile system—a joint project developing an aerial defense system for naval vessels. Moreover, since Modi took power this summer, New Delhi has purchased a whopping $662 million worth of Israeli arms.

So is the Indo-Israeli strategic relationship likely to be fundamentally different now that Modi is in power? Although Indo-Israeli ties are undoubtedly on the upswing, history suggests that Modi is not likely to have a fundamental impact on the substance of the bilateral relationship. During the early part of the Cold War, Indian Prime Minister Jawaharlal Nehru briefly considered inviting Israel to the 1955 Bandung Conference, but eventually decided against doing so in order to appease Arab and Middle Eastern states. While this carved out India's Cold War foreign policy of opposing Israel and siding with Palestine, New Delhi's military ties with Tel Aviv, however modest, began by the 1960s. Not only did Israel provide military assistance to India in its wars in 1962, 1965 and 1971, but Tel Aviv was also one of the first countries to recognize Bangladesh following India's victory in its 1971 war against Pakistan. When the traditionally pro-Israel and Hindu, right-wing, Jan Sangh-led government was briefly in power from 1977 to 1979, Israeli foreign minister Moshe Dayan paid a secret visit to New Delhi in August 1977 to further expand bilateral ties.

While Prime Minister Indira Gandhi mostly maintained her father's pro-Palestine position, her son and successor Rajiv Gandhi met his Israeli counterpart in September 1985 during the UN General Assembly's annual meeting, which was the first such open meeting between the prime ministers of the two states. Indian concerns over the fast-advancing Pakistani nuclear program are believed to have facilitated these improved ties. However, it was not until 1992—after the end of the Cold War and India's 1991 economic liberalization—that New Delhi formally established diplomatic relations with Israel. Nevertheless, it is important to note that even without formal diplomatic relations, Indo-Israeli military ties existed during the Cold War. These ties have certainly increased in volume since the 1990s.

However, a constant theme in the history of Indo-Israeli relations has been that their public visibility has been conditioned on which party holds powers in New Delhi. Specifically, each time a Hindu nationalist coalition led by the Bharatiya Janata Party (BJP) is in power in New Delhi, the visibility of the bilateral ties increases, but not the substance. On the other hand, the Congress Party has tended to downplay

India's ties to the Jewish state whenever it holds power. In this sense, the Modi government's proximity to Israel harkens back to the previous BJP-led National Democratic Alliance. In 2000, for instance, BJP leader L.K. Advani was the first senior Indian minister to visit Israel since the 1992 establishment of diplomatic ties between the two countries. An Indo-Israeli joint working group on terrorism was formed that year, and in 2003, then national security advisor Brajesh Mishra delivered a speech at the American Jewish Committee underlining the potential for cooperation among India, Israel and the United States in fighting Islamist extremism.

Once the Congress Party–led United Progressive Alliance government came to power in 2004, however, Indo-Israeli ties mostly disappeared from the headlines. This was by design; in 2010, the Indian Ministry of External Affairs refused to allow Congress Party MP Mani Shankar Aiyar to ask questions about the Indo-Israeli defense relationship in parliament on the grounds that it pertained to a "state secret." At other points during the UPA's tenure, Israel and India openly clashed. This was the case, for instance, when Indian president Pratibha Patil called on Israel to withdraw from Golan Heights as a primary condition for peace. Despite this public bickering, Indo-Israeli strategic ties remained rock solid. In fact, in the wake of the Mumbai attacks, India's defense purchases from Israel increased so much that Tel Aviv briefly replaced Russia as New Delhi's largest defense supplier in 2009.

In other words, the key difference between the secular Congress Party-led coalition and the one led by the Hindu nationalist BJP lies in their public-relations management of the bilateral relationship. The former publicly downplays strategic ties between India and Israel, while the latter loudly champions its defense and strategic cooperation with Tel Aviv. Beyond these semantics, however, the Congress Party and the BJP maintain largely similar ties with the Jewish state.

Not surprisingly, then, as Narendra Modi prepared to take office, think tanks in Washington and New Delhi predicted that Indo-Israeli relations would once again become more visible.

After all, the Modi government's anti-Islam, anti-Pakistan, anti-terrorism and pro-business positions are compatible with its public enunciation of deeper defense, strategic and economic ties with Tel Aviv. Furthermore, given his historic win and the weak and fractured nature of the opposition, Narendra Modi is nearly able to single-handedly coordinate the future direction of India's foreign policy. This allows him and his government to magnify Indo-Israeli relations in public.

Which isn't to say that Indo-Israeli ties aren't currently expanding, as they are and are likely to continue to do so for the foreseeable future. New Delhi is currently Israel's largest arms customer, and talks are underway for the conclusion of a free-trade agreement that would increase bilateral trade many times over.

In addition, Israel has hailed India as a strategic partner in Asia, while China as merely a trading partner. With Modi entrenched in power, and strategic interests aligned, we are poised to see India and Israel expand on their already-strong relationship.

Narendra Modi's plan to visit Israel is just dangerous for India's foreign policy

Prime Minister Narendra Modi's proposed visit to Israel, confirmed by External Affairs Minister Sushma Swaraj on 31 May, may sound like an idea that sounds like the government is 'thinking out of the box', but it's a dangerous foreign policy move.

A solid argument in favour of Modi deciding to become the first-ever Indian PM to pay an official visit to Israel stems from the fact that the Indian foreign policy in favour of the Palestinians in the Israel-Palestine conflict has yielded zilch so far for New Delhi. Moreover, the Arab world has stymied India routinely and over the years repeatedly taken Pakistan's side on the Kashmir issue.

The Arab nations has done this through the platform of Organisation of Islamic Conference (OIC), a body of 56 Islamic states and the argument is that through these periodic anti-

India resolutions passed at the OIC platform it has repeatedly cocked a snook at India. Some believe it is time for New Delhi to rework its foreign policy vis-a-vis the Islamic nations and take sides with Israel openly.

But this is not only a flawed way of looking at the complex relations between India and the Muslim world but is also fraught with dangerous diplomatic, economic and strategic consequences that we can ill afford.

Congress leader Anand Sharma on 3 June in Hyderabad has said that PM Modi's proposed visit to Israel is "worrisome" as it undermines India's position on Palestine and also "destroys balance" in India's foreign policy. But even Sharma failed to elaborate why such a step would be bad for Indian foreign policy and Indian national interests.

It was the Congress government of PV Narasimha Rao which had dared to establish diplomatic relations with Israel in 1992. Incidentally, China too had established diplomatic relations with Israel in the same year.

Since 1992, both India and China have invested a lot in their diplomatic engagements with Israel, overtly as well as covertly. Both India and China have consistently counter-balanced their relations with Israel and stepped up their outreach to Islamic nations simultaneously.

But by deciding to pay an official visit to Israel, PM Modi has threatened to do away with the traditional diplomatic balance between Israel and the Islamic nations.

The Modi government must not lose sight of the fact that Israel is a trigger-happy state. It has routinely 'punished' the Palestinians and the Arab world for their attacks on Israel. Most often, the retaliatory attacks have been disproportionate. So much so that if one Israeli is killed in a terror attack, reprisals from Tel Aviv often claim far more lives.

Israel has routinely gotten away for its trigger-happy, aggressive foreign policy largely due to two reasons: One, it is a de facto nuclear weapon power . Two, it is not only tolerated but also encouraged by the world's sole superpower the United

States, thanks to the perennially strong Jewish lobby in the US. The 'exploits' of Israel and the fact that this small Jewish state has survived all these decades may inspire jingoists, but the fact is that an overtly strong relationship with Israel will inevitably trigger a much bigger and costlier backlash for India from Islamic nations.

India continues to rely heavily on oil imports from the Islamic nations. Moreover, more than seven million Indians are living and working in Islamic countries. By becoming the first Indian PM to visit Israel, Modi may unleash an irrevocable damage.

Such a step will also impinge badly on Indian trade with the Islamic nations. For example, India has annual bilateral trade worth $75 billion with a small country like the United Arab Emirates. India must also consider its relations with two major Islamic powers – Saudi Arabia and Iran – if it were to decide to take its relationship with Israel to another level with a prime ministerial visit. Both Saudi Arabia and Iran will be fuming and India will lose its strategic grip on these important nations which it has carefully developed and nurtured over the past decade.

As for China, one must not forget that China and Israel have a very strong military relationship. Israel is China's second largest foreign supplier of arms, second only to Russia.

But at the same time, Israel is of utmost strategic importance for India. There are certain relationships which are seldom or never put out in the open – and should not be. The India-Israel relationship falls in this unusual category. It is good to intensify relations with Israel, a country which has helped us immensely in countering Pakistan's proxy war over the past decades. This relationship needs to be nurtured and strengthened, but covertly.

'CONSTITUENT DIPLOMACY' IN INDIA'S FOREIGN POLICY

After over a decade, the British Government in a major policy shift has decided to give up its boycott of the Gujarat

Government headed by Narendra Modi. The UK High Commissioner shall be visiting Gujarat and interacting with Modi and senior officials of the state. In 2002 during his chief ministership, the state was witness to ghastly communal riots. As a consequence of which many Western governments, including the UK, kept him at arms length for a while. In 2005, he was also rejected for a visa by the US Government and has not been issued a visa ever since.

In the recent past however, many foreign governments have been cozying up to Modi, and he has received accolades from overseas. A report published by the Congressional Research Service (CRS) in September 2011 showered praise on the Gujarat Chief Minister for being an efficient administrator who has the ability to deliver. This report was followed by a write-up titled "*India's Most Admired and Most Feared Politician*" in March 2012 by William Antholis, Managing Director and Senior Fellow in Governance Studies at the Brookings Institution. While the write-up did draw attention to Modi's ambiguities on issues pertaining to foreign policy, itwas laudatory when it came to his economic policies, efficient governance, and foresight. Many believe that Britain is making attempts to build a rapport with a future Prime Ministerial candidate; however, the British High Commissioner's Gujarat visit is not the first example of a foreign government wooing aState Government. In May 2012, Secretary of State Hillary Clinton visited West Bengal even before she visited New Delhi and met up with the Chief Minister Mamata Banerjee to discuss the possibility of US investments in West Bengal. Last year, Clinton visited Tamil Nadu and met up with the Chief Minister Jayalalitha.

What explains this increasing engagement between foreign and local governments?

First, ever since the 1990s in the immediate aftermath of economic liberalization, local governments have been aggressive in pursuing economic diplomacy with both the US and other countries. Some clear examples of this point being Andhra Pradesh and Karnataka. In recent years, even other states such as Maharashtra, Gujarat, Tamil Nadu, and Bihar have been pro-active and wooed foreign governments. State governments such as Gujarat and Bihar have in fact started global summits where potential investors from other parts of the world are present.

The second reason for the ever increasing role of local governments in foreign policy is the trend of coalition politics, in which regional parties have an important role to play. These regional parties have been able to exercise a considerable influence over foreign policy, especially with regard to the neighbourhood. In certain cases, they have even intervened on issues which in the past would be considered the exclusive domain of the central government.

This participation of regional governments in foreign policy is a global phenomenon and has been defined as 'constituent diplomacy' by American scholar John Kincaid, who attributes a mix of factors arising out of globalization, such as economic liberalization, diffusion of technology, and politics and local economic incentives.

Two prominent examples of assertive regional parties in India's foreign policy include West Bengal Chief Minister and Trinamool Congress Supremo Mamata Banerjee (who until recently was an ally of the incumbent Congress-led UPA regime in Delhi but left due to differences on issues such as the introduction of Foreign Direct Investment (FDI) in multi-brand retail) and the DMK of Tamil Nadu (which is still a constituent of the UPA).

Mamata's pressure on the UPA Government resulted in India's last minute decision to back out of the Teesta River sharing agreement which was to be signed with Bangladesh in September 2011, during Prime Minister Dr. Manmohan Singh's visit to Bangladesh. Similarly, pressure from DMK leader Karunanidhi, an important ally of the UPA and the ruling AIADMK regime headed by Jayalalitha, have dictated India's Sri Lanka policy. As a result of pressure from both these parties, New Delhi was compelled to vote against Sri Lanka at the UNHRC in March this year. In the resolution, India sought credible investigations into substantial allegations of heinous crimes committed against the Tamil minority in Sri Lanka, during the war against Tamil Tiger separatists in 2009. It should be mentioned that the DMK, a crucial ally of the UPA alliance, threatened to withdraw support in case New Delhi did not vote against.

Aggressive posturing on Sri Lanka did not end here. In July, both the DMK and ruling AIADMK, which hardly see eye to eye on any issue, expressed their displeasure at the presence of Sri Lankan army personnel in the Defence Staff College in Coonoor. A few days before this, Sri Lankan airmen under training in Tamil Nadu had to be shifted to Bangalore due to pressure from the Tamil Nadu government.

In the third week of August, both Karunanidhi and Jayalalitha again expressed their displeasure with New Delhi, saying that it needed to take a tougher stance vis-à-vis Colombo on issues pertaining to the Tamil minority there and also the killing of fishermen by Tamil navy. The DMK leader in fact wrote a letter in which he put forward a range of demands such as moving a resolution in the UNHRC for giving greater political rights to the Sri Lankan Tamils.

Karunanidhi also urged New Delhi to provide asylum to Sri Lankan Tamils in India. In September, a soccer team from Sri Lanka, which had come to play a friendly match in Chennai was forced to leave by the chief minister, and a stadium official was suspended for allowing the Sri Lankan team in. It would be unfair to say that their concerns were totally false.

Mamata did not want to go against public opinion since the earlier left dispensation in West Bengal, which was taken into confidence when the Ganges water treaty was signed between the two countries in 1996, still faces criticism from certain quarters.

Similarly, Sri Lanka's record on its treatment of Tamils is not acceptable, but the way in which they have compelled the UPA Government to take a stand is detrimental to India's interests. Apart from coalition partners pressurizing New Delhi in the realm of foreign policy, certain state governments which are not allied to the Central Government have also been batting for a better relationship with the neighbours, and have ironically backed the Central Government. Two examples are those of Punjab (which neighbours Pakistan), Tripura (which borders Bangladesh), and Manipur and Arunachal (which border Myanmar).

In Punjab, such is the desire for peace with Pakistan due to shared culture and the economic benefits of a potentially cordial relationship, that the ruling Shiromani Akali Dal has been more than supportive of New Delhi's peace initiative towards Islamabad. Both the Congress and the ruling Akali Dal have been pressurizing Delhi to open up more trade routes, increase the number of commodities through the Attari-Wagah land route, and ease vise restrictions. Punjab's role in the Indo-Pak relationship is also especially interesting considering that Punjab was always a problem, not a bridge, with Pakistan.

The increasingly pro-active role of states in foreign policy raises some interesting questions. First, state intervention in foreign policy is not always obstructionist, and examples of Tripura and Punjab clearly reiterate this point. Second, many times allies are more troublesome in the foreign policy realm than those who are not part of the coalition, as is evident from the examples discussed. Third, some leaders are very aggressive when it comes to wooing countries outside the immediate neighbourhood but fail to do so within it.

A good example of this point is Gujarat Chief Minister, Narendra Modi who has visited countries such as Japan and China to attract foreign investment to his state, but has not extended an olive branch to neighbouring Sind in Pakistan. This is in spite of the two regions having old trade linkages and also the fact that one of the biggest beneficiaries of trade with Pakistan would be Gujarat.

Interestingly, Modi has spoken about cooperation with Sind in the realm of energy, apart from encouraging investment from across the border in his state, but this has been downplayed by him individually and the Indian media. Trade delegations from Pakistan have also been visiting his state; the Karachi

Chamber of Commerce has in fact invited him to visit Pakistan but so far he has been non-committal.

INDIA IN THE MODERN WORLD/ INDIAN FOREIGN POLICY: PRIORITIES AND IMPERATIVES

One year has passed since a momentous election brought to power a right wing, Nationalist party—the Bharatiya Janata Party (BJP). For the first time in decades, India has a single party majority government. Its leader the Prime Minister, Mr. Narendra Modi is credited with this victory. However, it would be wrong to discount the contribution to this victory made by the general public disenchantment with the preceding coalition government led by the Congress Party.

There are very high expectations, some probably unattainable, of the new government quickly addressing the challenges of poverty alleviation, political and social reform. Incidentally, these high expectations of India are not limited to its population. Most of its international partners are also rooting for her success, even if with different motivations, hoping that India's emergence will enhance international stability and security.

There is little doubt that the Modi government has introduced a great amount of new energy in the conduct of foreign policy with several high-profile prime ministerial visits to neighbouring countries, meetings with leaders of the great powers and participation in multi-lateral forums. Nevertheless, any analysis of whether this zest is creating significant change requires a look at the domestic challenges facing India. After all, foreign policy flows from the need to protect and enhance a country's national interests as determined by domestic objectives.

Challenges

India today is home to more than a third of the world's poor. According to the UN and Indian government, it is 21.9% (defined based on an income of less than $1.25 per day). According to the World Bank, it is 23.6 %. This is approximately 300 million to 400 million people. To make matters worse, India has the largest number of malnourished children—one third of the world's total. India, unlike most countries is experiencing a "youth bulge" or "demographic dividend". Sixty five percent of India's population is below the age of 35. While this is seen to be a positive trend

SECRET AND SCARY SEA-BASED AMBITIONS

India and Pakistan are intertwined in an absolute longstanding security competition. Although, nuclear parity does not exist in the region neither both states are conventionally parallel but action-reaction or tit-for-tat cycle is rapidly enhancing the nuclear capabilities in Southern region, specifically of India and partially of Pakistan. Nevertheless India's conventional superiority and nuclear advancements strongly influence Pakistan's threat perceptions and nuclear strategies, resultantly boosting the region's nuclear developments. The two most recent developments in South Asia have critically hoisted the danger of an accelerated nuclear arms race between India and Pakistan. First, the predominant development in region is the production and modernization of ballistic and cruise missiles by both states, along with the deployment of Ballistic Missile Defense (BMD) by India; Second, the developments related to sea-based nuclear warheads, that are shaping naval nuclear regime in South Asian region.

Currently, both Pakistan and India have enough nuclear capable bombers, warheads and ballistic and cruise missile. Notwithstanding these aspects, the robust modernization and enlargement of India's military arsenals has significantly increased the size of its conventional and nuclear weapons. India's pursuit of BMD will undermine the prevailing paradigm of mutually assured destruction or strategic equilibrium because the BMD shield system will make India believe that it can launch a nuclear strike while successfully defend itself against any retaliation. Evidently, it will become requisite for Pakistan to seek strategic partners who could provide the capability to counter BMD. Second, asymmetry will pressurize Pakistan to develop an assortment of nuclear missiles and delivery systems in view of amid reality that deployment of BMD would assist Indian ambitions to launch a conventional military operation such as through cold start.

Conversely, the evolving naval nuclear dynamics in South Asia would start a new competition in the region with alarming future prospects. Both states are said to be developing their naval nuclear forces. India, the world's largest weapon importer, has a while back approved $16 billion for nuclear powered submarines and naval warships. Reportedly, India plans for developing more than 160 ship navy, 3 aircraft carriers and more than 40 warships and submarines that includes anti-submarines corvettes and stealth destroyers. India is one of the three Asian countries to maintain aircraft carriers.

The above mentioned naval concerns are surfacing more vehemently as India has finally tested the long awaited the indigenously-developed, nuclear capable K-4 ballistic missile lately. According to various sources, the Defence Research and Development Organization (DRDO) has not yet made public its recent test of nuclear capable submarine launched ballistic missile (SLBM) K-4. Although the missile is yet to get its actual name, it was being developed under a secret project, code named K-4. The name is said to have been derived from Missile Man of India Abdul Kalam. The test has been declared as 'roaring success' and according to the revealed details "the K-4 missile was fired at a depressed trajectory, starting from successfully clearing the launch tube and breaking the water surface to stage separation and maintaining the ballistic trajectory.

The missile was launched from a submerged pontoon, replica of a submarine, from water 9 meters deep". Reportedly, the missile achieved all parameters before zeroing in on the pre-designated target with high accuracy. Presumably, it has been confirmed that the missile has been tested at its full-operational range. The K-4 is an intermediate-range nuclear-capable submarine-launched ballistic missile with an alleged range of up to 3,500 km. During a previous test in March 2014, the K-

4 was only tested to a range of 3,000 km. However, as the technical details on the top-secret K-4 remain scarce, purportedly, it is 12 meters long, weighs around 17 tons, can carry a nuclear capable warhead of up to 2 tons, and is powered by solid rocket propellants.

Moreover the missile is capable of cruising at hypersonic speed, also features an "innovative" system of weaving in three dimensions during flight as it approaches its target.

According to DRDO officials the missile will have to undergo at least two more developmental trials before it will be test-fired from the ballistic missile nuclear submarine (SSBN) INS Arihant. The INS Arihant was slated to be commissioned this month, but like several delays yet again a delay seems likely. The submarine is equipped with four vertical launch tubes, which can be armed with four K-4 missiles or K-15 missiles, another member of the K-series of missiles.

On other hand Pakistan last year approved a proposal from China to purchase eight diesel-electric submarines. However viewing India's naval ambitions, Pakistan will look to neutralize developments with India and it may prove an initiative for having permanent sea-based deterrent equipped with submarine launched variant of cruise missile.

Evidently, the pursuit of sea-based nuclear strike force is the next step towards India's quest for an assured retaliatory capability and Pakistan's naval nuclear ambitions are fueled primarily with growing conventional asymmetry rather than strategic imbalance between both countries.

Nonetheless, an imperative issue is missing in debate that what a new command and control model will be adopted by Indian strategic forces and what challenges it would pose to the security of region. However evidently, these two recent developments in South Asia affect three foremost components of strategic stability that includes deterrence stability, arms-race stability and crisis stability. The recent trends show that India is shaping the regional security domains and Pakistan will be bound to be shaped.

INDIA'S FOREIGN POLICY: CHALLENGES AND ACHIEVEMENTS

Strategies are never revealed, they are reflected in the person's tasks. The Modi government has been working on the strategy of bringing foreign investment and enhancing economic cooperation with the strategically located, powerful, and developed countries of the world. The exploitation of the Indian market by China's marketing experts had been a matter of concern for Indian government since last 5-6 years. The Modi government has come up with a planned agenda of convincing the countries of Indo-Pacific region to deal with the China's increasing dominance in the Asian economy.

Modi's foreign policy and his agenda of "MAKE IN INDIA" to bring foreign direct investment (FDI) in the manufacturing sector have been the prime issues trending in Indian economic and political domains. Modi has inherited foreign policy legacy of the NDA government led by Atal Bihari Vajpayi. Modi's mind has been playing many tricks in these two years of his government and his decisions are not clearly understood by the common people of India. Since the work has not been on the ground, it appears to be only virtual.

But for the sake of the country's development, Modi's efforts to enhance trade and economic co-operations with neighboring countries have been outstanding and his "ACT EAST POLICY"has gained an unexpected success till now.Modi's foreign visits have been very much strategic and his visit to Japan, South Korea, US, etc. has given his government a lot to praise.

Modi's intention to balance the economic upliftment of China in the Asian context has compelled Modi to work with China, which is the reason behind the Strategic and Economic Dialogue (SED) between the two countries. Moreover, China, being the leading exporter of capital and technology and second largest economy of the world can never be ignored by any government in New Delhi. Modi's focus on Japan is an important step in the Asian context as Japan is the leading country in the field of technology which India needs. Moreover, Japan is the only way for India to enhance its economic importance and its dominance in Indo-Pacific region without any strategic alliance with China. The Indo-Pacific region has its own significance in the economic development of India and the visits of foreign minister Sushma Swaraj to the neighboring countries located on the bank of Indian/Pacific ocean (for instance Vietnam) shows how important are they for India to strengthen its hold on the region.

India has often been confused regarding the path it should chose in dealing with the prominent economic giants. Whether to align with Japan-US or to go with China-Russia has been the dilemma facing the Indian foreign policy makers. India guards the sanctity of national sovereignty almost as zealously as China and Russia do. But Indian economic experts are more "tending" towards US-Japan because of their dominance on the world and their economic stability.

Only with time, one may be able to make a judgment regarding the success or failure of Modi's foreign policy, but it is undeniable that world's economic powers have taken note of India's emergence economically and have recognized the fact that India is politically stable enough to maintain its economic progress.

NARENDRA MODI TO VISIT BHUTAN IN FIRST FOREIGN VISIT AS PRIME MINISTER

In a signal that his foreign policy priorities include South Asia first and foremost, India's new prime minister, Narendra Modi, will visit Bhutan later this month. According to reports from several Indian sources, the prime minister will likely visit Thimphu in the third week of June. Bhutan and India have friendly relations, with India being Bhutan's largest trade partner and a huge source of development assistance. Given Modi's decision to invite the leaders of all the South Asian Association for Regional Cooperation (SAARC) to his inauguration on May 26, the decision to make his first foreign trip to Bhutan underscores his commitment to ameliorating

India's neighborhood relations before focusing on the world abroad. Modi's second known foreign visit will be to the United States in September.

According to government sources cited by *The Indian Express*, the decision to go to Bhutan was not immediately obvious. The prime minister also considered trips to Nepal, Bangladesh and even Afghanistan. For Modi, Bhutan is an important Indian partner. Given Bhutan's dependence on India's economy, the nation has largely been compliant with India's national interests and has not taken any action in contravention of New Delhi's will. In addition to commercial matters, Modi may enlist Bhutan's assistance in internal security matters.

In the early 2000s, the Royal Bhutanese Army weeded out anti-state insurgents, including the United Liberation Front of Assam, that were using Bhutan as a base. In 2007, India and Bhutan renegotiated the basis of their bilateral relationship and signed a new treaty of friendship which has formed the basis of their relations ever since.

Former prime minister Manmohan Singh visited Bhutan in 2008, pledging support for Bhutan's gradual shift from monarchy to democracy. Furthermore, energy cooperation is an important issue in India-Bhutan relations. India has pledged to import 10,000 megawatts of electricity from Bhutan by 2020 and the two countries plan to cooperatively work on four hydropower projects that would together generate 2,120 megawatts, according to the *Times of India.*

Indian Ministry of External Affairs spokesman Syed Akbaruddin drove home the idea that Modi's foreign policy would prioritize India's immediate neighbors; he notes that while the "the prime minister's inbox relating to foreign policy is very crowded ... India's foreign policy priorities are in the neighborhood." Bhutan's foreign minister Rinzin Dorji noted, following Bhutanese Prime Minister Tshering Tobgay's visit to India for Modi's inauguration, that Modi "is a prime minister who delivers and from the interaction, we could sense he has concerns for Bhutan and the region."

Modi Visits Bhutan on First Step of Bid to Assert Regional Sway

Prime Minister Narendra Modi assured Bhutan on Sunday of India's support during his first trip abroad, a move seen as an attempt to assert his country's influence in south Asia where China is steadily making inroads. His decision to make tiny Bhutan his first destination was the latest in a series of unconventional policy choices by the new prime minister who came to power last month on the promise of making his country an economic and military power.

He previously invited South Asian leaders to his inauguration and has exchanged friendly letters with Pakistan's Prime Minister Nawaz Sharif in a bid to re-establish India as the dominant power in the region. While India has struggled recently with policy paralysis and a slowing economy, China has been building ports in Sri Lanka, Bangladesh and its "all-weather ally", Pakistan. It overtook India as the biggest foreign investor in Nepal in the first six months of this year.

Modi, given a ceremonial welcome in Bhutan's capital Thimphu nestled in mist-covered mountains, opened a Supreme Court building constructed with Indian assistance. On Monday he will lay the foundation for a 600 megawatt hydroelectric power station, part of an energy cooperation plan to feed demand in Bhutan, and also India. "PM underlined that he would not only nurture strong bonds but would also strengthen them," a government official said after Modi's talks with Bhutan's King Jigme Kesar Wangchuk and Prime Minister Tshering Tobgay. Bhutan, wedged in the Himalayas between India and China is the closest India has to an ally in South Asia, a region home to over 1.5 billion people but held back by bristling rivalries.

Modi's Bhutan visit shows an astute sense of the region's critical importance to India's economic dynamism and strategic strength, said Alyssa Ayres, a South Asia expert at the New York-based Council on Foreign Relations. "Of course, India is also closely watching China's border talks with Bhutan and China's recent efforts to establish stronger ties with Thimphu," she said.

On Sunday, hundreds of school children dressed in traditional red and green tunics lined the route from the airport to wave the Indian flag as Modi's motorcade arrived in the kingdom which for centuries was closed to outsiders. "Bhutan and India share a very special relationship that has stood the test of time," Modi said before he left New Delhi. "Thus, Bhutan was a natural choice for my first visit abroad." Modi's government aims to make India the dominant foreign investor across South Asia as well as the main provider of infrastructure loans, in the same way China has done in much of the rest of Asia and in Africa.

Clout

"Although India would like to have a greater say in South Asian matters beyond trade, so far we have not been able to exercise substantial political clout," said P.D. Rai, a lawmaker from the state of Sikkim, which shares a border with Bhutan. "Modi's first visit to Bhutan will have to be looked at in this light." Bhutan, the size of Switzerland and with a population of 750,000, has only recently emerged from centuries of isolation.Its first road was built in 1962 and television and the Internet arrived in 1999. It is the first country to monitor gross national happiness, an alternative to gross domestic product, to balance a tentative embrace of modernity with an effort to preserve traditions.

But Bhutan, which made the transition from absolute monarchy to parliamentary democracy in 2008, is struggling with high unemployment and a growing national debt. The government that took power in 2012 says it wants to focus on obstacles to happiness. "It is good that we are being connected to the world, we are all on Facebook," said schoolgirl Tenzin Lamsang, as she and a group of friends prepared to greet the Indian leader.

PM Modi Wows to Nurture 'B2B' Ties on Primary Foreign Visit to Bhutan

Making Bhutan his first foreign destination, Prime Minister Narendra Modi today vowed to nurture bilateral relations which he described as "B2B – Bharat to Bhutan" as he held talks with the Bhutanese King and the Premier, discussing an entire gamut of ties. Embarking on a two-day trip here to display "special and unique" status forBhutan in India's foreign policy, Prime Minister Modi also inaugurated the Supreme Court complex built by India as part of the developmental cooperation. "The primary focus of both the meetings was the extensive development cooperation between the two countries and measures to enhance the economic ties," official sources said.

Modi described the bilateral relations as "B2B relations – Bharat to Bhutan relations," the sources said on his meeting with Bhutanese King Jigme Khesar Namgyel Wangchuk and Prime Minister Tshering Tobgay. Modi announced doubling of scholarships being provided to Bhutanese students in India which will now be worth Rs two crore. Prime Minister Modi also promised to assist Bhutan in setting up a digital library which will provide access to Bhutanese youth to two million books and periodicals. The fact that the Prime Minister chose Bhutan as his first foreign destination assumes significance since China has lately intensified efforts to woo it and establish full- fledged diplomatic ties with Thimphu.

Modi, accompanied by External Affairs Sushma Swaraj, National Security Advisor Ajit Doval and Foreign Secretary Sujatha Singh, was accorded a grand welcome as he arrived at the Paro airport and was received by Tobgay and several of his Cabinet colleagues. The Bhutanese government rolled out the red carpet as Modi was given a ceremonial guard of honour. The Prime Minister drove down from Paro to Thimphu, a distance of about 50 km, traversing through the picturesque mountainous ranges. Common people, including children, in colourful attire lined up most of the road between Paro and Thimphu, waving Indian and Bhutanese flags. Big hoardings carrying Modi's photographs also could be seen en route. Modi's meeting with the Bhutanese King lasted for nearly an hour and then he held talks with Tobgay. Modi expressed satisfaction at India being considered as a privileged partner of Bhutan and underlined that his government "would not only nurture these strong bonds but would also strengthen them."

Bhutan-India Ties Role Representation Political Relationship: Bhutan PM

From Lalit K Jha Washington, Mar 19 (PTI) Describing ties between India and Bhutan as a "model relationship", Bhutanese Prime Minister Tshering Tobgay said trust, cooperation and confidence have helped build close relations between the two neighbours. "We have a role model relationship politically, but in terms of economic cooperation, the center piece is hydropower, so we work together, we invest together to build our power stations," Tobgay said in a first ever interview to a popular American talk show on Public Broadcasting Service. India is our immediate neighbour and we are extremely close. Our friendship is based on good will, trust, understanding, very good cooperation," he said.

"Our relation with India transcends political parties. The architecture of our friendship is our leaders and from the Bhutanese part it is our kings." "Bhutan was the first foreign country that the Prime Minister Narendra Modi visited within three weeks of his swearing in," said Tobgay.

Tobgay said Bhutan has a "good relations" with China, but not as deep as India. "We have a 420-kilometer border that has not yet been finalised with China. We are discussing the border and we need to finalise the border" he said.

Responding to questions, Tobgay said the country's problem is youth unemployment which is about 9.6 per cent. "So we need to create jobs, we need to have industries.

We need to have investment to create jobs for them. So while this is a problem, I acknowledge it as a problem, and I don't want to see a single Bhutanese boy or girl unemployed," he said during the interview.

Corruption is not a problem more than it is a risk, he added. Our economy is small, but we have been given everything — health, education, infrastructure, social security which is very important, he said.

"We have to work hard to ensure that our future generations also enjoy free education and free healthcare and that we have an economy that can support all this," he said. Tobgay said in 10 years he would like Bhutan to be self-reliant in a manner that our economy is green and sustainable. "72 per cent of our country, as you know, is under forest cover. The constitution requires 60 per cent. We've declared that owe will be carbon neutral for all time to come," he said.

Bhutanese Clap to Make an Exception for Modi

People of Bhutan do not clap as a congratulatory gesture as they believe that clapping is done only to ward off evil spirits. But on Monday they made an exception for Prime Minister Narendra Modi who gave a rousing speech at the joint session of Bhutanese parliament. As Modi finished his extempore speech, delivered in Hindi, which the members of parliament including the Bhutanese PM Tshering Tobgay and other important dignitaries listened to in rapt attention with the help of interpreters, the gathering broke into spontaneous applause.

The clappings began in one corner of the national assembly — the lower house where the joint session was held — and it soon spread among the VVIPs seated at the chamber, as also the visitors' gallery where a large number of Indian and Bhutanese journalists and other officials as also some meritorious students were present. As the applause reverberated from almost all corners of the assembly, some of their countrymen smiled embarrassedly. In fact, an advisory issued to the media on Sunday itself had referred to the custom. "It may kindly be noted that there will be no clappings/applause in the Bhutanese parliament during the PM's address to the joint session of the Bhutanese parliament. "This is because of the Bhutanese religious belief that clapping is done only to ward off evil spirit," said the notice posted at the media centre set up here for Modi's two-day trip.

4

India's Security Policies Under Modi Government

As the new National Democratic Alliance (NDA) government forms its cabinet, it is worth considering the implications of the electoral verdict on India's security calculations. Importantly it can be expected that India's strategic and security calculations will be driven by nationalist and more decisive political leadership revolving around enlightened self interest. What this means is that India centric concerns and imperatives on larger global or regional issues will be the hallmark of a new BJP-led NDA government.

In practical terms, relations with the U.S. as well as major Asian players like China, Japan, South Korea and ASEAN will be driven by perceptions of their impact on long-term Indian economic and security interests. This implies that the U.S. pivot to Asia and Chinese assertiveness will be evaluated in terms of how they affect Indian interests, with the policy responses shaped accordingly, rather than being driven by the demands of larger collective security or economic groupings.

This does not mean that India is suddenly going to chart an independent course; rather, what it implies is that all options within the broader strategic framework of the Asia-Pacific will be closely analyzed from Indian perspectives and the policy response crafted accordingly. This is hardly unprecedented, but the emphases will shift, backed by greater political conviction and in concert with a defined national agenda and Indian vision. There is every likelihood that the new government may go ahead and issue a white paper on India's national security strategy.

In the initial phases of an NDA Government, relations with the U.S. will remain largely transactional, implying greater quid pro quo: attempts at trade restrictions, visa issues, transfer of technology etc. will all be evaluated at the altar of strict reciprocity. Strategic partnership will also be evaluated on its long term regional impact and understandings of long term US regional commitments. While there is no doubt commonality of interest in maintaining peace and stability in the Asia-Pacific and preventing the emergence of a Sino-centric Asia, India is unlikely to blindly follow U.S. strategic calculations. Rather, it will shape its responses on its own understanding of the state of play and the long-term consequences. Issues like natural allies and concerts of democracies will be downplayed in favour of a more pragmatic approach to relations.

Economic and political relations with Japan could see an upswing, although the new government will not enter into strategic partnerships or arrangements that are manifestly aimed at containing China. With Japan, the accent will be on greater economic partnership and developing a joint strategic vision – such as sea lines of communication – that helps secure the global commons. Improving the domestic investment climate by revoking or revamping archaic laws, the new Modi government will go all out to woo Japanese investors, making economic rather than security and strategic relations the underpinning of bilateral relations.

With China, India will seek a different kind of relations. The new government will be less paranoid when it comes to Chinese investment, although restrictions and caution in sensitive sectors will remain a hallmark. Closer economic partnership implies investment and trade on more equal terms (a reduced trade surplus and equal investment opportunities). Strong political leadership shorn of political compulsions is likely to be more decisive in moving China toward greater reciprocity.

In strategic terms, India will seek to avoid unnecessarily needling China with any explicit or implicit containment strategies, implying that New Delhi will not be party to any quadrilateral or multilateral initiatives that have containment in mind. In fact, the new leadership is more likely to push an agenda for greater strategic cooperation to encourage more balanced Chinese behavior, acting as a regional moderator rather than balancer. Yet even while pursuing a policy of more engagement, the new government will act to enhance and modernize military capabilities and improve infrastructure in border areas. To be sure, dealing with China will be an incremental process underpinned by comprehensive economic engagement backed by credible capability development dictated solely by core Indian interests.

In terms of regional security, the NDA/BJP manifesto makes an interesting commitment of working towards strengthening regional forums like SAARC and ASEAN. The new government is likely to focus and push toward greater economic integration and the resolution of outstanding bilateral issues. Two broad perspectives can be envisioned. First, the new Indian government will attempt to improve both political and economic relations. It will clearly define its core interests and respect those of its regional partners. Effort will be made to resolve outstanding issues in the spirit of mutual accommodation with greater Indian investment and trade, aspects relating to trade concessions, and investment in infrastructure projects as inducements. The concerns of Indian federal states neighboring these countries will be taken up in a spirit of mutual accommodation.

Second, on contentious issues such as illegal immigration, river sharing, the rights of fishermen, and the growing Chinese footprints, New Delhi will seek resolution without the internal politics. In other words, the new government will tell Bangladesh about its concerns regarding illegal immigration without being overly worried about West Bengal or Assam politics.

Similarly, Sri Lanka will be told in clear terms about Tamils and fishing rights and their impact on India. The center will not allow states to hijack the policy agenda, although they will be consulted. What this implies is a freer hand in shaping regional policies, greater engagement, and enhanced economic relations. In short, more sensitivity.

With Pakistan, as in the era of Atal Bihari Vajpayee, every effort will be made to have a constructive relationship, with two clearly defined redlines. First, cross-border terror will have to stop. Second, attempts by Pakistan to play the jihadi card, ratchet up border tensions, or use its deep state to undermine Indian interests in India and Afghanistan will elicit a strong Indian response. In short, another Mumbai 26/11 will not produce a tepid response. Nor will India tolerate major military or nuclear inroads that pose a critical challenge to India.

Nonetheless, as with China, effort will be made to build a new partnership based on trade, commerce, and transit rights. There will in the initial stages be strict reciprocity with Pakistan unless the new government sees Islamabad as willing to move forward in easing its fixation on Kashmir and helping to improve bilateral tensions. A policy of cautious optimism without the emotional baggage is likely to be the hallmark of the Modi government's Pakistan policy. Afghanistan and Iranian policies are likely to see less change, although engagement could deepen if the strategic environment is conducive.

Economic projects like Chabahar Port and greater investment in mining, and the Turkmenistan-Afghanistan-Pakistan-India pipeline will all be on the table. Indian concerns will be dictated by maintaining peace and stability, undermining radical movements, and its increasingly critical energy requirements. Pakistani efforts to intimidate Indian interests will draw a much sharper response.

The government will hope that a robust Pakistan policy backed by strong political leadership will produce a tangible impact and restrain Pakistan from following an anti-Indian agenda. Whereas boots on ground are not anticipated, India could at a future date take over some training duties from the British as part of a larger international effort to bolster the capabilities of the Afghan security forces.

Relations with Russia will remain high on India's foreign policy and security agenda, principally because of the changing geo-strategic environment and the continued dependence of Indian armed forces on Russian weapons. India-China-Russian engagement could see a major shift if Modi's engagement with China begins to bear fruit. This will deepen trilateral relations which would then need to be balanced with strategic partnerships with both the U.S. and Japan. Post-Ukraine crisis Russia is looking to deepen its energy commitments; how these play out will also be important and will help shape policy options.

Overall, expect to see a more robust policy shaped by a strong and self-confident leadership. Policy formulation will largely be centred on greater economic engagement, safeguarding core Indian interests backed by credible military power. A gradual shift from a sole dependence on soft power to a mix of soft and hard power is likely.

INDIA'S SECURITY NEEDS

India's security needs have always played a dominant role in the formation of its foreign policy. Its threat analysis was based on nuclear China in the North East and the everlasting conflict with Pakistan in the Jammu-Kashmir region. Nuclear China led India to go nuclear in 1974. Emergence of China as the fastest growing country in the world once again perceived as a competing power in the region. This is similar with USA's perception of China as a possible rival power in the 21st century. This competition is especially based on the needs for energy resources in order to sustain growing economy. These energy resources will be supplied from the Persian Gulf and the Caspian Sea region however the statistics demonstrates that although the Caspian Sea resources will be important at the margins, the Persian Gulf will continue to exist as the dominant supplier. Thus in this context, US can need India to balance China in the region in long term.

Therefore US-Indian relations are interpreted as having a potential to be a strategic partnership. Another dimension of this cooperation is the mutual grievance from terrorism. After September 11, India is one of the first countries that declared its support to USA's war on terrorism. In the last decade, Islamic fundamentalist groups have attacked India more than a dozen times. Most of these groups are based in Pakistan and they are receiving moral or economic support from Pakistani institutions. The basis of the conflict is the conflict over Jammu and Kashmir which lasts since the Independence of India from Britain in August 1947. However, a major obstacle that prevents the development of Indian-American relations to a next level is the strategic position of Pakistan for US's war against Taliban and Al-Qaeda. Pakistan gave full permission to USA to operate in its borders against Al-Qaeda. Although Indian officials interpret this relationship as shortsighted, in the short-term Pakistan is very important for US to achieve its goals in Afghanistan. Since January 2004, Pakistani-Indian relations are changing in a positive way. Since November 2003, there is ceasefire between the two states and in September 2004, leaders of the both states declared their intentions to achieve real results because of this dialogue. Improvement in Indian-Pakistani relations may enhance Indian-American relations into a next level.

EMERGING SECURITY CHALLENGES

Even as India grapples with diverse external and internal threats to its security, many new challenges are emerging on the security horizon. Before the dangers evident in them can be addressed, the emerging threats need to be identified and understood. The major emerging threats are outlined below:

- Increasing demands for electric power to meet the requirements of industry and the growing population will make energy security a primary concern. Energy security will be particularly important in future, as fossil fuels will become more and more inadequate for the nation's increasing energy needs. Domestic oil production has been declining while the demand has been rising steadily. Hence, oil will continue to be a strategic resource and the security of India's oil supplies from abroad as well as that of all oil reserves and installations will need to be ensured.

- India's growing population and the likelihood of mass migrations into India, for example from Bangladesh, will threaten the existing food reserves and endanger food security. The nation will find it extremely difficult to cope with successive failures of the monsoon, if they occur, and the consequent famine-like conditions that are likely to prevail. For almost a decade now, the monsoon has been bountiful in most parts of India. Quite obviously, this cannot continue for long and the law of averages will catch up sooner rather than later.
- The ravages of global warming and changing monsoon patterns are likely to deplete India's water sources and threaten water security even as the increasing population, rapid industrialisation and the enhanced requirements of irrigation raise the demand for water. The Tata Energy Research Institute has estimated that the demand for water will almost double from 564 billion cubic metres (bcum) in 1997 to 1,048 bcum in 2047.14 The situation will be further exacerbated when the Himalayan nation-states begin drawing more water for their own consumption. The amicable sharing of the Ganga River waters between India, Bangladesh and Nepal has already been posing problems. Successive droughts have ravaged some of India's western states during 1999 and 2000 mainly due to groundwater levels having fallen to extremely low levels.
- Information warfare is another emerging threat through which, besides nation-states, non-state actors, individual terrorists and even disgruntled elements within a state can play havoc with a nation's telecom, banking, stock exchanges, power grids, railways and air traffic control infrastructure, besides military communications and networks. The prevention of large-scale damage through a complex cyber-security system requires an inter-

departmental approach in concert with industry and private entrepreneurs and can only be undertaken by a duly empowered apex organisation.

- The threats to India's maritime security are increasing exponentially as the world turns more and more towards the exploitation of ocean resources for food, energy and raw materials. This long- neglected aspect needs to be incorporated in the management of national security so that India's ocean resources in its exclusive economic zone (EEZ) are not poached at will by state and non-state actors. Increasing piracy at sea and the possible use of India's island territories by terrorist organisations and for trade in contraband goods are other serious maritime threats.
- Security of the environment is another emerging challenge. The continuing increase in the population will threaten the already depleted forest resources as the area of cultivable land comes under pressure. Also, over exploitation of the oceans may upset the delicate marine balance. Increasing urbanisation is causing its own environmental problems. Soil erosion in some areas, specially in hill states due to the impact of deforestation, and the irreplaceable loss of vital nutrients due to the tendency to harvest three to four crops a year in some other states, will eventually lay waste vast areas of cultivable lands and severely curtail agricultural production.
- In future, the Indian government will have to increasingly plan for the security concerns of the vast Indian Diaspora, particularly the migrant Indian population employed on temporary work permits in the Gulf countries. The Gulf War in 1990-91 had resulted in the most massive airlift since the Berlin airlift as over 100,000 Indian workforce personnel had to be evacuated from Iraq. The increasing persecution of ethnic minorities of Indian origin in countries like Pakistan will create its own tensions and may force India to

intervene in future. The May 2000 coup in Fiji, where the Indian minority was specifically targeted, may be a pointer of the shape of things to come.

Still newer challenges that are emerging include those from organised crime and narco-terrorism. India is flanked by two of the most notorious narcotics producing regions in the world - the Golden Crescent (Afghanistan, Iran and Pakistan; annual production approximately 2,500 tonnes) on the west and the Golden Triangle (Laos, Myanmar and Thailand; 1,500 tonnes) on the east. Money laundering and the issue of fake currency by inimical neighbours are new problems to be contended with. The Asian financial crisis demonstrated that a nation's currency can be undermined through external intervention and its economy can be de-stabilised. The Ministry of Defence (MoD) Annual Report 1995-96 listed several other non-military 'pressures' on the national security environment which could not be ignored. These included "...those relating to trade, intellectual property rights, environment, human rights..." The existing and emerging threats to national security are becoming more and more complex to evaluate and manage in the prevailing era of strategic uncertainty.

Need for a Formal Defence Policy

These threats and challenges to national security require systematic evaluation by an apex body and the formulation of a comprehensive national security strategy to ensure that they are managed well and not allowed to spin out of control. Indian defence analysts have for long lamented the lack of a national security vision and strategy. With his characteristic frankness, K. Subrahmanyam minces no words in bluntly stating that, "It is now well recognised all over the world that India does not have a tradition of strategic thinking... mainly due to the incapacity of our political leaders and top civil servants to take a long-term view of national security. This is compounded by their consequent failure in giving a lead to the armed forces in preparing the country to face its long-term need for defence preparedness." In Brahma Chellaney's view, "The lack of an integrated, long-term national security approach stands out as the biggest failure of nation-building in the half-century that India has been independent. In the absence of such an approach, national security policy-making has been characterised largely by ad hoc decisions to meet new threats and realities." M. D. Nalapat says that national security policy has generally been one of reacting to threats and events and, "A holistic view was avoided as this would have reduced the powers of the separate bureaucracies (in the home and defence ministries especially) dealing with the problem... this uncoordinated response to security threats is a major failing in the system." And, K. N. Daruwalla asks, "Can a country have a military doctrine if it does not posses a strategic one? If your overall objectives and goals are ambiguous and undefined, how can you lay down objectives for your armed forces? How can a military doctrine be embedded in such amorphousness?.... Since the armed forces are required to safeguard national interests, foreign policy objectives should go hand in hand with the development of the military machine." However, Jasjit Singh has expressed the view that, "... the reality also must be recognised that (despite the absence of a formally articulated defence doctrine) the country has managed its defence and military affairs well during the past half century."

Indian policy planners have traditionally fought shy of formally articulating the country's defence and national security policies. Perhaps this reticence owes its origins to an innate sense of refraining from hurting the sensibilities of India's adversaries and neighbours. In its Nineteenth Report, the Estimates Committee had recommended that the country should have a formal National Security Doctrine. When the Standing Committee on Defence (1995-96) in the Tenth Lok Sabha enquired about the action taken on this recommendation, the Defence Secretary replied: "... there is a policy; the only thing is that it is not written down as a separate document and published as such... As a matter of policy we have not published such a document and the Government has not been in favour of publishing a separate document. It is only the United States in my knowledge which annually publishes a document called

National Security Doctrine. Non-publication of the document does not mean in any way non-existence of policy." Replying to the debate in the Lok Sabha on the Demands for grants of the MoD, on May 10, 1995, Prime Minister P. V. Narsimha Rao, who was also the Defence Minister, stated: "We do not have a document called India's National Defence Policy. But we have got several guidelines which are followed, strictly followed and observed... This policy is not merely rigid in the sense that it has been written down, but these are the guidelines, these are the objectives, these are the matters which are always kept in view while conducting our defence policy..."

Similarly, the Ministry of External Affairs (MEA) avers in its Annual Report 1998-99 that, "We view foreign policy as an integral part of the larger effort of building the nation's capabilities: through economic development, strengthening social well-being and the quality of life and of protecting India's sovereignty, territorial integrity and security, not only in its defence and economic aspects, but in the widest strategic sense of the term." It says that India's external relations are guided by "well-established principles" which have formed the "basis of our foreign policy for decades" and "enjoy a broad national consensus, thus providing a strong foundation of stability and continuity." However, the report does not spell out what those principles are in specific terms and how they translate into practical execution in furthering national interests and objectives.

It is due to this lack of a long-term national security perspective and the failure to initiate a public debate for the formulation of a national consensus on the vital interests, national security objectives and a synergised national security strategy, that the security pendulum has swung between the interventionist "Indira Doctrine" of the 1970s and 1980s on one end and the conciliatory "Gujral Doctrine" of the mid-1990s on the other. The Indira Doctrine stated that, "India will neither intervene in the domestic affairs of any state in the region, unless requested to do so, nor tolerate such intervention by an external power. If external assistance is needed to meet an external crisis, states should first look within the region (that is, to India) for help." The ill-conceived IPKF intervention in Sri Lanka, as also the stand-off with Nepal on the trade treaty and the successful crushing of the coup in the Maldives could be attributed to the practical application of the Indira Doctrine (dubbed as a "muscular" foreign policy by some non-Indian South Asian commentators). The Gujral Doctrine reflected the recognition that India's policies towards its smaller neighbours within Southern Asia should show greater concern for their security perceptions, instead of sticking to hard-line attitudes that have created tensions in the past. The essence of the doctrine was that India would not insist on reciprocity and would be prepared to go more than half way to improve its relations with its smaller neighbours. Inder Gujral, India's Minister for External Affairs, expected the implementation of his ideas to result in a "fundamental recasting of South Asia's regional relationships... to create a climate of greater confidence and close and mutually beneficial co-operation." The two doctrines would require fundamentally different national security strategies to implement though these would not be mutually exclusive and would even overlap in certain areas. Radically different approaches to national security from decade to decade can only lead to a mismatch between capabilities and intentions and must be resolved through wider national debate.

The closest that government documents in India come to articulating national security and foreign policy objectives are the annual reports of the MoD and the Ministry of External Affairs (MEA). In fact, it was only with the 1997-98 annual report that the MoD for the first time spelt out India's national security objectives. Commenting on this interesting development, Raja Menon wrote recently: "The Annual Defence Report of 1997-98 has many welcome changes and for the first time, the notion of 'sacred territory' has been watered down. In all the previous years the role of the armed forces was depicted purely and solely as the 'defence of our territorial integrity', exhibiting a mindset that was not conducive to understanding coercive diplomacy, the manipulation of risk and the threat of military action."

In its opening chapter entitled "National Security Environment", the Annual Report of 1997-98 stated that India's national security objectives are served by:

- Defending the country's borders as defined by law and enshrined in the Constitution and protecting the lives and property of its citizens against terrorism and insurgencies.
- Promoting further co-operation and understanding with neighbouring countries and implementing mutually agreed confidence-building measures.
- Working with countries of the Non-Aligned Movement to address key challenges before the international community and engaging in co-operative security initiatives such as the ASEAN Regional Forum (ARF).
- Pursuing security and strategic dialogues with major powers and key partners.
- Following a consistent and principled policy on disarmament and international security issues based on universality, non-discrimination and equal security for all.
- Having a secure and effective deterrent against the use or the threat of use of weapons of mass destruction against India.

Post-Pokhran II in May 1998, in the 1998-99 Annual Report, the issue of deterrence against weapons of mass destruction was moved up from the last place to the second place in the national security objectives and was re-worded as follows: "Having a secure, effective and credible minimum deterrent against the use or threat of use of weapons of mass destruction against India. The profile of this deterrent, including accurate and refined delivery systems, will not be circumscribed in range and payload by any outside pressure or influence but will be determined by the country's threat perception at any point of time." Also, a new sub-para on technology control regimes was added: "Insulating the country from the effect of individual or group restrictions on the transfer of material, equipment and technologies that have a bearing on India's security, particularly its defence preparedness. This involves a greater emphasis on in-house research, development and production of the nation's requirements and recourse to feasible alternative sources." In the 1998-99 Annual Report, in the objective on the country's disarmament policy, the phrase "based on the principles of supreme national interest" has been added after the words "and international security issues". Curiously, the report refers to the territorial dispute with China as a "boundary" dispute. A careful reading of the national security objectives enunciated in the annual reports of the MoD reveals a tendency to mix objectives with policy in some cases and shows that the objectives are mere statements of intent in others.

According to the MoD, "... although there has been no specifically written document called India's National Defence Policy, yet it has been articulated clearly and unambiguously through various policy statements over the years. The policy articulated since independence is as follows:

"That our military capability is to be so directed to ensuring the defence of national territory over land, sea and air encompassing among others the inviolability of our land borders, island territories, offshore assets and our maritime trade routes. Government have repeatedly made it clear that it is not our objective to influence/interfere/dominate (the) region on the basis of military strength."

In a submission made by the MoD to the Standing Committee on Defence, it was stated that the following aspects "fully depict the national security interests":

- Defence of national territory over land, sea and air, encompassing among others the inviolability of our land borders, island territories, offshore assets and our maritime trade routes.
- To secure an internal environment whereby our Nation State is insured against any threat to its unity or progress on the basis of religion, language, ethnicity or socio-economic dissonance.
- To enable our country to exercise a degree of influence over the nations in our immediate neighbourhood to

promote harmonious relationship in tune with our national interests.

- To be able to effectively contribute towards regional and international stability.
- To possess an effective out-of-the-country contingency capability to prevent destabilisation of the small nations in our immediate neighbourhood that could have adverse security implications for us.

Though national security interests and objectives have been spelt out in bits and pieces by the Government, in annual reports and while answering the queries of the Standing Committee on Defence, as brought out above, these have tended to change from time to time and have not been subject to direct parliamentary oversight.

These policy statements are of a transitory nature and could sometimes even be based on the personal predilections of policy makers who may be in power at a given point in time. A case in point is the question of whether or not China poses a threat to India. It is well known that while the Defence Minister was reported to have named China as India's number one threat, the Minister for External Affairs subsequently ruled out such an assessment. Hence, these transitory policy statements do not amount to a comprehensive, nationally debated approach that is sanctified by parliamentary consensus transcending the political divide.

Brahma Chellaney has written: "... it needs to be recognised that national security is much more than defence policy. The defence of India means the defence of its national interests. National security demands integrated planning and co-ordinated use of India's political, military, diplomatic and scientific resources to advance its core interests... Unfortunately, India lacks a long-term national security strategy despite the pressing problems it confronts. There is no integrated policy-making process that seeks to make specific policies compatible with each other... serious efforts have (not been) made to establish institutionalised methods so that policy-making is driven less by personalities and more by long-term integrated planning.

A host of functional inefficiencies continue to burden Indian policy-making constricting any government's ability to manage national security in a prudent, cost-effective and result-oriented manner..."

Even the Kargil Review Committee Report has recommended an overhaul of the present system: "The Committee strongly feels that the Kargil experience, the continuing proxy war and the prevailing nuclearised security environment justify a thorough review of the national security system in its entirety."

It clearly emerges that the manifold existing and emerging external and internal threats to national security demand a comprehensive and mature system for their handling and management.

Present Government policies appear to reflect individual ministerial approaches rather than a holistic integrated approach. Coherence in application can only flow from a synergised national security strategy. Only an all-encompassing national security management system can take into account all the prevalent inter-ministerial, inter-departmental and civil-military diversities. The emerging asymmetric threats require systematic evaluation and meticulous planning, so that long-term projections can be made in respect of military force structures and the development of the necessary capabilities.

Only when a comprehensive national security strategy is formulated to deal with the existing and emerging threats on a long- and mid-term basis, can the responsibilities of the armed forces and concerned government departments be clearly visualised. Based on the security objectives and the responsibilities assigned, the Services can review their organisational and force structures and make recommendations to the government to institute the changes necessary to translate policy into action. The virtues of long-term defence planning cannot be over-emphasised. Ad hoc functioning on a year-to-year basis leads to imperfection in decision-making and tends to result in avoidable waste.

FOREIGN POLICY CHALLENGES FOR MODI

The massive mandate that Indian Prime Minister-designate Narendra Modi has managed to secure for the Bharatiya Janata Party (BJP) is certainly a verdict against the status quo in India. The buoyant stock market demonstrated the confidence of the business class over his promises regarding the economy. And, the speed with which world leaders, including Pakistani Prime Minister Nawaz Sharif and Bangladeshi Prime Minister Sheikh Hasina congratulated him meant they were eager to engage with his government. With the leash of coalition politics gone, Modi is expected to pursue a more proactive foreign policy, maybe one driven by economy. In fact, he has demonstrated his intent by extending invitations to the heads of states and governments of the SAARC countries for his swearing-in ceremony on May 26.

The US obviously had an inkling of the verdict weeks ago, and had therefore dispatched its then Ambassador to New Delhi, Nancy Powell, to call on him and smoothen ruffled feathers, especially over the visa row. The US President Barack Obama too spoke with Modi soon after the results saying he was looking forward to working closely with him.

However, one must realise that the key to India's emergence as a regional and global power lies in New Delhi's ability to calibrate a policy that succeeds in improving relations with its immediate neighbours—particularly, Pakistan, Bangladesh, and China. If Modi is to rewrite the India story by reviving the economy and accelerating the growth rate, his government will have to make sure India's neighbourhood is politically stable and economically sound. Only a stable neighbourhood can make India expand its footprint beyond the sub-continent and let it pursue its big power ambitions.

What could Modi's policy towards Pakistan be?

Over the course of the election process, he stated that there can be no talks amid the din of gunfire and bomb explosions. Many in Pakistan, rightly or otherwise, sought to interpret this as a pre-condition set by Modi. The challenges before Modi are manifold. First, he has to demonstrate that he is a tough leader who will not let India be regarded as a soft power by anyone. Second, he has to prove that he has the foresight and the statesmanship to actually take India-Pakistan relations beyond what his predecessor Atal Behari Vajpayee could achieve.

Most importantly, if Modi is to prove he is different, he has to deal with the 'K' word, and try and settle the Kashmir issue; and not just retain the status quo. The key question here is whether Modi will be able to enjoy the trust and cooperation of the stakeholders in Jammu & Kashmir – particularly after the BJP, in its 2014, election manifesto stated that it would like to revoke Article 370 that gives special status to the state. The silver lining is that Pakistanis have expressed hope about a thaw in the long-fraught ties between the two neighbours under Modi. Sharif has already invited Modi to visit Pakistan and Islamabad has been quick to talk about granting India the 'Most Favoured Nation' status to set the ball rolling.

The tragedy of the Manmohan Singh era in Indian diplomacy has been its failure to forge strong ties with smaller neighbours such as Bangladesh. The Bangladeshi economy is not really buoyant, although Dhaka talks about a good growth rate, and, therefore, trade and business is important for the country. The balance of trade is heavily tilted against Bangladesh, and until recently, New Delhi did not do much to set in motion measures to reverse the trend.

Modi, in the course of his campaign did refer to Bangladesh in not so pleasant terms. He stated that after his government takes over, Bangladeshis will have to leave India. This is not a controversial remark because Modi was referring to illegal Bangladeshi immigrants and most parties and groups in Border States like Assam want illegal immigrants from that country to be detected and deported.

This had been a good election-time rhetoric, but Modi's biggest challenge will be to detect illegal Bangladeshi immigrants who have to be confirmed as illegal aliens by the due process of law. With Dhaka firm in its stand that its citizens have not illegally migrated to India, dealing with the issue will be difficult. However, such sensitive issues can be dealt with in a more comfortable manner if ties between the two nations improve with a good measure of trust.

China is another country that Modi referred to, rather aggressively, during his campaign in Arunachal Pradesh, the Indian state that Beijing has set its eyes on. He had actually warned China to shed its "mindset of expansionism" and pledged to "protect my country." In fact, India's China challenge will continue even under Modi, and dealing with Beijing will require more engagement in diverse fields; and, of course, a strong deterrence. Going by Modi's 'vikas' or development mantra, his immediate challenge along the Chinese frontier will be to improve the infrastructure of our armed forces to get a level playing field during critical times. Modi's China challenge will be to reduce the gap with that country – something that India can actually do. Retention of the current status quo cannot achieve any of this and Modi is unlikely to continue with old approaches.

INDIA'S SECURITY CONCEPT ON ITS CHINA POLICY

India's post-Cold War security concept and adjustments to its China policy. In the process of this discussion, we have distinguished two phases of adjustment to both the post-Cold War India security concept and China policy, and established that these changes were more or less simultaneous. We have also found that India's China policy reflects its security concept; in other words that adjustments to the content of India's China policy correspond to continuities and discontinuities in India's security concept. It may be said that this consistency demonstrates the important influence India's security concept has had on its China policy. Policy-making, in any event, is the linking of concepts and policy; in other words, concepts, through government policy-making, crystallize into policy. Exploring the evolution of the Indian policy-making class and mechanisms, therefore, also benefits understanding of the manner in which security concepts of different eras and phases have influenced India's China policy.

India's foreign policy behaviour during the Cold War was largely determined by a few predominant personalities, both its foreign and security policies having long been dominated by Nehru and Indira Gandhi. The two leader's views on China had decisive influence on India's China policy. When considering India's defeat in the 1962 Sino–Indian Border Conflict and the open wound it represented to both the Nehru family and the INC, their adoption of an unyielding tack toward China was the sole political means of saving face. Sino–Indian relations consequently remained in stalemate for nearly 30 years. When Rajiv Gandhi replaced his mother in 1985, he seemed at first to follow her line on foreign policy.

The rapidly changing international situation, however, forced him to veer from it, and specific improvements in Sino–Soviet relations compelled his adjustments to India's China policy. Soviet leader Mikhail Gorbachev urged Rajiv Gandhi during a visit to India in 1986 to improve relations with China, saying it would suit Soviet interests, and hinting at a press conference that the USSR would no longer be willing to provide support to India in the event of Sino–Indian conflict. In this situation, Rajiv Gandhi considered that India on its own would be powerless against a threat on two fronts. He was hence forced to change his preparations for a two-front war, as it was apparent that dispelling tensions along the eastern front through reconciliation with China would allow him to concentrate India's energies on the western front with Pakistan.

The Nehru family's stately bearing was absent after the Cold War, and the INC's power had declined. The insularity that had characterized India's foreign policy-making process since independence, however, did not change. The nation's foreign and security policy stayed in the hands of the prime minister and cabinet from 1991 to 1996, during which time the views of Prime Minister Rao and leaders of the INC government on security and foreign policy matters were decisive, and the influence of parliament, think tanks and academic institutions was negligible. It is notable, however, that Rao's background as home minister, defence minister and external affairs minister throughout the 1980s, as well as his status as the Congress Party's elder statesman, signified that he was a loyal adherent of Nehruvianism, and unrepresentative of any new type of thinking. The transformation of India's security concept during the Rao administration, therefore, can be understood as entirely the result of external forces.

As earlier mentioned, changes in the international and domestic situation compelled Rao to change his understanding of national strength. He began emphasizing the strategic influence of economic strength and promoting restoration of the economy as a matter of urgency in withstanding security threats in the aftermath of the Cold War.

This passive reaction to a complex situation gave the impression of India's overall foreign policy as passive and defensive.

India adopted a focused approach to diplomacy during this period, directing its energies towards restoring the economy but maintaining a low profile in international affairs, as expressed in its China policy. Rao continued and furthered Rajiv Gandhi's adjustments by focusing on stabilization of Sino–Indian political relations and establishing tranquil borders as means to ensuring the recovery of India's domestic economy.

Two major changes occurred in India's foreign policy-making process during 1998. The first was the BJP's assumption of office that ended the long-standing INC power monopoly, and established foundations for a clean break with the traditional security concept. Although the BJP's domestic policies had a relatively ideological slant and promoted a Hinduist revival, the party was pragmatic as regards foreign policy.

In contrast to the Congress Party, it dared to confront history, criticise India's previous foreign policy and introduce new thinking. Jaswant Singh, successively the Vajpayee government's External Affairs Minister and Finance Minister, published early in 1999 a book entitled *Defending India* in which he systematically describes his new security concept. Various views were thereafter expressed in government-issued articles.

The BJP was obviously preparing to move on from the passive security concept of the Rao era. The second major change was India's refinement of its foreign policy-making mechanism. The November 1998 establishment of the National Security Council symbolized India's casting off of the influence and control of personality-based policy-making in favour of scientific research, inquiry and decision-making, and comprehensive long-term planning. The introduction by National Security Advisory Board subordinated to the National Security Council of scholarly authorities, reporters and former government and military officials demonstrated how much more open India's foreign policy-making process had become.

The BJP differed in its approach to China policy from both that of the Cold War era Nehru family, with its 1962 complex, and the early 1990s Rao government, which had been wearied and bound hand and foot by domestic and international pressure. The BJP's seizing of this historic opportunity confirmed India's rise as the nation's long-term strategic goal and placed its relationship with China on the strategic level. In other words, the BJP saw the Sino–Indian relationship as an important influence on India's rise. Although the two nations would be dealing with historically significant problems, they could be seen as a starting point.

The gradual opening of India's foreign policy-making process, moreover, made way for a vibrant exchange of ideas regarding China policy, which fell roughly into three groups: the first held that Sino–Indian cooperation suits both sides' interests and that post-Cold War China has no intention of making an enemy of India, desiring instead friendly relations and strategic partnership; the second that China is a long-term strategic threat to India because China's strategic objectives lie in establishing hegemony over Asia, which necessitates India's containment and, therefore, limitation of Indian influence. India, therefore, should adopt diametrically opposed policies; and the third group, situated between the two, held that the two nations could simultaneously rise to become main Asian powers and that competition and cooperation could coexist. Discussions on how to evaluate and understand China by Indian scholars and strategic circles are ongoing. After frequent debates among Indian National Security Council groups, the third, middle-ground viewpoint seems to be gaining acceptance.

When the INC regained power in 2004, a variety of factors led the new government to carry on with the previous administration's security concept. The new INC government's China policy was its predecessor's legacy, because the rise of India's international status during the BJP coalition government left the INC powerless to dispute the success of the previous government's foreign policy. The INC's democratized and more youthful leadership team was also willing to jettison historical baggage and look to the future. Although the Nehru family's leadership role within the Congress Party remained uncontested, the influence of Prime Minister Manmohan Singh and Foreign Minister Mukherjee on foreign and security policy could not be disregarded. Moreover, the liberalization of India's foreign policy-making process was superimposed against a long-standing civil service system which ensured continuity of policy. In other words, many masterminds of BJP foreign policy still active in the external affairs ministry, defence ministry and other relevant functional departments under the INC, as well as in consultative committees, the media, think tanks and other non-functional departments, continued to exert influence.

Substantial changes occurred in India's China policy after the end of the Cold War whereby the nation's long-standing (1962–1988) antagonistic approach became one of reconciliation and engagement. These adjustments originated to a great extent in changes in the sub-continent's post-Cold War security concept, manifest in two major shifts which effected two major phases of adjustment in India's China policy. The new post-Cold War China policy nonetheless retained traces of the former, programme, imbuing it with a duality that reflected the overlap of India's old and new security concepts.

A change in India's security concept first became apparent during the period from the end of the Cold War to 1998. The first phase of adjustments this change triggered in India's China policy was evident in the sub-continent's extended concept of military might as national strength to one encompassing economic factors, and acknowledgement of the strategic value of economic strength in countering what it perceived as the looming threat of marginalization within the international community. Restoration of the domestic economy hence became a main measure through which to resist security threats in the post-Cold War era. Having made this shift in foreign policy objectives towards economic recovery, India set about creating a favourable environment within which to achieve this goal. Overall implementation of a China policy of preserving stable Sino–Indian relations by guaranteeing border tranquillity was vital to achieving this strategic objective. India consequently focused on the feasibility of reconciliation and, in view of China's reflective, inward-looking mood, no longer viewed China as an enemy. As regards India's specific policies, while focusing on the establishment of a progressive means to guaranteeing tranquil borders, thereby stabilizing Sino–Indian relations, India at the same time sought communication and cooperation in other areas. To avoid provoking China, the Indian government made tactical adjustments to its approach to Tibet from that of exploiting the issue and causing uproar to handling the matter in a low-key manner.

The new developments apparent in India's security concept in 1999 brought with it the second phase of adjustments to India's China policy. Indian leaders considered that the nation's security environment had improved to the extent that it constituted a strategic opportunity for India to rise to global-power status. This change in thinking and understanding caused the second shift of objective in India's foreign policy from that of improving the economy to the grand goal of global-power status. It corresponded to India's acknowledgement of the crucial nature of the Sino–Indian relationship and change of focus from border tranquillity and stable political relations to comprehensive considerations of how the two nations' relationship would strategically affect India's; rise. These insights compelled a shift of objective in India's China policy towards making China a positive factor in the sub-continent's rise; also recognition that this objective could be accomplished only by maintaining a stable basis for Sino–Indian relations. Official introduction during this phase of a comprehensive security concept signalled India's adoption of a more pragmatic, comprehensive handling of its relations with China.

The specific steps it adopted were: increasing economic cooperation with China, thus benefiting India's economic development and stabilizing bilateral political relations; strengthening military communication and security dialogue, thus deepening understanding of China's strategic intentions towards India, increasing mutual trust, minimizing misunderstandings and avoiding conflict; and seeking Chinese support in its quest for a permanent seat on the UN Security Council, which would expand India's political power and international prestige.

In the course of research, however, it became apparent to the author that India's security concept did not undergo a thoroughgoing change after the Cold War ended, as elements of the Cold War approach remained in place. Although India's security concept extended after 1988 to include both military and economic security, the ultimate purpose of national defence as regards a fundamental guarantee of security nonetheless remained that of increased military strength to safeguard national unity and territorial integrity. India abandoned its strategy of pursuing security through alliances, yet still viewed parity and the principle of checks and balances as hallmarks of its national defence. Influenced as it was by traditional concepts, post-Cold War India's China policy was imbued with vigilance. Even though India did not perceive China as a threat in the short term, it was nevertheless concerned that the swing in balance of power between the two was not in its favour, and that China constituted a potential obstacle to India's rise. Indian leaders consequently embarked on a race against China to expand comprehensive national strength, particularly military force, including India's nuclear capability, as the means to a balance of power. India at the same time sought to offset Chinese influence both regionally and globally through development of strategic relationships with the United States, Japan and other nations. The sub-continent also remained vigilant in the long-standing issues of border disputes and Sino–Pakistani relations, and maintained pressure on China in this regard.

Changes in post-Cold War India's security concept were thus the result of both domestic and foreign factors. The first change during the early post-Cold War period was triggered by passive reactions to transformations in the nation's domestic and international situation that, in turn, prompted a passive transformation of thinking and understanding, manifest in passive defensiveness of India's foreign policy, specifically its China policy.

The security concept that appeared during the late 1990s was comparatively proactive. The expanded strength of India's domestic economy and improvement of its external environment compelled a new understanding of security issues, as expressed in the proactive change in its security concept. This assertiveness was manifest in strategy and in an active, enterprising foreign policy. Seizing the historic opportunity to realize India's rise had become the common security objective of both major Indian political parties. Decentralization of political power and expanded openness of the foreign policy-making process, however, caused India's old and new security concepts to bind into one, and the resultant duality of India's hybrid security concept since the Cold War's end is reflected in its China policy. As India's dual security concept will continue into the foreseeable future, the duality of its China policy will be difficult to change.

5

Modi's Foreign Policy of Pakistan

SOCIAL RELATIONS WITH PAKISTAN

Cultural Links

India and Pakistan, to some degree have similar cultures, cuisines and languages which underpin the historical ties between the two. Pakistani singers, musicians, comedians and entertainers have enjoyed widespread popularity in India, with many achieving overnight fame in the Indian filming industry Bollywood. Likewise, Indian music and films are very popular in Pakistan. Being located in the northernmost region of the South Asia, Pakistan's culture is somewhat similar to that of North India. The Punjab region was split into Punjab, Pakistan and Punjab, India following the independence and partition of the two countries in 1947.

The Punjabi people are today the largest ethnic group in Pakistan and also an important ethnic group of northern India. The founder of the Sikhism religion was born in the modern-day Pakistani Punjab province, in the city of Nankana Sahib. Each year, millions of Indian Sikh pilgrims cross over to visit holy Sikh sites in Nankana Sahib.

The Sindhi people are the native ethnic group of the Pakistani province of Sindh. Many Hindu Sindhis migrated to India in 1947, making the country home to a sizable Sindhi community. In addition, the millions of Muslims who migrated from India to the newly-created Pakistan during independence came to be known as the Muhajir people; they are settled predominantly in Karachi and still maintain family links in India.

Relations between Pakistan and India have also resumed through platforms such as media and communications. Aman ki Asha is a joint venture and campaign between *The Times of India* and the *Jang Group* calling for mutual peace and development of diplomatic and cultural relations.

Geographic Links

The Indo-Pakistani border is the official international boundary that demarcates the Indian states of Punjab,Rajasthan and Gujarat from the Pakistani provinces of Punjab and Sindh. The Wagah border is the only road crossing between India and Pakistan and lies on the famous Grand Trunk Road, connecting Lahore, Pakistan withAmritsar, India.

Each evening, the Wagah border ceremony takes place at the Wagah border in which the flags are lowered and guards on both sides make a pompous military display and exchange handshakes.

Linguistic Ties

Hindustani is the linga franca of North India and Pakistan, as well as the national language of both countries, under the name Hindi and Urdu, respectively. Standard Urdu is mutually intelligible with Standard Hindi. Both languages share the same Indic base and are all but indistinguishable in phonology and grammar. Most linguists consider them to be two standardized forms of a same language; when speaking colloquially, a speaker of Urdu has no trouble understanding a speaker of Hindi. Apart from Hindustani, India and Pakistan also share a distribution of the Punjabi language (written in the Gurmukhiscript in Indian Punjab, and the Shahmukhi script in Pakistani Punjab), Kashmiri language and Sindhi language.

Matrimonial Ties

Some Indian and Pakistani people marry across the border, particularly with present generation of relatives who had migrated from India at the time of partition. In April 2010 a high profile Pakistani cricketer, Shoaib Malik married the Indian tennis star Sania Mirza. The wedding received much media attention and was said to transfix both India and Pakistan.

Sporting Ties

Cricket and hockey matches between the two (as well as other sports to a lesser degree such as those of the SAARC games) have often been political in nature. During theSoviet invasion of Afghanistan General Zia-ul Haq traveled to India for a bout of "cricket diplomacy" to keep India from supporting the Soviets by opening another front. Pervez Musharaff also tried to do the same more than a decade later but to no avail. In tennis, Rohan Bopanna of India and Aisam-ul-Haq Qureshi of Pakistan have formed a successful duo and have been dubbed as the "Indo-Pak Express."

Diasporic Relations

The large size of the Indian diaspora and Pakistani diaspora in many different countries throughout the world has created strong diasporic relations. British Indians and British Pakistanis, the largest and second-largest ethnic minorities living in the United Kingdom respectively, are said to have friendly relations with one another. It is quite common for a "Little India" and a "Little Pakistan" to co-exist in South Asian ethnic enclaves in overseas countries. There are various cities such as Birmingham, Blackburn andManchester where British Indians and British Pakistanis live alongside each other in peace and harmony. Both Indians and Pakistanis living in the UK fit under the category ofBritish Asian. The UK is also home to the Pakistan & India friendship forum. In the United States, Indians and Pakistanis are classified under the South Asian Americancategory and share many cultural traits. The British MEP Saj Karim is of Pakistani origin. He is a member of the

European Parliament Friends of India Group, Karim was also responsible for opening up Europe to free trade with India. He narrowly escaped the Mumbai attacks at Hotel Taj in November 2008. Despite the atrocity, Mr Karim does not wish the remaining killer Ajmal Kasab to be sentenced to death. He said: "I believe he had a fair and transparent trial and I support the guilty verdict. "But I am not a supporter of capital punishment. I believe he should be given a life sentence, but that life should mean life."

Trade Links

Trade across direct routes has been curtailed formally, so the bulk of India-Pakistan trade is routed through Dubai. Re-evaluation

The insurgents who initially started their movement as a pro-Kashmiri independence movement, have gone through a lot of change in their ideology. Most of the insurgents portray their struggle as a religious one. Indian analysts allege that by supporting these insurgents, Pakistan is trying to wage a proxy war against India while Pakistan claims that it regards most of these insurgentgroups as "freedom fighters" rather than terrorists

Internationally known to be the most deadly theatre of conflict, nearly 10 million people, including Muslims, Hindus, and Buddhists, have been fighting a daily battle for survival. The *cross-border firing* between India and Pakistan, and the terrorist attacks combined have taken its toll on the Kashmiris, who have suffered poor living standards and an erosion of human rights.

INDIA-PAKISTAN RELATIONS: HISTORICAL BACKGROUND

Shortly after 3:45 PM on May 11, 1998 at Pokhran, a desert site in the Indian state of Rajisthan, groups of local Bishnoi herders—whose customs forbid killing animals or cutting trees—heard a huge explosion, and watched in amazement as an enormous dust cloud floated in the sky. What the Indian farmers did not realize, but the diplomats in Washington and around the world soon grasped, was the fact that India had just joined the United States, Russia, England, France and China as the newest member of the nuclear club. On that warm May afternoon, Indian nuclear scientists successfully exploded three atomic devices amounting to about six times the destructive power of the American bomb dropped on Hiroshima in 1945. The next day, as the world tried to absorb the frightening news, India ignited two more nuclear explosions.

Even as ninety percent of Indians applauded then-Prime Minister Vajpayee's decision to go nuclear, then-U.S. President Clinton immediately reacted to the explosions with shock and criticized India's nuclear testing. The American President argued that India's actions violated the Comprehensive Test Ban Treaty endorsed by 149 nations and the 1970 non-proliferation treaty signed by 185 nations. Despite the fact that neither India nor Pakistan has signed the treaties, the President, citing the 1994 Nuclear Proliferation Prevention Act, immediately called for economic sanctions against India including cutting off $40 million in economic and military aid, and all American bank loans. The President also asked the International Monetary Fund and World Bank to cancel all new loans which could cost India around $14.5 billion worth of public projects, including a major modernization of India's often failing electrical system. Moreover, Japan and other industrial nations soon followed the U.S. example and froze on-going projects in India worth over a billion dollars in aid.

Pakistan Responds

As the five nuclear powers, all permanent members of the United Nations Security Council, discussed ways to punish India as well as ways to prevent Pakistan from testing its own nuclear devices, the leaders of Pakistan were busily moving forward with their own nuclear plans.

On May 28th, Nawaz Sharif, Pakistan's prime minister at that time, announced that following India's lead, Pakistan had successfully exploded five "nuclear devices." Not content to equal India's five tests, Pakistan proceeded on May 30th to explode yet a sixth device and at the same time the Prime Minister announced that his government would soon be able to launch nuclear war heads on missiles.

Both President Clinton and a majority of the world community condemned Pakistan's nuclear testing, although China was much less harsh in its criticism of Pakistan, its close ally. Following the sanctions policy after India's tests, the United States, Japan, Britain, Canada and Germany ended their aid to Pakistan and asked the International Monetary Fund (IMF) and World Bank to place a moratorium on loans to Pakistan. However, despite President Clinton's wish to impose a world-wide system of economic sanctions on India and Pakistan, a vast majority of western nations have refused to join the effort.

The Story Behind the Headlines

Despite the seeming suddenness of India's and Pakistan's decisions to test nuclear devices and in so doing seek to join the other five world nuclear nations, the headlines following the explosions "heard round the world," had a fifty-year history. Since their independence as new nations in 1947, India and Pakistan have followed a path of mutual animosity. Pakistan was created as a national homeland for the Muslim-majority areas of the subcontinent, while India proposed to become a secular nation that included about 85 percent Hindus, but also more than ten percent Muslims as well as large numbers of Sikhs, Christians and members of other religions.

Soon after the partition of the sub-continent into the two nations, about 17 million people fled their homes and journeyed to either Pakistan or India. In one of the largest exchanges of populations in history, violence soon broke out with Muslims on one side and Sikhs and Hindus on the other. The resulting blood shed in the Punjab and West Bengal regions left more than one million people dead in its wake.

In the midst of this refugee movement and open violence, the governments of India and Pakistan hastily tried to divide the assets of British India between the two new countries. From weapons and money, down to paper clips and archaeological treasures, all had to be divided. The British had left behind, besides about half of the subcontinent that it directly governed, some 562 independent or "princely" states. The provision was that each state could remain independent, join Pakistan or accede to India. A violent competition soon resulted as the two new nations sought to win to their own nations the largest and most strategically located states, such as Hyderabad and Kashmir. Because Kashmir was more than 70% Muslim, Pakistan insisted that a vote be taken in the state. However, India argued, since the Maharaja of Kashmir was Hindu, he had right to take the state into India. Even as independence was being celebrated, India and Pakistan began a covert war in Kashmir and the struggle for that state still goes on today.

In 1947, 1965 and 1971 India and Pakistan fought wars that did not change the status of Kashmir, but did result in the 1971 further partition of West and East Pakistan into the two nations of Pakistan and Bangladesh.

Not only did the architects of Indian foreign policy fear Pakistan, but in 1962, after China's sudden invasion of northeast India, they suddenly realized the ancient protection of the Himalayan Mountains had vanished. India now would have to build sufficient military power to protect itself from both Pakistan and China, the largest country in the world and a major military power armed with nuclear weapons.

Soon after the China war of 1962, Indian scientists began developing its nuclear capability. Under Indira Gandhi's Prime Ministership in 1974, India successfully exploded a nuclear device, announcing to the world its scientific capacity to develop nuclear bombs. Because of the strong world opinion against nuclear testing, India did not undertake additional nuclear testing until May, 1998. However, this fourteen-year moratorium on nuclear testing did not mean Indian scientists and political leaders were not planning to join the nuclear club.

India in the 1990s: the Moratorium Ends

Although Prime Minister Rajiv Gandhi reversed his mother's policy of nuclear development, when a new prime minister

Narasimha Rao assumed power in 1991, India resumed its plans for nuclear development and in December, 1995, Rao was ready to authorize a nuclear test—only to be discovered by CIA spy satellite and discouraged by President Clinton from going forward with the tests. With the election of the Hindu Nationalist, Bharata Janata Party in 1998, Prime Minister Atal Vajpayee ordered Indian scientists to proceed with plans for testing as soon as possible. This lead to the series of detonations in May, and the subsequent quick response by Pakistan.

Foreign Policy Relations

The United States has treaties which provide nuclear umbrella to Japan and NATO nations. At present, the United States has cordial relations with China. American policy is worked out in tension between those who insist on expanded human rights in China, and those who favor opening markets and investments in China and downplaying human rights issues. The United States was closely allied with Pakistan until end of Cold War. Pakistan provided bases for U-2 flights and conduit for arms to Afghanistan rebels. The United States provided most of Pakistani military aid from 1954 to the 1980s. China is now the major military supplier to Pakistan. The United States has maintained cool relations with India because of its refusal to join the west during the Cold War, its pursuit of a non-alignment foreign policy and for its tight controls on American investment and business enterprise in India.

China is the premier military power in Asia and considers Pakistan its oldest and most powerful Asian ally. China continues to occupy areas inside of India's borders as a result of the Indo-China war of 1962.

China has nuclear-armed missiles positioned against India along the Himalayan border and in Tibet, in addition to being Pakistan's main military weapons provider. Russia has had close relations with India since Indira Gandhi became prime minister in 1966. Russia provides most of India's military sales. After the demise of the Soviet Empire, Russia is unable to provide economic or military aid to India. India has pursued a policy of non-alignment with Soviet Union and United States since its independence. India's planned economy was not open to U.S. investment until change of policy toward free market in 1991.

India would not accept American military aid or join alliances, thus alienating U.S. leaders and majority of Americans. Under President Kennedy, the United States supported India in its war with China. Under Nixon, the United States supported Pakistan in 1971 in the war that led to creation of Bangladesh (the former East Pakistan). America sent a nuclear-armed aircraft carrier to Bay of Bengal, which helped motivate India to go nuclear. Now that Russia is weak, India feels isolated and alone in world community. India has felt that the United States has also been hostile to India and that we now are promoting China as the major power in all of Asia. Pakistani testing of Gauri missile on April 6th, 1998 was a major factor in India's decision to undertake nuclear testing. India will suffer from the end of economic aid, but its leaders have calculated that that the nation can survive the sanctions.

Pakistan relied on its close alliance with the United States from 1954 through the 1980s. During the 1990s, leaders looked more to China for support and military technology and hardware; China is currently a major supplier of these components to Pakistan. The Pakistani foreign minister traveled to China for consultations ten days before Pakistan conducted nuclear tests. Pakistan will suffer far more than India as a result of economic sanctions by world community. Loss of aid will result in undermining of currency, great increase in debt and increase in poverty.

In the hunt for Osama bin Laden in Afghanistan and Pakistan in early 2002, U.S. relations with Pakistan and its leader, President General Pervez Musharraf, improved, which further aggravated India-Pakistan relations.

While economic sanctions were lifted, Pakistani militants staged several attacks and bombings; in one occassion, targeted Indian and Kashmiri legislatures. The United States feared possible nuclear retaliation and advised Americans to evacuate both South Asian countries. Today, U.S. relations with India and Pakistan are strong. In March 2006, when U.S. President George W. Bush visited South Asia, he remarked that we "are now united by opportunities that can lift our people." In India, he commented that "The United States and India, separated by half the globe, are closer than ever before, and the partnership between our free nations has the power to transform the world."

INDIAN AND PAKISTANI IDENTITY FORMATION

In analysing the role of identity in India-Pakistan relations, it is crucial to recognise the socially constructed, as opposed to primordial or instrumental, quality of identity formation. Many adopt a primordialist interpretation and attribute the enduring rivalry to the irreconcilable worldviews of, and entrenched hostilities between, monolithic 'Muslim' Pakistan and 'Hindu' India—essentially explaining the conflict as an offshoot of Hindu-Muslim communalism. While superficially appealing, this argument fails to account for the centuries of relative coexistence and inter-social, cultural and religious connections and exchanges between generally pluralistic Hindu and Muslim communities prior to the twentieth century. More fundamentally, it ignores the *socially constructed*, rather than natural, quality of both states' national and state identities; something this section aims to address, beginning with India. Much of 'modern' India's self-conception was originally formulated around Indian nationalist discourse and spearheaded by the highly-dominant Congress party before and following independence.

In particular, Jawaharlal Nehru was pivotal in helping to articulate the central features of Indian identity—not in a liberal-individualist sense, but as a purposeful agent embedded in a social structure consisting of the intersubjective ideas of the wider Indian nationalist movement. The first core element of India's self-conception was *Sarva Dharma Samabhava* (secularism), which was key in distinguishing India from the 'communal' and 'reactionary' Pakistani 'other,' highlighting the in-group/out-group differentiation element of identity formation. Indeed, Nehru himself defined India's self-image as 'a secular nation' by differentiating it with ' two-nation theory which Pakistan is sponsoring.'

The 'exceptionalism' of Indian democracy in South Asia as well India's espousal of non-alignment and its claim to moral leadership in the developing world were the other core 'differentiating markers' from the Pakistani 'other' in India's self-image. In addition, India was deemed a *modern* 'major power'; a successor to the British with a powerful regional and global mission that reflected its 'national greatness.' Narratives and frames were utilised to reify this self-conception; history was interpreted anew and multiculturalism presented as a natural feature of Indian civilisation, while 'pacific' ancient cultural and social traditions coupled with stories exalting the glories of India's past civilisations helped legitimise its 'benign' global role in the international system. Moreover, 'India' was transformed from a vast land of disparate provinces and princely states—described as a 'porridge of irregular and improbable jigsaw puzzle shapes' —into an 'imagined community' whose territorial borders were naturalised and embedded into the national consciousness through 'the popular sacralisation of territory,' embodied in the metaphor of *Bharat Mata*('Mother India').

While India's self-image has been based on secularism, Pakistan's identity was constructed on the mythical narrative of the 'two-nation' theory, popularly articulated by the Muslim League, which posited that the Muslims and Hindus of India represented two monolithic, incompatible civilisations who were based, as Jinnah declared, 'on conflicting ideas and conceptions.' Crucially, Pakistan's national (and state) identity as the homeland of India's Muslims and its self-image as an advanced, *modern* Islamic state was (and continues to be) constructed against the perceived threat of Hindu (the 'other') domination and majoritarianism. Thus, the notion of*parity* between 'Muslim' Pakistan and 'Hindu' India has been central to Pakistan's self-conception. As former Prime Minister Zulifkar Bhutto wrote:

One of the dominant urges for Pakistan has been to dispel the notion of seniority or superiority of Hindu India over Muslim India by creating a Muslim State equal and sovereign to the other State.

Moreover, being different from the Indian 'other' has been essential in providing 'a rationale for the two-nation theory and for Pakistan's battle for a separate identity.' Narratives have thus emphasised Pakistan's Islamic-Arabic roots and '[rejected] everything that was Indian' about Pakistan. Some have suggested the narratives and cultural symbols associated with the 'two-nation' theory were merely instruments in the power struggle between elites (and thus without normative content). However, while the 'two-nation' theory was certainly employed strategically by political entrepreneurs, such activity took place within a normative structure influenced by a mass, broad-based movement, and arose from a genuine fear of 'Hindu domination,' as elements of the Congress-led 'nationalist-secular' movement increasingly incorporated 'Hindu' symbols and policies. Similarly to India, Pakistan was socially constructed as an 'imagined community,' based on the narrative of the two-nation theory. This was achieved not merely through territorial state/nation-building, but more importantly through 'representational practices,' that 'in various ways attempted to inscribe something called India [and Pakistan] with a content, history, meaning, and trajectory.'

The identities of the two states, however, have not been stable and unchanging. Beginning in the 1980s, India's secularism began to decline and its conception of 'self' and 'other' was increasingly informed by the discourse of Hindu nationalism framed by the *Hindutva* movement, which attacked the 'pseudo-secularism' of the Congress for purportedly empowering religious minorities, particularly Muslims (the 'other'), at the expense of Hindus, and sought to 're-imagine' India as a virile and masculine Hindu *rashtra* (state). Narratives were employed to reconstruct Hindus as a homogenous in-group, with India's identity being re-articulated on the principle of *akhand bharat*, or 'one nation, one people, and one culture.'

Critically, Hindu nationalism was invigorated by the 'Muslim question' and Pakistan; the Hindu *rashtra* was constructed in contradistinction to the Muslim and Pakistani 'other.'

Hindutva was further empowered by the formation of BJP governments, notably in 1998. Nevertheless, Hindu nationalist parties were compelled to moderate their agendas to remain in power because of the constraining effects of India's liberal-democratic structures. Thus, rather than forging a Hindu *rashtra*, India's self-conception has been defined by the tensions, compromises and even convergences between secular and Hindu nationalist narratives.

Pakistan also underwent 're-imagining' in the 1980s, as processes of *Islamisation*, particularly under Zia-ul Haq, sought to redefine Pakistan's identity on the basis of orthodox Islam. *Madrassas* and *Jihad* symbolised the new discourse, and fresh narratives about the nation's birth were employed to reconstruct Jinnah and the anti-colonial freedom struggle as Islamists that aimed to establish an Islamic state.

Moreover, protecting Pakistan's Islamic identity and defending its 'ideological frontiers' became crucial for achieving national unity and stability in Pakistan's self-conception. As Zia-ul Haq declared, the 'preservation of [Pakistan's ideology] and the Islamic character of the country ... as important as the security of the country's geographical boundaries.' Islamisation has also been considered vital to the core aim of distinguishing Pakistan from the Indian 'other,' which is reflected in the fear that 'if Pakistan does not become and remain aggressively Islamic, it will become India again.'

Role of identity in shaping actors and foreign policies

The conceptions of identity discussed above have played a pivotal role in shaping both states' actions and understandings of their material and instrumental geopolitical and strategic interests—or their *social purposes*and *cognitive models*—as well as their foreign policies. As Gupta argues, 'cultural and ideological factors [have been] enmeshed with strategic calculations' of both states, which is reflected in their respective*strategic cultures*, which Ken Booth defines as perceptual frameworks entailing the 'traditions, values, attitudes [and] patterns of behaviour' of nations—or in Alistair Johnston's words their 'integrated set of symbols' —that shape states' security discourses and interactions (which are not merely determined by the 'rational' pursuit of instrumental interests). Within this context, one of the 'key elements of Pakistan's strategic culture,' notes Peter Lavoy, has been opposition to Indian hegemony.

This is characterised by what many describe as Pakistan's primary foreign policy goal; to achieve *parity*—politically, diplomatically and even militarily—with India, and to eventually balkanise 'akhand bharat' (united India) in order to make it more manageable and less threatening. This *purposive goal* is not merely a prudent geopolitical strategy arising from threats to state survival by a hegemonic neighbour in an anarchic world, but has been intimately shaped by Pakistan's long-standing self-conception as a strong 'Muslim' state that is equal to 'Hindu' India and must challenge 'Hindu' majoritarianism and domination. For its part, India's own security and strategic discourses have centred on—even 'obsessed' over—the Pakistani 'other.' While realist analysts have derided the 'irrationality' of this preoccupation with a far smaller power, the strategy has been motivated by India's self-image as a secular nation that needs to challenge and demonstrate the artificiality of Pakistan's two-nation theory. The disputed territory of Kashmir attests to the centrality of identity to both states' geostrategic understandings, for the meaning and significance attached to it has been defined by their respective self-conceptions rather than narrow material incentives. For Pakistan, Kashmir is crucial to its 'Muslim' (and pan-Islamic) identity and the two-nation theory, while for India, as former Prime Minister Vajpayee commented in 2002, 'Kashmir is not a piece of land; it is a test case of secularism.' Identity has also played a fundamental role in the most significant security issue—the nuclearisation of the subcontinent. As Das and others have demonstrated, India and Pakistan's nuclear trajectories have been—to a considerable degree—shaped by their self-images.

Thus, by pursuing a nuclear capability, India sought to act out its identity as a *modern* post-colonial state (and indeed a major power) established on the *modernist*principles of secularism, democracy, and scientific and technological progress. Similarly, Pakistan's nuclear programme sought to confirm its 'scientific and technological greatness' and self-image as 'the most advanced Muslim country,' while also being 'a symbol of defiance' to the Indian 'other,' and furthering its goal of *parity* with 'Hindu' India. Indeed, Pakistan originally contextualised its nuclear policy around its 'Islamic' identity, with Bhutto coining the term 'the Islamic bomb' and reasoning that:

> The Christian, Jewish, and Hindu civilizations have [a full nuclear capability]... Only the Islamic civilization was without it ... but this was about to change.

The 1998 nuclear tests further demonstrated how conceptions of 'self' and 'other' have shaped both states' security discourses. For India, the tests reflected the increasing salience of *Hindutva* as a source of Indian identity, as the Hindu-Right BJP government overturned India's longstanding policy of nuclear ambiguity to showcase the nation's 'nuclear teeth,' dubbing the tests 'Operation Shakti' as Hindu nationalist discourse situated it in the context of 'the cult of manliness and virility' that defined the Hindu *rashtra*—in contradistinction to the Muslim and Pakistan 'other.' Realist analysts explained the tests as instances of instrumental power politics vis-a-vis Pakistan, and especially China, but this fails to appreciate that the tests were actually strategically counter-productive and *not* constructed against 'the China threat.' Rather, the tests most importantly represented what Talbot terms the 'Hindutva bomb'—aimed primarily at the Pakistani/Muslim 'other.' Pakistan's subsequent 'tit-for-tat' explosions were also framed within the context of its Islamic identity as an advanced Muslim state reacting to the domineering threat of the Hindu 'other.' Thus, the tests were constructed as the 'Islamic bomb' responding to the 'Hindu bomb,' which also reflected the increasing importance of an orthodox Islamic identity to Pakistan's strategic culture and its foreign policy and security discourses. In India, *Hindutva* was further energised by the post-September 11th security context, as the 'cult of manliness and virility' informed India's new, more aggressive, policy of 'coercive diplomacy' vis-a-vis Pakistan. The Pakistani/Muslim 'other' was now constructed as a despotic *Jihadi* state and 'the epicentre of world terrorism'; as well as a threat to Indian civilisation.

As the preceding discussion has shown, India and Pakistan's identities have shaped their respective understandings of the material world, informed their interests and influenced their foreign policy and security discourses.

NEW FACETS IN INDIA-PAKISTAN RELATIONS

The terrorist attacks of September 11, 2001 in New York and Washington have had profound implications on developments in India-Pakistan relations. The American led offensive against the Taliban resulted in an end to Taliban rule and the installation of a democratically elected Government headed by President Hamid Karzai in Afghanistan.

But, the Taliban, the Al Qaeda and their allies affiliated to the "International Islamic Front" formed by Osama bin Laden in February 1998, retreated into safe havens across the Afghanistan-Pakistan border. They set up base in Baluchistan and the tribal areas (North and South Waziristan) of Pakistan's Northwest Frontier Province. While Pakistan assisted the US and its western allies in tracking down some Al Qaeda leaders, the Taliban leadership was not touched.

It has now regrouped and commenced attacking American led NATO forces in Afghanistan's Southern and Eastern Provinces, adjacent to Afghanistan's borders with Pakistan. One major impact of the removal of the Taliban from power and the passage of UN Security Council Resolution 1363 was the decision by western powers to ban all those organizations affiliated with Osama bin Laden's "International Islamic Front".

The organizations that were thus banned included four extremist Islamist groups backed by Pakistan's Inter Services

Intelligence (ISI) that were playing a leading role in terrorist violence in Jammu and Kashmir (J&K) The terrorist organizations banned internationally included the *Lashkar e taiba*, the *Harkat ul Mujahidee* n, the *Harkat ul Jihad ul Islami* and the *Jaish e Mohammed*. While these organizations continue to operate under new names, the Pakistan Government came to realize that mere resort to terrorist violence in an attempt to force India out of J&K was proving counterproductive and that political initiatives had to be undertaken, if the international community was to be persuaded of Pakistan's commitment to ending terrorist violence and normalizing relations with India.

These developments have resulted in a sustained dialogue between India and Pakistan over the past three years, to enhance cooperation and promote confidence. An agreement has been signed on prior notification of missile tests and measures to avoid incidents at sea between the two navies are being finalized.

New border routes have been opened for travel between the two countries and travel between the two sides of Jammu and Kashmir between Srinagar and Muzzafarabad has resumed after lapse of nearly half a century. It has been agreed for the first time to promote trade across the LOC in J&K. Similar travel arrangements are envisaged between Poonch in the Jammu Region and Rawalkot across the LOC. India has proposed further easing of restrictions for travel between the two sides of Jammu and Kashmir by opening bus routes between Kargil and Skardu in the isolated "Northern Areas" of the State. Most importantly, a cease fire across the Line of Control has been observed by both sides since November 2003.

It was in this background that President Musharraf stated that progress could be made in resolving the issue of J&K only if both sides explore mutually acceptable proposals. He has proposed that J&K should be divided into seven different regions, followed by the "demilitarization" of identified regions. He has specifically demanded that Indian forces should be withdrawn from the urban centres of Baramulla, Kupwara and Srinagar. President Musharraf has also advocated "self governance" in

J&K without clarifying whether such "self governance" would be equally applicable to areas under Pakistan's control. Finally, he has proposed that there should be a system of "Joint Management" of Jammu and Kashmir by India and Pakistan. While welcoming "new ideas" from President Musharraf, India's Prime Minister Dr. Manmohan Singh has proposed that while borders cannot be changed they can be made "irrelevant" or just "mere lines on a map".

He has said that people of both sides of the Line of Control (LOC) in J&K should be allowed to move and trade freely across the LOC. Responding to General Musharraf's proposal of "Joint Management", Dr. Manmohan Singh has suggested that India and Pakistan should devise "cooperative and consultative mechanisms" to promote cooperation across Jammu and Kashmir. Discussions between India and Pakistan on these proposals have been taking place in recent months. Measures to resolve the issue of J&K figured prominently for the first time when the Foreign Secretaries of India and Pakistan met in New Delhi in November 2006. New Delhi appears to be ready to discuss General Musharraf's proposal for "selfgovernance" and would be quite prepared to discuss greater devolution of powers and autonomy in a manner under which there is harmonization in the nature and extent of self-governance and devolution of powers on both sides of the LOC in J&K. At the present moment, the State of J&K under Indian Administration enjoys far greater autonomy than the regions of "Azad Kashmir" and the "Northern Areas" under Pakistan's control. Both "Azad Kashmir" and the "Northern Areas" are directly administered by governing "Councils" presided over by the Prime Minister of Pakistan who wields his authority through the Federal Ministry of Kashmir Affairs. Local representatives of these areas have virtually no powers, even in the appointment of Government functionaries.

Given Pakistan's continuing assistance to armed terrorist groups functioning out of Muzzafarabad in "Azad Kashmir" under the banner of a "United Jihad Council" India cannot obviously agree to any proposal for the "demilitarization" of areas it presently governs in J&K. Moreover, J&K lies on the vital lines of communications to India's western borders with China. Free movement and deployment of India's forces in J&K is, therefore, essential for the security of its frontiers with China. But, should Pakistan effectively ban and disarm groups waging *"Jihad"* in Jammu and Kashmir from territory under its control, India could consider redeployment and reduction of its forces in J&K, provided Pakistan takes corresponding measures on its side of the LOC, both in "Azad Kashmir" and the "Northern Areas'.

These are issues that appear to have figured in both formal and informal discussions between India and Pakistan in recent months. While these "new ideas" for resolving Jammu and Kashmir have figured prominently in discussions and have been the focus of extensive media attention, one has to inject a sense of caution and realism on the path ahead.

President Karzai has made no secret of his conviction that the Musharraf Government is actively aiding, arming, training and providing safe haven for the Taliban on Pakistani territory. There are, similarly, strong sentiments in India that the Pakistan Government continues to use terrorism as an instrument of State policy to promote its interests and territorial ambitions. The revival of the Taliban has encouraged Pakistan based terrorist groups like the *Lashkar e Taiba* that the climate is ripe to promote *Jihad* not merely in Jammu and Kashmir, but in other parts of India also.

Further, if borders are indeed to be made "irrelevant" as proposed by Dr. Manmohan Singh then Pakistan will have to remove existing trade and economic restrictions on relations with India and join with other South Asian countries in SAARC to make South Asia and Economic Community for the free movement of goods, services and investment within the next fifteen years. Pakistan appears to be totally averse to moving in this direction. There is thus a climate of continuing uncertainty about the directions Pakistan's policies will take in coming months. Much will depend on political developments within Pakistan in coming months. Both India and Afghanistan will have to wait and see whether the post-election political scenario in 2007 in Pakistan results in moderate elements opposed to religious extremism taking over the reins of Government, or whether the Islamist elements in the army and in the political set up will retain their hold over the conduct of Pakistan's policies.

PAKISTAN-INDIA RELATIONSHIP IN 2015

To date, it seems premature to talk about qualitative changes or significant adjustment behaviour of India and Pakistan in relation to each other. But over the last year, during the rule of Narendra Modi in the Indian government, each of the parties has had the opportunity to define its position.

The Bharatiya Janata Party (BJP), that came to power following the results of the parliamentary elections in May 2014, sharply criticized the previous government led by the Congress, stating that "a cursory look at a lost decade demonstrates the deviation and loss of direction in its relations with its neighbours, misguided diplomacy towards Pakistan and short-sightedness in the determination of foreign policy with the island states of the Indian Ocean." Exactly from this standpoint the government of Prime Minister Narendra Modi built relationships in the region.

2014 was characterised by another round of tension in relations between the two countries. Islamabad emphasised the presence of "...some fundamental differences with New Delhi". According to statements of its foreign minister, "... the process of normalization was hampered by the lack of composite dialogue between the countries, but we are striving to renew it on all unresolved questions".

Adjustments of the approaches of the general line of foreign policy of Pakistan and India in 2014 – 2015 are connected with several reasons:

- Firstly, the accession to power of new leaders in Pakistan (Prime Minister Muhammad Nawaz Sharif – May 2013), and in India – Prime Minister Narendra Modi as a result of the parliamentary elections in May 2014, and subsequent changes in their foreign policy vectors;

- Secondly, the modification of the general geopolitical content in the region after the completion of the combat mission of the International Security Assistance Force in Afghanistan (ISAF) and the withdrawal of the major part of the coalition forces in December 2014;
- Thirdly, the military establishment of Pakistan had an impact on the development of foreign policy, particularly in the Indian direction.

In 2014/2015 Islamabad adjusted its approaches on the Kashmir issue in comparison with the former administration headed by the president Asif Ali Zardari.

The Kashmir sovereignty issue was again included as a major point in the agenda of Pakistani-Indian relations. The former ruling in 2008-2013, the Pakistan Peoples Party (PPP) avoided to raise the issue as a priority in its dialogue with New Delhi in 2011-2013.

On the contrary, the government urged to "freeze" this and settle some technical issues, visas (providing expedited visa regime for certain categories of citizens of the both countries), transportation (bus routes in Kashmir), etc.

Muhammad Nawaz Sharif and Narendra Modi met in May, 2014 for the first time when the head of the Federal Cabinet of Ministers of Pakistan was invited to the inauguration in New Delhi. But the first political battles were turned by them against each other at the end of September 2014 at the UN General Assembly.

Pakistan severely criticized the position of India directed at blocking the execution of a referendum in Kashmir. The main accusation of the Indian party came down to the characterisation of Pakistan, as a "main source of terrorism". A little later, in January 2015, this point was again voiced during the visit of President Barack Obama in New Delhi. Several traditional and new "painful points" appeared in the relations between Islamabad and New Delhi in 2014 and the first half of 2015:

- armed conflicts along the Line of Control and Working boundary in Kashmir from September, 2014 to March, 2015;
- strong statements of Pakistan with the purpose of blocking plans of India for the construction of new settlements in the Indian part of Kashmir;
- further delay by Pakistan of the issue of granting India the status of most favoured nation;
- Islamabad once again accused New Delhi of using Afghan territory for terrorist attacks in Pakistan, as well as the involvement of the Indian intelligence agency (RAW) to the activities of terrorist organizations in Pakistan;
- the strengthening of confrontation between India and Pakistan for influence in Afghanistan, or so-called "proxy war".

The process of reforming the UN Security Council In 2014, Pakistan called on the UN General Assembly to prevent the creation of new permanent seats in the Security Council and at the same time emphasized the need to strengthen the role of the 193 members of the Assembly. Pakistan opposed granting India the status of a permanent member of the UN Security Council.

Reforming the Security Council, according to Islamabad, should reflect the interests of the wider membership of the United Nations. He pointed out two major obstacles to India in the UN Security Council: firstly, the idea of new permanent members of the Security Council will create additional centres of power, and, secondly, India, according to Pakistan, is not eligible for special status in the Council, as it violated UN Security Council resolutions on Jammu and Kashmir, and the right of the Kashmiri people to self-determination. Pakistan believes that a country that has violated the UN Charter is not entitled to a permanent seat in the UN Security Council.

During his visit to New Delhi in January 2015, the US President Barack Obama expressed support for India's candidature to the UN Security Council, a privileged international forum. Pakistani media very sharply reacted to this statement. Pakistan is not opposed to civil nuclear cooperation and membership of the Nuclear Suppliers Group -NSG, which have not joined the Treaty on the Non-Proliferation of Nuclear Weapons. But at the same time it opposes granting membership to India in the NSG, believing that it will be a severe blow to the non-proliferation regime. The US-Indian nuclear deal in 2008, according to Islamabad, is aimed at building up the nuclear capabilities of India, that has not done much for its transparency.

Islamabad expressed concerns about the capacity growth of Indian military potential Its defence expenditures have increased by 12% in 2014-2015 and up to $38.35 billion US. According to Pakistan, the US-India defence agreement for a period of ten years will further strengthen the existing imbalance of conventional and nuclear weapons and therefore lead to a destabilization strategy in South Asia.

In February 2015, the government of the BJP joined the rush for a conventional arms race. The Prime Minister N. Modi announced the reforming of its defence procurement policy with the priority on domestic production and cancelled restrictions on foreign investments in the defensive area.

In response, Pakistan stated that "... it has never been a part of an arms race with India and will adhere to this policy in the future. However, bearing in mind the situation in the region, Pakistan has the right to maintain a balance of conventional weapons ... and, despite financial difficulties, for the government to meet the needs of their armed forces, will continue this strategy in the future."

Islamabad has expressed concerns at the deterioration of the strategic imbalance during heightened Pakistan-India tensions, the violation by India (according to Pakistan) of the ceasefire along the Line of Control and Working boundary.

But on a high note of the discussion of military budgets, on February 13, 2015 India made the first step towards: Prime Minister Narendra Modi called Prime Minister Muhammad Nawaz Sharif. The next step of India is the visit to Islamabad in March 2015 of the Indian Foreign Subrahmanyam

Jaishankar. In other words, the parties started negotiations on the level at which they had been "frozen" in August 2014 (on August 25, 2014 a meeting was planned at the level of secretaries of the foreign ministries. But the planned scenario was disrupted. Preceding the Indian side was a meeting of the High Commissioner of Pakistan in India, Abdul Basit (the Pakistan envoy to India Abdul Basit) with leaders of Kashmir (Hurriyat Leaders), despite protests from New Delhi. In response, India unilaterally cancelled the talks. Pakistan put the responsibility for the failure of negotiations on its eastern neighbour.)

In March 2015, the main attention was paid to the discussion of bilateral issues: Jammu and Kashmir, Siachen, Sir Creek and water issues.

They confirmed that for in order to find their solutions concerted efforts are required and the resumption of the dialogue process, maintaining the ceasefire (2003), the main mechanism for the stabilization of the situation on the Line of Control and the Working boundary between the two countries.

The visit of the Secretary Ministry of Foreign Affairs of India in Pakistan was generally formal and was held on the eve of the SAARC summit, which will take place in Islamabad. Analysts pointed out that it had not brought much hope for a qualitative breakthrough, improvement of bilateral relations. At the same time, according to the Pakistani side, it opened the way for future negotiations. However, without a specific date of the event.

And in May 2015, the Prime Minister of India, Narendra Modi confirmed his intention to "break the ice" in relations with neighbouring countries through the "cricket diplomacy": "... We have decided to start a series of games of cricket between the teams of the two countries, and it will be the first step towards normalization of relations."

The games are planned in the United Arab Emirates, away from the unpredictable behaviour of the majority of the fans. "Cricket diplomacy" is a return to the positions of the parties in 2011-2012, when former Pakistani Prime Minister

Yousuf Raza Gilani arrived in India on an unofficial visit, and together with the former Prime Minister of India M.Sindhom watched a cricket match. And so all the years of these relationships – one step forward, two steps back.

MODI MADE PAKISTAN IRRELEVANT IN INDIA'S FOREIGN POLICY

For years, the centre of India's foreign policy was Pakistan. Love it or hate it. This was the country that the external affairs ministry had to break its head over most of the times. You can't brush off four wars (1947-48, 1965, 1971 and 1999), two conflicts (Rann of Kutch and Siachen), militancy in Kashmir that claimed tens of thousands of lives and terrorist attacks all over India.

More importantly, Pakistan held the trump cards when it came to America, China, Afghanistan and the entire Arab world. All these countries would always favour Pakistan over India. We had Russia on our side but even it became neutral with the collapse of communism in 1991.

Detractors are laughing at how Prime Minister Narendra Modi is touring one country after another like a mere tourist. He is being ridiculed as a non-resident Prime Minister. However, his visits are already paying rich dividends. Here's how. For one, Modi is snatching away Pakistan's allies one by one. The first is America. Ever since US President Barack Obama took over, he didn't care two hoots for India. That has drastically changed. The Obama-Modi bromance is being talked about all over the world. In one meet, Obama ran to Modi, held his hands and called him a "man of action". Modi's stance at the recently concluded climate talks in Paris was greatly appreciated by Obama and one environmental news website even called Modi as the "Man who saved the world".

More importantly, the results are already coming in. The dead Indo-US nuclear deal was revived and hectic parleying over both strategic and economic ties are taking place.

China is similarly being engaged and trade deals are being inked left, right and centre. India has taken an aggressive stand against border incursions and China is known to respect a tough adversary. Afghanistan is being engaged too and Modi's recent visit was a landmark.

Tweeted Habib Khan Totakhil, a Wall Street Journal reporter in Kabul... That's the kind of change happening which is changing the perception as far as India is concerned.

A watershed event is our engagement with the Arab world. A red carpet welcome awaited Modi in UAE, where more than one of the rulers of the Emirates came to receive him, a rarity. Trade ties were taken forward and terror was discussed.

Don Dawood Ibrahim may have his home in Pakistan, but his office is in Dubai. Modi has conveniently bypassed Pakistan and got UAE to squeeze Dawood's operations in Dubai. A few terror suspects have already been deported to India and an accused in the AugustaWestland scam has been located. Bangladesh (which shares a love-hate relationship with Pakistan) is being engaged and they have started extraditing militants. Shutting Pakistan's terror camps will go a long way in neutralising Pakistan. (Again we are bypassing them).

For that, National Security Adviser Ajit Doval has to be given due credit. He is discussed more on Pakistani TV channels than Indian ones. Modi has visited other Muslim countries like Turkey, Kazakhstan, Kyrgyzstan, Tajikistan, Turkmenistan and Uzbekistan. Modi is isolating Pakistan in the Muslim world itself and that's a big handicap for our neighbour.

Interestingly, we are making progress with every country in West Asia. What are the chances that a country can significantly hike ties with both Israel and Muslim countries? Modi is doing just that. They may be rivals, but both of them want to do business with India. That's just the way Modi is engaging both America and China, despite their rivalry.

Modi has thrown the zero sum game in the dustbin which had been plaguing the sub-continent. He can engage with everyone simultaneously. This is without mentioning countries like Australia, Germany, Canada, Brazil etc, where our ties are way ahead of Pakistan. If you analyse the way we are engaging with countries like Myanmar and Bhutan, the encirclement of Pakistan is complete. It is a classical strategy of surrounding your enemy and isolating it. Of course, it's not a military tactic but a diplomatic one!

Modi's biggest trump card is trade. Both the British Empire and the US superpower dominated not on military might alone, but trade too. It's the economy stupid! India has overtaken China in GDP growth rate and Modi is making India irresistible for every country in the world.

The Chabahar Port in Iran is just one small example. In the future, Pakistan may be forced to make peace because, potentially, India could be Pakistan's biggest trading partner.

It's not all Modi. He has dollops of luck on his side. India-hater Mahinda Rajapaksa lost in Sri Lanka and India is weaning the island nation away from China towards itself. Russian president Vladimir Putin is flexing his muscles on the world stage and counting on India.

After the spat with Turkey, a top official flew down to India to offer Turkey-related business to India and we accepted. Indo-Russia ties could go back to the pre-1991 days without any problems with America and China.

Pakistan is no longer what it was. Pakistan occupied Kashmir is witnessing protests for reunification with India. The Balochistan independence movement is gaining ground. The war in North Waziristan has claimed the lives of 6,000 Pakistani military personnel and 30,000 terrorists and rages on without an end in sight. Thanks to this, the Pakistani Army is jaded and for the first time in ages has agreed to join Indo-Pak talks should their representatives be called. More than 60,000 Pakistani civilians have been killed in terrorist attacks since 9/11.

The death-rate in Kashmir militancy has crashed in the 2010s, thanks to all of the above. There is a famous saying which first appeared in the essays of Francis Bacon, "If the mountain won't come to Muhammad then Muhammad must go to the mountain." The way our foreign policy is shaping up, we won't have to go to Pakistan. Pakistan may well be forced to come to us with a workable peace offering. For that Modi has already shown that he is accessible. He invited Pakistan prime minister Nawaz Sharif to India for his swearing in, met him on the sidelines of summits and recently visited Lahore when he was invited at extremely short notice.

The sight of Modi and Sharif hugging and then walking hand in hand like a couple of schoolboys was a sight to behold. Our foreign policy is working and Modi should just keep at it!

IT'S TIME FOR MODI TO DIRECTLY ENGAGE WITH PAKISTAN

Almost two decades after the India-Pakistan Composite Dialogue was invented, both the frame-work and the relationship face a stalemate of sorts. India will not resume that dialogue, which has eight boxes of bilateral issues, until Pakistan shows good faith in curbing terror, particularly by punishing the perpetrators of the 26/11 attack in Mumbai; Pakistan continues claiming it too is a victim of terror, including that sponsored by India, and that resolution of the Jammu and Kashmir issue is key to better relations.

Pakistan's paranoia emanates from its western border with Afghanistan i.e. the Durand Line established in 1893, being porous and unacceptable to Afghanistan. This feeds into its approach to its eastern border with India where, to quote their Chief of Army Staff Gen Raheel Sharif, there is the "unfinished agenda of partition". The Afghan link to India-Pakistan relations goes back to 1948 itself, when the raiders pushed into Kashmir by Pakistan were largely Pashtun. Once again, terrorism commenced in J&K only after the Soviet withdrawal from Afghanistan in 1988, freed-up Punjabi militants for exporting terror to India.

The decade-long US presence in Afghanistan ensured that India-Pakistan rivalry there was contained. It also constrained Indian retaliation to Pakistan-sponsored terror attacks as Washington wanted to keep the Pakistani army focused on their western front. India, in turn, stuck in Afghanistan to development projects, committing nearly $2 billion of aid. Pakistan kept imagining an Indian hand in the Baluchistan militancy and the rise of Tehrik-e-Taliban Pakistan, which targeted the Pakistani state. The intemperate remarks of the Indian Defence Minister Parrikar, about fighting terror with terror and then likening Pakistan's reaction to imbibing sharp chillies, have only provided Pakistan the peg they needed to hang their charges on.

A good start...

Narendra Modi's penchant for the dramatic and non-conventional conduct of foreign policy became evident at the very start when he invited the leaders of the other seven SAARC countries for his swearing-in.

Prime Minister Nawaz Sharif's presence and seemingly positive meeting with Modi seemed to herald a new beginning to a stalled relationship. But since then, bilateral relations have been up and down, the latter being more pronounced.

The announcement that the foreign secretaries of the two countries would meet to take the process further was seen as a sign from the Modi government that the fundamental problems stalling the relationship and preventing the resumption of talks had been overcome.

Within Pakistan, however, the political situation deteriorated from mid-2014 as Imran Khan of Tehrik-e-Insaaf party and the Canada-returned activist Tahir ul Qadri sought dissolution of the National Assembly and the resignation of the Nawaz government alleging electoral fraud. The Pakistani army too decided to escalate tension across the Line of Control and even the international border by increasing breaches of the cease-fire which had held since the last part of Musharraf presidency. The Pakistani army's role in domestic affairs enlarged as Sharif sought their help to quell the civil disturbance.

While both the LoC situation and the political standoff in Islamabad constituted valid grounds for postponing the Indian foreign secretary's visit, the government chose to call off the talks citing the Pakistani High Commissioner's meeting with

Hurriyat leaders. The Hurriyat meeting, though provocative on the eve of bilateral talks, was not unprecedented. A perception was created that Modi was playing to the domestic gallery as elections were around the corner in the crucial state of Maharashtra and, subsequently, in J&K.

Lack of clarity

Since then, the government has talked of fighting cease-fire violations by heavier counteraction. The PM dodged his Pakistani counterpart at the UN, ignored him on the first day of the SAARC summit in Kathmandu only to relent and talk to him during the retreat, and finally sent the new foreign secretary, S Jaishankar to Islamabad under the alibi of a SAARC outreach by combining the Pakistan visit with trips to other South Asian nations. Cricketing links were resurrected as a possibility but quickly dropped after the public furore in India over a Pakistani court's decision to allow the master conspirator behind 26/11, Zaki-ur Rahman Lakhvi, to walk out of jail.

What then should India's Pakistan policy be? First, it is generally accepted that the Composite Dialogue in its present form is unworkable or even outdated. Issues like terror, water and Afghanistan assume greater prominence today than was given to them in the old format.

Moreover, the simultaneous discussion of confidence-building measures and disputes is like a three-legged race but with the two runners out of sync. Pakistan holds back on doable items that can build mutual trust i.e. trade, people-to-people engagement etc and India cannot yield to the Pakistani desire for immediate resolution of disputes likeSir Creek, Siachen and particularly J&K. In the meanwhile, Pakistan being both a victim and a perpetrator of terror, wallows in self-pity rather than facing the demon in all its manifestations, including regime-friendly groups like the Lashkar-e-Taiba.

Simplistic view

One view is to ignore Pakistan, harden Indian defences against terrorism, bypass Pakistan via Iran for Central Asian and Afghan connectivity, build a missile defence and nuclear triad as nuclear deterrent and let Pakistan wrestle with its demons till the outcome is clear. This is premised on the belief that Pakistan faces inevitable economic decline and unsustainable ethnic crises which may either force its army to sue for peace with India or simply keep it embroiled in debilitating internal wars.

This simplistic approach ignores the revival of Pakistani economy, the impact that $46 billion of Chinese infrastructure building may have on Pakistani finances, the rebalancing by Afghan President Ashraf Ghani of his nation's relations with India and Pakistan, and the Saudi unhappiness over Pakistan tilting towards the Iran-China axis and not militarily responding to its urging for Pakistani intervention in Yemen. The Taliban summer offensive in Afghanistan, despite the Pakistani commitment to bring the group to the negotiating table, may mark the beginning of a new kind of militant leadership in Afghanistan that could be utilising the Al Qaeda-ISIS rivalry.

Combined with this is the renewed attempt by Pakistan to pump LeT operatives into the Kashmir valley to tap the emerging militant and pro-Pakistan public rhetoric after BJP's dalliance with the Peoples Democratic Party. As in the 1990s, the external in Af-Pak is meeting the internal in J&K, with the additional danger of ISIS influence finding hold elsewhere in India where a section of Muslim youth is alienated.

Outflank, but engage

The appointment of a former Director, Intelligence Bureau as envoy for Af-Pak and West Asia indicates that the Modi government is looking at the entire Islamic world to India's West through an intelligence-security prism and not a diplomatic-cultural construct. Modi's Pakistan policy is conditioned by a similar mind-set of talking but not negotiating, while building security pressure points and counter alliances.

Inevitably, such a policy will have flip-flops like the yes-no on cricketing ties, as the PM lurches between his pragmatic instincts and the logic of Hindutva nationalism.

What is needed is a clear political outreach to Iran, Saudi Arabia, the UAE, Egypt and Israel. That can only be done by Modi himself and not by envoys. Into this has to be fitted the Afghanistan-Pakistan sub-set, as that region has great influence on Pakistani thinking and financial security. China alone will not be able to balance the combined might of the GCC-plus in conditioning Pakistani behaviour.

However, this outflanking move has to be underpinned by direct engagement with Pakistan – to reconstruct the dialogue format with innovative ideas on both CBMs and dispute resolution. For instance, it is inadequate to simply decry elections in Gilgit Baltistan. India must raise awareness of the demographic invasion of the Shia-dominated areas and link this to the resolution of the Kashmir issue. Can Pakistan even think of a UN-sponsored plebiscite there, minus the intruding Sunni population? Strategically, that part of Kashmir is even more vital than the Kashmir valley as it connects Pakistan to China and cuts off India from Central Asia.

That is why Indian policy makers who talk of a new Asian security order must not limit themselves to the Asia Pacific. It is time they expanded the field of play to include Central and West Asia.

PAKISTAN'S POLICY IN THE CHANGING SCENARIO

The events of 9/11, the attack on the Indian parliament, and the following war-like situation between India and Pakistan not only greatly impacted the Kashmiri resistance movement but also compelled Islamabad to change its track on Kashmir. Moreover, the unfriendly international environment and Pakistan's deep involvement in Afghanistan forced Islamabad to rethink its relations with India and its Kashmir policy. The decision of General Pervez Musharraf to join the US-led War on Terror was also a factor in changing Islamabad's strategic position on Kashmir, particularly in terms of its ideological foundation. The economic condition of the country, unrest in the tribal areas, and — allegedly externally sponsored — violence in some parts of Balochistan, and the growing engagement along the Afghan border also played an instrumental role in bringing about a paradigm shift in Islamabad's thinking towards India. It is also said that Pakistan's trusted friends, like China and Saudi Arabia, advised it to seek an unconventional way out for a lasting deal with India over the Kashmir issue and bilateral relations; besides, constant persuasion from the United States also continued.

Pakistan's capacity to protract the low cost conflict in Kashmir is beyond any doubt. Although the likely spillover effects of this on Pakistan's polity are obvious, they will be, to a great degree, manageable. On the other hand, despite its conventional military superiority and strong diplomatic backing from the world, India could not subdue the resolve of Pakistan to support Kashmir's right to self-determination and its demand for sovereign equality with India. Pakistan's ties with the United States, and its role as an ally of the West, are considered advantageous for seeking a settlement of the Kashmir issue. As the country's former Foreign Secretary Shamshad Ahmad observed:

We cannot deny the post-9/11 reality that our "friends," the Americans, now have deeper than ever stakes in India-Pakistan rapprochement as a factor of stability for regional and global peace.

The 'covert' US engagement with Islamabad, Delhi and Kashmiris is no longer a secret. Washington has expressed its desire at a number of times to help settle the Kashmir issue within the existing territorial parameters but with minor realignment. It views India as a potential rival to China, not only in the region but also in global affairs. Siddharth Srivastava, a New Delhi-based journalist, observes:

The US is striving to build India as a strategic counterweight to China, along with Japan and Australia.

Termed as naïve by critics, Pakistan's calculations of the ground realities are optimistic, being based on the belief that India will never be able to bring normalcy into Kashmir because

Kashmiris are highly skeptical towards it, and that India will need Pakistan's support and will ultimately make tangible transformations in its current stance over Kashmir. The majority of Kashmiris do not trust the Indian government and, ever since the eruption of the resistance, their aspiration for the right of self-determination has multiplied manifold and now cuts across even the hardcore pro-India circles in the Kashmir Valley. India's carrot and stick tactics and the brutalities of its forces have alienated the local population and invoked armed resistance, which may not die down easily. It is this assessment of the situation that emboldened Islamabad to make tangible concessions on Kashmir and bring India to the table for talks. Some also believe that the personal ambition of the President Musharraf — his wish to be regarded in history as a statesman who settled one of the world's most complicated disputes — is a driving factor that has brought essential changes in Islamabad's policies.

Besides various other factors that caused India and Pakistan to change their policies on the Kashmir issue, back channel diplomacy led by the US played a major role in alleviating the crisis and creating a viable atmosphere for initiatives towards a comprehensive normalization process.

Change in India's Approach

For a long time, India's approach for dealing with Pakistan had revolved mainly around zero tolerance in any concerns related to India's security or political ideology. However, its inability to 'punish' Pakistan and to break its back economically (by creating a war-like environment in the region) had a sobering impact on the Indian mindset and led New Delhi to conclude that its conventional policies vis-à-vis Pakistan and Kashmir were getting nowhere. In the past, New Delhi had publicly pronounced several times that it would take punitive action and destroy what it alleged were militant training camps inside Azad Jammu and Kashmir (AJK) by air strikes. However, its hostile attitude did not yield the desired results and Islamabad did not succumb to its pressure.

At the same time, economic tycoons and multinational companies were pressuring the Indian government to normalize relations with Islamabad as hostile relations between the two neighbors and the constant fear of war had a negative impact on business activity and international investment. New Delhi needed peace in the region and internal stability to continue its current annual growth rate of 8-10 percent and obtain further foreign investment. As one researcher on the peace process put it:

Improved relations would lead to improved trade: there was money to be made, and this had become a strategic objective for both Islamabad and New Delhi.

India realized that its successful economic journey would cease if it did not settle disputes with Pakistan. It had to think about the immense potential in bilateral trade and in trade with landlocked Afghanistan and Central Asia via Pakistan. Besides, India aspires for a permanent seat in the UN Security Council for which it had to ensure friendly relations with neighbors and settle the Kashmir issue in the context of which India is regarded among those countries that did not comply with the UNSC resolutions. Moreover, the Kashmir resistance poses a huge financial burden on the Indian treasury. It is also acknowledged that the Indian security forces do not have the capacity to fix the problem; rather, they invite anger by frequently committing severe human rights violations that aggravate the already complex situation.

After the withdrawal of Indian forces from the Pakistani borders, Pakistan made a chain of unilateral concessions pronounced by President General Musharraf himself. It began with a unilateral ceasefire on LoC announced by Prime Minister Zaffarullah Khan Jamali in November 2003. In the following month, speaking to *Reuters*, General Musharraf said he had "left aside" the 55-year-old demand for a UN mandated plebiscite on Kashmir and wished to meet India "halfway" in a bid for peace in the subcontinent.

These multiple pulls created a sense of obligation among the Indian ruling elite to at least take some measures to show that they were serious about settling the problems. Eventually, the Indian Prime Minister Atal Behari Vajpayee went to Kupwara in the south of the Kashmir Valley and offered a hand of friendship to Pakistan in April 2004. This was regarded a departure from the conventional Indian thinking on Kashmir and Pakistan, and paved the way for further initiatives on Kashmir. It also created a palatable environment for Vajpayee to visit Islamabad to attend the South Asian Association for Regional Cooperation (SAARC) summit.

Musharraf's 'Out of the Box' Thinking

Islamabad has consistently said that it supports the resistance in IHK diplomatically and politically, and has nothing to do with the armed struggle. It has also invariably linked talks with India with progress on the Kashmir settlement. But it relinquished both of these stands in the quest to find a compromised solution. Pakistan accepted the responsibility to rein in militants operating from areas under its control. It also pledged to stop all kinds of cross-border activities from Azad Kashmir. Pakistan had never acknowledged the armed resistance in IHK as terrorism, but astonishingly, it ceded even this stance and conceded to the Indian interpretation of the movement. As a retired former Ambassador aptly commented: This amounted to an admission of its guilt and was unprecedented in that Pakistan unilaterally took on a responsibility that was not only almost impossible to honor, but even more importantly, it was given without any reciprocal obligation by the other side. To further the shift in policy, the Pakistani President articulated his ideas on Kashmir for the first time while speaking to journalists during an *iftar*dinner held in Islamabad in October 2004. Although he said these were "off the cuff" ideas, the nature of the proposals on the Kashmir settlement that he forwarded suggests that he had in mind a well-conceived and thought-out plan, on which he was gauging feedback. The crux of the proposals is outlined below:

- Identify seven regions, demilitarize them, and change their status before looking for possible options to resolve the dispute.

- The status quo in Kashmir is unacceptable and the LoC cannot be a solution to the lingering dispute.
- As a starting point for a step-by-step approach on the option of demilitarization, the regions on both sides of the LoC need to be analyzed for local culture and demographic composition. After identifying these regions, there could be gradual demilitarization, following which the two sides could discuss who should control these areas.
- Pakistan and India could also have joint control of these areas or the United Nations could be asked to play a role.

Later, Musharraf dilated upon his ideas with the *CNBC* anchorperson, Karan Thapar, on January 8, 2006. He suggested the concept of self-governance and joint management of the entire Kashmir area. In his words, "self-governance is more than autonomy but less than independence. In other words, both India and Pakistan will keep the parts of Kashmir they control but under their joint management. Self-governance is devolved to the Kashmiris, independence being firmly ruled out." The interviewer, Karan Thapar, afterwards elaborated this concept in his article, saying, "...The self-governance would apply to the full state of Jammu and Kashmir as it existed in 1947. This means it would be implemented in Northern Areas (Gilgit Baltistan). Additionally, the border within old Kashmir state would be open and thus irrelevant."

Subsequently, Musharraf had a comprehensive discussion on his proposals with the noted Indian lawyer and journalist, A. G. Noorani, who published it in the Indian magazine*Frontline* on August 12-25, 2006. Later on, President Musharraf also spoke to *NDTV* on similar ideas, going further to clearly articulate his position as follows:

- Kashmir will have the same borders but people will be allowed to move freely back and forth in the region;
- The region will have self-governance or autonomy, but not independence;

- Troops will be withdrawn from the region in a phased manner
- A joint supervision mechanism will be set up with India, Pakistan and Kashmir represented in it.

The proposals offered by Musharraf sent clear signals that: a) Islamabad was ready to compromise its traditional stance that the people of Kashmir will decide their destiny through free and fair plebiscite; b) Indian and Pakistani sovereignty would remain as it currently was at the end of the day; c) The LoC would be irrelevant, except as a line on a map to demarcate both parts of the state; d) Self-governance or self rule would be granted to both parts of Kashmir and joint management established.

Pakistan's proposals paved the way to move forward on a slightly faster track as India did not view them as being against its strategic or political interests. Previously, Pakistan had banked on the UNSC resolutions that guaranteed the right of self-determination to the Kashmiris, besides recognizing Pakistan as a principal party to the dispute. Musharraf relinquished these positions unilaterally without seeking any quid pro quo. In other words, he came close to almost acknowledging the Indian claim that Kashmir could not be receded from the Union. India also tactfully rephrased its traditional stance that "J&K is its integral part" in more acceptable language, now asserting that "Borders cannot be redrawn but any kind of solution could be acceptable to India." Musharraf agreed to this proposition while rejecting the status quo and showed willingness to embrace some kind of joint management of the state.

Moreover, Pakistan accepted the pro-Indian Kashmiri leadership's role in the future dispensation and changed its position that only the All Parties Hurriyat Conference (APHC) should be the representative of Kashmiri people in the negotiation process. President Musharraf said that the President of the National Conference, Omer Abdullah, and Mahbooba Mufti had a role to play in the Kashmir political landscape. This gesture comforted the Indian establishment as Pakistan's demands were in line with their own views and interests. These major departures from the traditional stance made Musharraf a good bet for India to deal with Pakistan on Kashmir and settle other issues broadly allied to Pak-India trade and access to markets in Central Asia and Afghanistan.

A Review of the Composite Dialogue

The dialogue process between Islamabad and New Delhi is slowly progressing despite several ups and downs. It is often said that the continuation of the process is in itself a success because, in the past, the two countries have been unable to remain engaged in a sustainable dialogue. However, the substance of the process and prospects of its success need to be analyzed.

Until February 1994, India and Pakistan were engaged in sporadic dialogues that always ended with zero progress. This is why both countries formally suspended dialogue in 1994. Islamabad's approach was to settle the Kashmir issue first, after which the other problems would get settled almost automatically, whereas India was interested in dilating first on other issues, such as trade and travel. Eventually, to bridge the gap between the two positions, both governments agreed to address all political and territorial issues simultaneously, including Jammu and Kashmir. Consequently, the foreign secretaries of the two countries met in Islamabad and resumed the stalled dialogue process in June 1997. They institutionalized the process by identifying eight areas to deliberate upon and established working groups to make progress on each issue separately but simultaneously.

This entire process was called off when the Kargil confrontation occurred. As discussed earlier, post-9/11 events also contributed in the stalemate between the two countries. Later, in 2004, India and Pakistan launched a renewed peace process aimed at resolving all their longstanding disputes. However, the Kashmir dispute still dominates over other issues. Even after voicing his new approaches, President Musharraf said that if progress on Kashmir could not make headway, the entire process would be back to square one. Recently, Prime Minister Shaukat Aziz has underscored the settlement of Kashmir as a precondition for further progress on other related disputes as well as for offering trade and business opportunities to India.

Since January 2004, both neighbors have been engaged on two different levels. The first is the official level, at which concerned officials from both sides meet periodically and report their progress to foreign secretaries, who meet to review the outcome and discuss the Kashmir, peace and security issues, before, finally, the foreign ministers meet to take stock of developments and set the rules for further dialogue. The second level of engagement is back-channel diplomacy. Pakistan's National Security Secretary, Tariq Aziz, who is known to be a close aide of President Musharraf, and India's S. K. Lamba, former High Commissioner to Pakistan, are engaged in a serious dialogue. However, it has been said that only five people in Pakistan are truly in the loop on the actual state of bilateral negotiations. Therefore, no one can really assess the behind-the-curtains activities or predict the contours of solutions.

So far, at the official level, both countries have completed four rounds of a composite dialogue. This process received a dent when the Mumbai train blasts on July 11, 2006 caused a postponement in the foreign secretary-level talks. India blamed elements from Pakistan for their involvement in the blasts but no evidence was provided by the Indian government to Pakistan. This decision was in violation of the joint statement, issued on April 18, 2005, by the leaders of Pakistan and India, which states that, "Terrorist acts would not be allowed to derail the peace process." Eventually, sanity prevailed and the stalled process was resumed in November 2006. Likewise, in February, the Lahore-bound Samjhauta Express became a target of bomb blasts that killed 68 passengers, most of whom were Pakistani.

Islamabad reacted with caution and did not allow the peace process to derail, despite the immense loss of its citizens' lives. The question does arise how New Delhi would have reacted had Indian citizens been the victims.

The fourth round of composite dialogue was held in Islamabad on March 13-14, 2007, with a focus on the Jammu and Kashmir dispute and peace and security. In the context of peace and security, the two sides discussed a wide range of issues relating to their conventional and nuclear military capabilities and reviewed the entire process. The Pakistani team sought India's response to President Musharraf's "ideas" on the resolution of the Kashmir issue and emphasized the need for forward movement on Jammu and Kashmir, saying it was time to move from confidence-building measures to dispute resolution.

Among related issues, Pakistan pushed for early finalization of the agreements on speedy return of inadvertent line crossers; quarterly flag meetings of the sector commanders at the LoC; and liberalization of the visa regime. Pakistan also proposed some new cross-LoC confidence building measures, including allowing sports activities and launch of helicopter and postal services between Srinagar and Muzaffarabad.

In addition, Pakistan tabled a new proposal on anti-ballistic missiles. Siachen, Sir Creek and economic cooperation were among the other issues discussed. Following are the significant consensus points of the fourth round of foreign secretary-level talks:

- After years of reluctance, Pakistan agreed to the Indian proposal of launching a bus service between Kargil and Skardu in the Northern Areas.
- It was agreed that a truck service between Srinagar and Muzaffarabad would be launched in a few months;
- It was agreed that the Joint Committee of Retired Judges, set up to look into the prisoners issue, would begin its work soon and suggest ways to ensure the humane treatment of Indian prisoners in Pakistani jails and Pakistani prisoners in Indian jails;
- The two countries agreed to conclude an agreement on "No Development of New Posts and Defense Works" along the LoC and proposed drafts for new border control guidelines along the International Border;

- The two sides agreed to work on finalizing a liberalized visa regime, including a proposal for group tourism.

Although the meeting could not settle the problem of demilitarizing Siachen, it was able to narrow down differences on some elements. The political leadership of both countries appears optimistic about resolving this issue in the days ahead.

Likewise, the formation of a Joint Counter-Terrorism Mechanism is also a significant development. India has long blamed Pakistan for any terrorist activities occurring on its territory.

The Mechanism offers an opportunity for thorough investigation of incidents prior to the pronouncements of conclusions. However, it was reported in sections of the Pakistani and Indian press that Islamabad seeks to keep the armed resistance in J&K out of the ambit of the Joint Anti-Terrorism Mechanism.

At a joint press conference with the Indian Foreign Secretary Shivshankar Menon, his Pakistani counterpart, Riaz Mohammad Khan, said that Jammu and Kashmir was "disputed" and should not be "mixed" with the initiatives that are between India and Pakistan only.

The visible achievement of the four rounds of foreign sectaries' level dialogue is the initiation of a Srinagar-Muzaffarabad bus service and, of late, the opening of entry points along the LoC for civilian crossing.

Although the 42-month dialogue process has not yielded the desired results, both the governments seem to be closer to agreements on a number of issues.

Besides, the two countries have also exchanged some proposals through the back channel on the settlement of the Jammu and Kashmir dispute. However, very few people of the two governments are fully aware of what is going on behind the scene. Concerned citizens and the general public on both sides know virtually nothing. This makes the back channel process vulnerable: nobody knows how stakeholders and the public will react when the solution is finally made public.

MODI AND SHARIF TAKE A GAMBLE

Prime Minister Narendra's Modi surprise visit to Lahore has revived once again the oft-desired hope that India and Pakistan will live as friends not adversaries. For that to happen, however, Pakistan's security establishment will need to stop seeing India as the existential threat.

This is not the first time an Indian Prime Minister has extended a hand of friendship towards Pakistan, what is different is the style: a sudden stopover in Lahore on the way back from Kabul. For many this is reminiscent of a phrase by former Indian Premier Dr Manmohan Singh in January 2007: "I dream of a day, while retaining our respective national identities, one can have breakfast in Amritsar, lunch in Lahore and dinner in Kabul. That is how my forefathers lived. That is how I want our grandchildren to live."

Every Indian Prime Minister has sought to leave an improvement in ties with Pakistan as their key foreign policy legacy. India's first Prime Minister Jawaharlal Nehru repeatedly offered his hand of friendship and so did his successors. Prime Minister Atal Behari Vajpayee, Prime Minister during the earlier BJP-led NDA government (1999-2004) sought to improve ties with Pakistan. In 1999 he went on a bus yatra to Lahoreand made it a point to write in the Visitor's book at the Minar e Pakistan that India and Indians have accepted the creation of Pakistan wish it well. Under Dr Manmohan Singh again India continued this policy and sought to reduce the trust deficit between the two countries. This is because a stable, civilian and democratic Pakistan is in India's national interest.

Mr Nawaz Sharif too came into power in June 2013 seeking to change Pakistan's policy with respect to India and Afghanistan. While in opposition he often spoke of the need for better relations between India and Pakistan. Unfortunately, as with previous Pakistani civilian administrations, this time too the Pakistan military-intelligence establishment that runs Pakistan's foreign and security policies has ensured that Mr Sharif is unable to change policies.

Mr Modi's foreign policy is a combination of pomp and show and behind the door secret negotiations. He has spent most of his eighteen months in power traveling around the world, visiting places Indian leaders have ignored and building personal relationships with fellow leaders. Mr Modi and his advisors understand the importance of South Asia to India. India's foreign secretary S. Jaishankar argued that India could not be a leading power if the neighborhood was not with India as "you need your region to root for you."

One of the Mr Modi's first decisions on winning elections in May 2014was to invite all South Asian heads of government, including Mr Nawaz Sharif, to attend his inauguration. Mr Modi and Mr Sharif have met at a number of international venues in the last eighteen months and attempted to restart the old cycle of rounds of talks and dialogues.

The background for Mr Modi's current trip to Pakistan appears to have been laid over the last few months with his meeting Mr Sharif in Ufa, the re-start of the talks between the two National Security Advisors that took place in Bangkok and the visit by India's External Affairs MinisterSushma Swaraj's visit to Islamabad in early December 2015 to attend the Heart of Asia conference which led to the resumption of talks between the two countries. Again one sees the use of both open and secret diplomacy: the meeting at Ufa was public whereas we were only told about the meeting of the two NSAs after the discussions had taken place.

For the last three weeks starting with the Bangkok talks and the Heart of Asia there have also been a succession of stories in the Indian media and comments by top BJP leaders, both federal and provincial, on how important it is for India to talk to Pakistan. Even leaders of the Rashtriya Swayam Sevak Sangh – a Hindu chauvinist organization and the ideological mentor organization of the BJP – have spoken of the need for India to talk to Pakistan.

Prime Minister Modi's surprise visit to Pakistan is reminiscent of the 2003 overture by his BJP predecessor Vajpayee. Two years after the failed Agra Summit of 2001 and the 2002 massive troop mobilization on the India-Pakistan borders, in April 2003 Vajpayee "extended a hand of friendship" and hoped that "both sides should decide to live together." This led to the revival of the 2004 composite dialogue process that continued till 2007 and stopped with the 2008 Mumbai terror attacks.

From the Indian perspective, a democratic and civilian-led Pakistan has multiple benefits. Since 2008 two civilian governments in Pakistan have attempted to improve ties with India. However, they have been unable to do so because of the veto of Pakistan's military-intelligence complex.

This time round Mr Modi's overture to Pakistan appears to be founded on the belief that Pakistan is facing tremendous international pressure not only from the United States and that at a time like this better ties with India would boost the civilian government by improving its global image.

From Delhi's perspective boosting a civilian government would help provide the civilians with leverage over the military-intelligence establishment at a time when the latter is facing pressure from radical groups both domestic and foreign. Restarting talks also opens the prospects of boosting economic and commercial relations and people to people ties that will help change the narrative and eventually lead to peace in the region.

That both Mr Modi and before him Mr Vajpayee chose to come to Lahore, not Islamabad/Rawalpindi, also needs to be pondered upon. By going to Lahore which houses the Minar e Pakistan, the message sent was that Indian leaders wanted Pakistanis to know that India had accepted the creation of Pakistan. Majority of Sindhis, Pashtuns, Baluch and Muhajirs prefer better ties with India. Punjabis are more likely to see India as an existential. The need to target the large Punjabi business community that seeks better ties with India is another reason for choosing Lahore.

However, what both Delhi and Islamabad need to ponder on is that both countries have been through this bonhomie at periodic intervals for almost seven decades. What is going to be different this time round and what will each side undertake to ensure that they deal with the issues critical to each, Kashmir for Pakistan and terrorism for India. Further, will firing across the Line of Control or a terror attack in India lead to suspension of the talks once again?

Meetings alone do not change policies; paradigm shifts are required to do that. For that to happen there needs to be a paradigm shift in how the Pakistani army views India.

In his memoirs Pakistan's first military dictator General Ayub Khan stated that Indian leaders sought to improve people to people ties arguing that this would help build the trust to resolve disputes like Kashmir. However, for Ayub, Pakistan could not allow this to happen because with time people may forget about key issues like Kashmir.

Sixty years later the Pakistani army leadership still believes that if they allow India and Pakistan to improve trade and commercial ties, people to people ties and easier visa policies over time the publics of both countries would forget about issues like Kashmir and war and they would lose their preeminent status in Pakistan as India would no longer be viewed as an existential threat.

NARENDRA MODI'S HARDLINE PAKISTAN POLICY

Islamabad learnt a bitter lesson in diplomacy during the dust-up over national security adviser talks with India —that once a side triumphs in the drafting of a text i.e., a joint statement, it can control the narrative about events.

There's little doubt that from Pakistan's vantage, the joint statement at Ufa was very badly drafted. It allowed India's external affairs minister Sushma Swaraj to point to elements in the brief 207-word text which suggest that both sides considered terrorism as a central theme of the NSA talks. Pakistan's NSA Sartaj Aziz could point to the part that said Prime Ministers Narendra Modi and Nawaz Sharif 'are prepared to discuss all outstanding issues' – which has traditionally been a euphemism for Jammu and Kashmir – but it is fairly clear that the Ufa statement, taken together, was loaded in favour of recognizing terrorism as a central to the NSA talks agenda.

Be that as it may be, there is reason to believe this was a pyrrhic victory, where India squandered bigger objectives and incurred bigger costs by getting into an ugly squabble over Kashmiri separatists and the talks agenda. It prompts questions about the way New Delhi handled the situation, it puts paid to well-circulated theories about Modi's foreign policy, evokes concerns about what this means for the future and raises doubts about the credibility of India's narrative internationally.

To begin with, many have already asked as to why the agenda was not sorted out by New Delhi well in advance, if terrorism was to be the singular agenda. Swaraj suggested that Pakistan did not respond for 22 days to India's call on NSA talks.

If that were true, were there no instruments at hand except feeding the media about India's strategy of sending out a strong message on terror, of handing over a dossiers on militant camps that were reviving, on presenting proof that Dawood Ibrahim lives in Karachi, and about handing an expanding list of Indian fugitives living in Pakistan? Once that public diplomacy agenda of projecting Modi and NSA Ajit Doval as strongmen was on, was there any surprise that Islamabad would trot out a meeting with Kashmiri separatists to burnish its own moral credentials by insisting on the "core issue"? Islamabad was, in any case, still very resentful of the way Modi peremptorily called off foreign secretary talks last year – and so India's posturing gave Islamabad the excuse to grandstand as well.

And even if Swaraj's reading of the Ufa statement is warranted, the question to ask is whether India can really expect Pakistan to discuss terrorism and nothing else? Even if Pakistan is a deeply unstable state wracked with internal challenges, and has long pursued wrongheaded policies on India, it still does remain a nation-state that has its own canons of status, dignity and prestige.

What is the incentive for Islamabad to participate in a dialogue where the agenda is structured to blame Pakistan, however warranted that blame is? Was not India's anger about terrorism, the proof thereof and the threats to convey by Doval better relayed in a private setting rather than played out in public leaving both sides little option but to posture? In any case, if India was supposed to have a dual strategy of engaging the civilian government of Nawaz Sharif while isolating the military establishment, how do stringent conditions for talks with a representative of PM Sharif square with such plans?

All told, Modi's posturing may have been good television that galvanised his base but it is completely out of step with the conventions of transaction between nation-states, however lopsided the balance of power is between two contending parties. If Indian policymakers argue that Pakistan does not deserve such courtesies as it exports terror, then why bother with Ufa in the first place?

Modi's Pakistan policy seems to stem from the belief that keeping Islamabad on a leash through hardened rhetoric and enforcing a circumscribed dialogue is the way to go. The problem is that it achieves little beyond beefing up his domestic legitimacy. For one, it does not guarantee an end to terror attacks. Clearly India's threats and a massive retaliation to cross-LoC firing last autumn has not deterred Pakistan from pushing terrorists into Gurdaspur or using artillery against civilians in the Poonch sector of Jammu and Kashmir. Pakistan has been steadily expanding its nuclear weapons programme and feels able to continue with sub-conventional warfare without too much of a cost. Modi's coercive tactics have not altered that calculus significantly yet as the increased attacks in J&K suggest. In fact, the principal reason why Pakistan is keen on resuming dialogue with India, is not because it quakes at the neighbour's military might, but because it sees engagement as a mechanism to contain escalation if a major terrorist strike does happen – a tool India has now deprived itself of.

Defenders of India's policy may argue that Modi is raising Pakistan's costs for proxy war through stringent conditionality and threatening 'hot pursuit' or implying covert action of its own. But we have just seen that Pakistan is unlikely to agree to pre-conditions since it has a competitive political landscape like any other country. The idea of hot pursuit of terrorists has also not been fully tested yet. Security experts say that aircrafts or commandos can execute an operation against militant camps in Pakistan but argue that returning to India may not be easy.

To restate, Modi's hardline approach has not yet achieved any of the outcomes that are in India's interests. All that this policy has yielded is a lot of anti-Pakistan sentiment, which has no policy utility beyond translating into a subliminal tirade against Indian Muslims on television on a regular basis. In effect, the policy is generating toxic effects in Indian society and on its public sphere rather achieving any strategic objective with Pakistan.

There are at least a couple of other policy implications to consider. The Modi government may well prefer not to deal with Pakistan but the current approach will have seriously undermined networks that will be handy for managing the next India-Pakistan crisis. If a non-state actor like the Lashkar-e-Tayyiba, decides to drive a wedge between the two countries — which is not inconceivable for figures with apocalyptic worldviews — it is not clear who Ajit Doval will lean on to prevent an escalation, especially when he is seen as a mastermind of the current strategy and a champion of hot pursuit of militants into Pakistan

In the aftermath of the next major terrorist strike, we will then have to rely on the Americans and the international community to defuse tensions, who will no doubt point out privately that India initiated this round of recriminations starting with the calling off of foreign secretary talks last August. In the meanwhile, if the Modi government is seen as egging on its hypernationalist media and embarrassing Pakistan's civilian government which desired talks, then the international community's indignation with the low-level terrorist violence that Pakistan sustains in India will wear thin.

This is not an argument for appeasement. Pakistan has, for sure, powerful actors who are implacably committed to destabilising India. There are, however, no military answers to the problem of terrorism. India would have tried them long ago if there were. India's policy must instead flow from a recognition that Pakistan is a nation of 182 million with a complex set of interests and motivations, both at the elite and popular plane.

India needs to have leverage all across Pakistani society to achieve its purposes, which for the moment includes rollback of terror and preventing escalation of conflict. The current policy is instead arraying all of Pakistan, including liberal elements of its civil society, against India, while the latter is also manufacturing animosity towards the neighbour. Effecting a social breach within and between both nations just to prove a point to a section of the Pakistan elite is neither sensible nor strategic. It is a dangerous place to be.

6

Modi's Foreign Policy of China

MODI'S LIKELY CHINA POLICY

While India is in the midst of a general election with leading political parties articulating their agendas before the people, foreign policy focus seems to be somewhat subdued. Yet, passing references have been made by the prime ministerial candidate of the Bharatiya Janata Party (BJP) Narendra Modi, poised to sweep the polls and be hoisted as the country's next prime minister as what his government's foreign policy priorities would be when he assumes office. While there shall be a general policy of continuity in India's neighbourhood policy, the policy under Modi's leadership under the banner of BJP-led National Democratic Alliance in particular towards China would be worth-watching.

India's stated foreign policy strategy boasts for its strategic autonomy but has often been criticised as meek, unclear and without focus. Indeed, if India aspires to be a regional power, it has to project its foreign policy that should look robust and muscular. Unless India does that clearly, merely having strategic partnership with many countries without defining what really those mean makes no sense. In particular, in view of China's assertive stances on regional issues and ongoing border disputes with India, how the next government handles the China challenge is worth examining. Even in the midst of the concerns over China's rise and suspect behaviour, India-China relations in the economic domain continue to improve. Even the issue of Dalai Lama and territorial issue in Arunachal Pradesh have not hampered the strategic and economic dialogues. Indeed, both the countries held the sixth round of strategic talks in Beijing on 14 April, discussing bilateral ties as well as expanding cooperation on common regional challenges. Coinciding with the ongoing general elections, China exercised restraint and played down the impact of elections in Arunachal Pradesh, which Beijing sees as a disputed region, and welcomed the foreign secretary Sujatha Singh who led a high-level delegation of diplomats for the sixth round of strategic dialogue. Comments in Chinese media did refer to the economic situation in the northeast region of India but did not mention Arunachal Pradesh.

After the foreign secretary met her counterpart vice foreign minister Liu Zhenmin, foreign affairs spokesperson Hong Liei observed that the dialogue is "an important activity under the China-India friendly exchanges of the year 2014" and believed that it will "enhance our strategic communication, friendly exchanges and practical cooperation and provide a strong boost to stable and sound relationship between the two countries". Singh also called on the foreign minister Wang Yi.

Since the dialogue took place amid the on-going general elections, it was expected that Beijing adopt a cautious, wait-and-watch approach before pushing any new major diplomatic initiatives until the new government takes charge in New Delhi in May. Not surprisingly, the main focus of the talks was expanding cooperation on common regional challenges such as the situation in Afghanistan.

China's position on territorial disputes with India, especially on Arunachal Pradesh on which it has made territorial claims, remains unchanged. However, when the state went to the polls in the second phase of the general elections, China preferred not to make any comment; neither did it express its uneasiness openly but maintained diplomatic disquiet. China has in the past issued stapled visas to students, athletes, bureaucrats and army officers from the State visiting China, which it calls South Tibet, to underline its position that the territory was disputed.

Contesting Arunachal Pradesh as an integral part of India, Beijing has often strongly criticised the visits of top Indian leaders, including President Pranab Mukherjee's November 2013 visit to the State. Beijing also protested when Dalai Lama, the spiritual leader of the Tibetans and a guest of India, visited the State in the past. The border in the State is one of the areas of dispute between the two countries with conflicting border claims.

Beijing is watching carefully what could be Modi's, if elected to power, policy towards China. There are two aspects of Modi's likely China policy, if he is catapulted to power, that Beijing would be analysing. One is economic and the other is political. Demonstrating his nationalistic posture, Modi observed in a rally at Pasighat in Arunachal Pradesh on 22 February: "Arunachal Pradesh is an integral part of India and will always remain so". He further asserted "no power can snatch it from us" and that "the people of Arunachal Pradesh did not come under pressure or fear of China". He had added, "China should shed its expansionist policy and forge bilateral ties with India for peace, progress and prosperity of both the nations."

Is Beijing worried by such Modi rhetoric? According to Hu Shisheng, a leading South Asia expert at the China Institute of Contemporary International Relations, China is not. He believes that Modi's stance on the border would not be harder as that would not serve India's interests. According to him, the only approach to resolve the border issue is by adopting the policy of give and take, and peacefully and diplomatically seeking mutually accepted solutions.

What happens if both fail to resolve the border issue in the near future? One way to address is to develop cooperation in some other more strategically important areas with strengthening the global and regional governance, while keeping the dispute pending resolution. But it would remain unclear if India would accept such a position, as that would mean admitting that a dispute does indeed exists, which is not the country's official position. Surprisingly, India did not raise any objection, which it should have, when the Chinese media criticised the Indian government's policies in the north eastern states, commenting that the north eastern states are isolated and neglected and that the unrest and insurgencies in the region geographically close to the disputed border were fuelled by New Delhi's continuous apathy towards the region. By not protesting to such comments to its internal affairs by a foreign country meant India's pusillanimity.

The other is economic, if Modi is going to imbibe the China model in the country's development strategy. During his visit to Beijing in the autumn of 2011, Modi as the chief minister of Gujarat addressed a crowd of 200 Chinese investors offering them "governance, transparency and stability", the three commodities that China Inc. would find difficult to locate elsewhere in India. Modi's pitch for the "Gujarat model" appealed the Chinese. Being an admirer of the "China model", the Chinese enterprises are likely to see Modi government with cautious optimism, though the Chinese official position would likely be complete indifference as outcome of elections is unlikely to influence either the Chinese government or its state-run enterprises and they will continue to engage with India irrespective of the outcome. It remains to be seen how Modi, if elected to power, would strike a balance between the country's stated stand on political issue while adopting the Chinese model of economic development in the country.

China seems to have sensed the possibility of Modi catapulted to the office of Prime Minister. The Chinese President and Communist Party General Secretary Xi Jiping is known to have expressed his desire to visit India later in 2014 to engage with the new government. This would be his first trip to India after taking over as President in March 2013. The proposed visit demonstrates that the Chinese leadership is keen to engage with the new government in India.

Though bilateral economic ties are on sound footing, India continues to face huge trade deficit to the tune of $35 billion and India is keen to address this issue and seek means to correct this imbalance. Increased investment from China and increased access to China of Indian IT and pharmaceutical products could mitigate to some extent to this imbalance. Both the countries are concerned over the return of Taliban and Al-Qaeda. In particular, Beijing is worried that their rise could have a destabilising effect on its Muslim Uygur Xinjiang province which is experiencing a spat of terrorist attacks.

The message that the strategic dialogue sends is both sides are committed to continuity in policies at a functional level, though political engagement must wait till a new leadership takes office in India. This dialogue will be followed by a high-level military-level dialogue in New Delhi in April itself. A PLA delegation led by the Deputy Chief of General Staff, L. Gen. Qi Jianguo will visit for DGMO-level talks on the boundary issue on 22 April. It will be during this time, the annual defence exercises to be held later in 2014 will be finalised. The forthcoming visit of Chinese Defence Minister Chang Wanquan later in 2014 is going to be equally significant. The participation of stealth frigate INS Shivalik in an international fleet review being hosted by China marking the 65th anniversary of PLA's Navy North Sea Fleet is yet another move to build cooperative relationship.

It is usual for the foreign investors in India, they often complain about lack of consistency in India's investment policy towards foreign firms. The Chinese are no exception. In particular, the Chinese investors in the power and telecom sectors complain that the investment environment offered by India is unfriendly. It is natural for a country with one-party political system to deal with the Centre and States in a democratic India that China sees as frustrating. Yet, the Modi government succeeded in wooing the Chinese in projects in Gujarat. In fact, between 2009 and 2012, three BJP Chief Ministers — including Madhya Pradesh's Shivraj Singh Chouhan and Karnataka's B.S. Yeddyurappa — visited China at the invitation of the Communist Party of China (CPC). On the other hand, no Congress Chief Minister visited the country during this period. The only other major visit by a State-level leader in this time was by Nitish Kumar from Bihar. During his visit to Beijing in 2011, Modi succeeded in signing an agreement for a Rs. 2,500 crore green energy park in Gujarat. This shows that Modi has already built up rapport with China, which will help in consolidating economic and political ties between the two countries when he takes over power in May.

China sees the likely outcome in the elections under Modi's leadership and policy towards China to be as "interest-oriented and not party-oriented. India-China ties are likely to rise above from purely bilateral level to the regional and global level as Modi told the Chinese investors that "the two countries will make Asia centre stage of the global economy". If this really happens, the new Modi mantra will be the buzz word for the coming decades.

If this is the likely scenario, how does one accept the argument that Modi advised China should shed its expansionist attitude, implying thereby that India will get tougher on territorial disputes with China? At a rally in Arunachal Pradesh on 22 February, Modi had said "I swear in the name of the soil that I will protect this country", implying that his policy towards India's neighbour would be more muscular. The likely policy of India towards its neighbour would be a policy that is economy-driven, which means to build the economy to put it on a sound footing so that one can deal with other countries on its own terms.

In this perspective, one can gauge that Modi is likely to adopt the Gujarat model for the rest of the country. While courting investment from China, Modi would steer a course between defending the country's security interests, while deepening economic links with the world's second largest economy. Being a great admirer and follower of the BJP stalwart and former prime minister Atal Behari Vajpayee who ordered a series of nuclear tests in 1998, thereby adopting a strategy on both Shakti and Shanti (power and peace), Modi is likely to adopt a similar approach to deter China from being adventurous.

NARENDRA MODI'S CHINA CHALLENGE

US President Barack Obama's recent visit to India has triggered a fresh debate on the old question: Will India join hands with the United States to contain China's rise? The Obama visit was otherwise welcomed by most Indian media and policy experts. The grand welcome Indian Prime Minister Narendra Modi offered to the visiting American leader, the "breakthrough" achieved by both leaders in the moribund civil nuclear deal and the decision to expand cooperation in defence production, all these point to, experts say, a renewed enthusiasm and confidence in bilateral relations.

The next question is obviously how this renewed enthusiasm in Indo-US ties will affect New Delhi's China policy. The joint strategic vision document released during Obama's visit lends credence to the argument that India will eventually be willing to play the American card in Asia.

The document calls for "safeguarding maritime security and ensuring freedom of navigation...especially in the South China Sea". Though it does not name China anywhere, it is beyond obvious who is being targeted when the United States and India are talking about freedom of navigation in the South China Sea. Beijing has increasingly been assertive in staking claims in the sea.

The joint statement is in line with the position India is taking vis-à-vis the South China Sea territorial disputes recently. In an earlier joint statement, issued when Prime Minister Modi visited Washington in September last year, both India and the United States "expressed concern about rising tensions over maritime territorial disputes, and affirmed the importance of safeguarding maritime security and ensuring freedom of navigation and overflight throughout the region, especially in the South China Sea." In the same month, while visiting Japan, Modi warned against countries with "expansionist policies", another reference to China. Importantly, New Delhi chose to articulate it in front of leaders from countries which are at odds with China.

The United States, though it enjoys strong trade and economic ties with China, is in a strategic competition to contain China's rise. It sees India, the third largest economy in Asia as a counterweight to China. During his visit to India in June 2012, then US secretary of defence, Leon Panetta, called India a "lynchpin" in the United States' strategic pivot to Asia. On the other side, India has its own problems with China, including a decades-old border dispute, security concerns as China is expanding its maritime reach, and a skewed trade balance. So, many experts believe there are objective conditions for both India and the United States to bond together against China.

This argument, however, has two problems. First, the United States is a declining superpower, while China is an emerging regional power whose influence is spreading in India's backyard. Aligning with a declining power against an emerging neighbour could become a strategic blunder. Secondly, joining the US strategic project could cost India its strategic autonomy and harm its standing in the region, much like what happened to Pakistan during the Cold War. It was a partner of superpower America and that partnership status did little to solve its problems. Indeed, it may have worsened them.

Indian policy makers seem to have realised this strategic trap. Look at how the Modi government is dealing with China. The Prime Minister had met Chinese President Xi Jinping during the BRICS summit in Brazil in July, a couple of months before he travelled to Japan. When Xi visited India, Modi offered him an unprecedented welcome at his home state Gujarat. Soon after Obama concluded his India visit, Foreign Minister Sushma Swaraj went to Beijing where she met her Chinese and Russian counterparts and issued a joint communiqué that took a diametrically opposite view from the West's on several global issues, from Ukraine to Syria. All these point to India's resolve to take a nuanced position vis-à-vis China.

But then, how do we explain the Indo-American joint statements that frequently take indirect jibes at China? India's China policy is multi-pronged. It has to accommodate both competition and cooperation. The disputes are largely territorial, while the areas of cooperation are related to the economy. India needs investments to develop infrastructure, which it could attract from China. During his India visit, President Xi had promised to invest $20 billion in India (in contrast, President Obama promised $4 billion investment).

On the territorial disputes, the strategy is to hold the line on the land frontier in the north and maintain the edge in the maritime south (Indian Ocean). To achieve the former, India is actively involved in talks with China and has developed several mechanisms for "resolving the border issue at the earliest".

On the other side, it's also in India's interest that China remains preoccupied with its immediate maritime theatre, the South China Sea or the Yellow Sea. Therefore, India taking up the issue of "free navigation in the South China Sea" with world leaders need not be seen as an effort of the country joining the China containment brigade. Rather, it could be a well calibrated attempt to strike a balance between competition and cooperation with China.

But the real challenge of this policy is the great game is Asia. The United States has already said that it is pivoting to the East. Australia and Japan are its strongest allies in the region.

It would like India to play a larger role in this pivot. On the other side, the strategic and economic cooperation between Russia and China is on the rise, which is what's called Putin's pivot.

Russia is angry with the West for reaching into its backyard in Eastern Europe, while China is concerned about US intentions. In other words, there are two pivots in Asia. And both sides expect India to play a role in favour of them. The challenge before Indian policy makers is to identify the areas of cooperation on both sides and limit the scope of partnership to those areas, irrespective of the pressure great powers exert on it. Only then maintain its strategic autonomy, which is imperative for its own rise.

SINO-INDIAN RELATIONS: A GROWING UNEASE

The dramatic rise of two Asian giants set against the backdrop of a troubled diplomatic history has propelled India and China into a trajectory that will likely prove difficult to navigate in the coming years. With the world riveted by Chinese aggression against Japan and Southeast Asian states in recent months, one country was not surprised: India. After all, New Delhi has been grappling with the challenge of China's rapid rise for some time. Bilateral ties between China and India nosedived so dramatically last year that Indian strategists were even predicting 'the year of the Chinese attack on India'; it was suggested that China would attack India by 2012 primarily to divert attention from its growing domestic troubles. This suggestion received widespread coverage in the Indian media, which was more interested in sensationalizing the issue than interrogating the claims.

Meanwhile, the official Chinese media picked up the story and gave it another spin. It argued that while a Chinese attack on India is highly unlikely, a conflict between the two neighbours could occur in one scenario: an aggressive Indian policy toward China about their border dispute, forcing China to take military action. The Chinese media went on to speculate that the 'China will attack India' line might just be a pretext for India to deploy more troops to the border areas.

A Growing Unease

This curious exchange reflects an uneasiness that exists between the two Asian giants as they continue their ascent in the global inter-state hierarchy. Even as they sign loftily worded documents year after year, the distrust between the two is actually growing at an alarming rate. True, economic cooperation and bilateral political, as well as socio-cultural exchanges are at an all time high; China is India's largest trading partner. Yet this cooperation has done little to assuage each country's concerns about the other's intentions.

The two sides are locked in a classic security dilemma, where any action taken by one is immediately interpreted by the other as a threat to its interests. At the global level, the rhetoric is all about cooperation, and indeed the two sides have worked together on climate change, global trade negotiations and demanding a restructuring of global financial institutions in view of the global economy's shifting centre of gravity. At the bilateral level, however, mounting tensions reached an impasse last year, when China took its territorial dispute with India all the way to the Asian Development Bank. There China blocked India's application for a loan that included money for development projects in the Indian state of Arunachal Pradesh, which China continues to claim as part of its own territory. Also, the suggestion by the Chinese to the US Pacific fleet commander last year that the Indian Ocean should be recognized as a Chinese sphere of influence has raised hackles in New Delhi. China's lack of support for the US-India civilian nuclear energy cooperation pact, which it tried to block at the Nuclear Suppliers Group (NSG), and its pro-Pakistan position on anti-India terrorist groups operating on Pakistani soil, including the orchestrators of the November 2008 Mumbai attacks, have further strained ties.

Sino-Indian frictions are growing, and the potential for conflict remains high. Alarm is rising in India because of frequent and strident Chinese claims about the Line of Actual Control in Arunachal Pradesh and Sikkim, where Indians have complained of a dramatic rise in Chinese intrusions into Indian territory over the last few years, most along the border in Arunachal Pradesh, which China refers to as "Southern Tibet". China has recently upped the ante on the border issue. It has been regularly protesting against the Indian prime minister's visit to Arunachal Pradesh, asserting its claims over the territory. What has caught most observers of Sino-Indian ties by surprise, however, is the vehemence with which Beijing has contested recent Indian administrative and political actions in the state, even denying visas to Indian citizens of Arunachal Pradesh.

The recent rounds of boundary negotiations have been a disappointing failure, with a growing perception in India that

China is less willing to adhere to earlier political understandings about how to address the boundary dispute. Even the rhetoric has degenerated to such an extent that a Chinese analyst connected to China's Ministry of National Defence claimed in an article last year that China could "dismember the so-called 'Indian Union' with one little move" into as many as 30 states.

Pakistan, of course, has always been a crucial foreign policy asset for China, but with India's rise and US-India rapprochement, its role in China's grand strategy is bound to grow even further. Not surprisingly, recent revelations about China's shift away from a three-decades' old cautious approach on Jammu and Kashmir, its increasing military presence in Pakistan, planned infrastructure linking Xinjiang and Gwadar, issuing stapled visas to residents of Jammu and Kashmir and supplying nuclear reactors to Pakistan, all confirm a new intensity behind China's old strategy of using Pakistan to secure its interests in the region.

India's Formidable Challenge

While it has not yet achieved the economic and political profile that China enjoys regionally and globally, India is increasingly bracketed with China as a rising or emerging power-or even a global superpower. Indian elites who have been obsessed with Pakistan for more than 60 years suddenly have found a new object of fascination. India's main security concern now is not the increasingly decrepit state of Pakistan but an ever more assertive China, a shift that is widely viewed inside India as one that can facilitate better strategic planning.

India's defeat at Chinese hands in 1962 shaped the Indian elite's perceptions of China, and they are unlikely to alter them anytime soon.

China is thus viewed by India as a growing, aggressive nationalistic power whose ambitions are likely to reshape the contours of the regional and global balance of power with deleterious consequences for Indian interests. Indian policymakers, however, continue to believe that Beijing is not a short-term threat to India but needs to be watched over the long-term. However, Indian defence officials are increasingly warning in rather blunt terms about the disparity between the two Asian powers. The Indian naval chief has warned that India neither has "the capability nor the intention to match China force for force" in military terms, while the former Indian air chief has suggested that China posed more of a threat to India than Pakistan.

China's recent hardening toward India could well be a function of its own internal vulnerabilities, but that is hardly a consolation to Indian policymakers who have to respond to an Indian public that increasingly wants the country to assert itself in the region and beyond. India is rather belatedly gearing up to respond with its own diplomatic and military overtures, setting the stage for a Sino-Indian strategic rivalry. Both India and China have a vested interest in stabilizing their relationship by seeking out issues on which their interests converge, but pursuing mutually desirable interests does not inevitably produce satisfactory solutions to strategic problems. A troubled history coupled with the structural uncertainties engendered by their simultaneous rise is propelling the two Asian giants into a trajectory that they might find rather difficult to navigate in the coming years. Sino-Indian ties have entered turbulent times, and they are likely to remain there for the foreseeable future.

The Indian and Chinese Experience

One of the cruel ironies of today's world is that India which is applauded as the world's largest democracy has the largest number of poor and destitute in any country, and China which has achieved, a steady rise in people's living standards and has also acquired the status of a world power has failed to develop democratic institutions and practices. It is also interesting to note that despite the absence of liberal democratic freedoms the West has a deep fascination with China which is reflected not only in the tourist inflow to China but also in the flow of foreign investment and government good will. Operation of democratic institutions such as free and fair elections, existence of competitive politics and dissent do not particularly attract either Western tourists or Western capital to India. On the contrary the geopolitics of South Asia has been governed by the US and other Western countries as compared by India's pre-eminent position and therefore they have followed by an large a policy of containment of India vis-a-vis its neighbours. The functioning democratic system of India has had little effect on their policy. The experience of India and China have put the theory of democracy to a severe test. Two old questions need to be asked again about democracy. In addition, two new questions have to be raised. Do formal political institutions and practices constitute democracy or does it involve appropriate socio-economic conditions which enable citizens to exercise their political rights. On this issue India scores poorly with nearly forty per cent of its people below what is statistically called a "poverty line". China has asserted that it is engaged in creating better living conditions for its people after overthrowing semicolonial and semifeudal domination. Today, however, this dichotomy between economic and political conditions of democracy is seriously questioned. Their mutual dependence is emphasised. Therefore both India and China have to achieve yet more conditions of democracy.

The other familiar question relates to equality and freedom. Western liberal democratic theory asserts the priority of freedom over equality even though the radical stream in liberalism stresses that gross inequalities are detrimental to the exercise of freedom. On this criterion pre-Reform China scored higher marks than India. Social inequalities were reduced in China to a very large extent with the abolition of landlordism and formation of cooperatives and Communes and also takeover of the bourgeoisie owned industries by the state. The wage system was directed towards promoting equality and limiting income differences within the six point grade system. In India too there were a number of measures taken in the early decades following independence to curb monopoly in industry, abolish zamindari system and carry out land reforms. In both the countries the stress on equality declined in the 1980s and almost disappeared in the 1990s. In the past decade or so equality has been a low priority in both China and India. The "equalitarianism", "theory of eating from the iron rice bowl" and such ideas of the Cultural Revolution were severely criticised by the Chinese reformers as being obstacles to the development of the productive forces. The perspective of the present day leadership in China is to "allow some people to get rich first" so that the general level of growth is raised steadily. In India the introduction of the Structural Adjustment Programme promoted the ideology of profit and the egalitarian programmes of social transformation took the back seat.

The two new issues arise from the great democratic upsurges of the past few decades, namely the social movements such as the women's movements, the environmental movement, the autonomy movement and the human rights movements. One question posed by them is to concretise freedom as freedom from multiple forms of domination so that freedom to realise the potentialities of the human being is advanced. Patriarchal domination continues substantially in all the countries of the world as evident from the deliberations at the Fourth World Congress of Women in Beijing and as documents in the 1995 *Human Development Report*. China and India have only marginal difference among them. As to ethnic self-determination there has not yet been a scientific measurement. But both the countries have fairly centralised regimes and both have regions manifesting popular discontent. The caste hierarchy and disabilities in India are targets of public attention and social action. There is no comparable social problem in China though new forms of social stratification have emerged in the recent years.

The other issue is response of the modern state to these expanding democratic demands. All ruling elites would like to have an appearance of being popular and responsive to the demands of the various unprivileged groups. And they engage in innumerable measures of legitimation to create a climate of acceptability among the people. Thus the modern state is coercive, responsive and legitimative at the same time. For this purpose it has developed sophisticated systems of management of society, complex methods of propaganda and innovative techniques of manipulation.

Today the technology of repression and the vast networks of communication allow the formal democracy to continue while the citizens remain helpless. There is a new authoritarianism in the modern societies including those of the West which make the basic notion of democracy nominal. The tragedy is that while failing on the scores of either political or socio-economic freedom both India and China have fast accumulated the resources of modern authoritarianism. These tools include modern capitalist preoccupation with consumerism promoted through advertisement. Sensate entertainment that commefcialises culture in the global scale on the one hand and building up security forces of all kinds to suppress democratic movements on the other. It is this process which is strengthened by the forces of capitalist globalization. The alliance of Western capitalists and the native elites has intervened to assimilate the rest of the third world into the Western model of capitalist political economy. The alternatives which the socialist revolutions and the anticolonial struggles had presented have been defeated in course of the battles of the recent decades. The socialist experiments adopted the same economic goals as capitalist systems and failed to promote socialist democracy. The anticolonial struggles such as India's which centred on the comprehensive concept of *Swaraj* failed to institutionalise after Independence.

The result was the crisis of the state and crisis of development in the third world to tackle which the elites leaned on the West. Thus today on the one hand there is an expanding demand for multidimensional freedom while on the other hand there is a an advancing tide of global hegemony by the capitalist West. The experiments in India and China are caught in this historical conjuncture. With these comparative notes let us look at the democratic prospects in China.

CHINA AND INDIA : DIFFERENT APPROACHES, DIFFERENT OUTCOMES

What the above discussion of the divergence and convergence between Sino-Indian interests reveals is the success of China in attaining its foreign policy objectives and the failure of India to preserve its vital interests vis-à-vis China. This cannot simply be attributed to China's economic and military strength. While China is definitely the bigger player in the region and the world at large but its success vis-à-vis India owes as much to its power as to the way that power has been cultivated and used. While realizing fully well that it would take China decades to seriously compete with the US, it has focused strategic energy on Asia. Its foreign policy is aimed at enhancing its economic and military prowess to achieve hegemony in Asia. China's recent emphasis on projecting itself as peaceful power is merely aimed at allaying the concerns of neighbours lest they try to counterbalance it. China's readiness to negotiate with other regional states and to be an economically "responsible" nation is also a signal to other states that there are greater benefits in bandwagoning to China's growing regional weight rather than opposing its rise in any manner.

However, while declaring that it will be focusing on internal socio-economic development for the next decade or so, China has actively pursued policies of preventing the rise of other regional powers. In case of India, this manifests itself in its cultivation of Pakistan as a close ally. From supplying it nuclear and missile technologies to building its military infrastructure, China has done all it can to build Pakistan as a counterweight to India. This policy has largely succeeded as India no longer enjoys its earlier conventional superiority vis-à-vis Pakistan possession of nuclear weapons by both nations ensures that any step that India takes to strengthen its nuclear weapons profile is viewed by the international community as highly destabilizing in the context of the "nuclear flashpoint" that South Asia has become for the world at large. China has thereby been successful in emerging as a "responsible" global player, despite its abysmal nuclear and missile proliferation record while the international community rails at India for making the world much more dangerous.

China's attempts to increase its influence in Nepal, Bangladesh, and Myanmar, its persistent refusal to recognize parts of India such as Arunachal Pradesh, its lack of support for India's membership to the United Nations Security Council and other regional and global organizations, all point towards China's attempts at preventing the rise of India as a regional and global player of major import. It is this strategy that China has consistently and successfully pursued without any apologies. In fact, this strategy has been so successful that today China no longer believes that India can be a serious rival for Asian hegemony and some have pointed out, India is off of China's diplomatic radar.

In contrast to China's well-laid out policy vis-à-vis India, India has from time to time oscillated from one extreme to another. George Tanham has famously pointed out that India has shown little ability to think strategically on national security. In the case of India's China policy, it needs to be realized that there is nothing really sinister about China's attempts to expand its own influence and curtail India's. China is a rising power in Asia and the world and as such will do its utmost to prevent the rise of other power centres around its periphery like India that might in the future prevent it from taking its rightful place as a global player. This is not much different than the stated US policy of preventing the rise of other powers that might threaten its position as a global hegemon. Just as the US is working towards achieving its strategic objective, China is pursuing its own strategic agenda.

There is also nothing extraordinarily benign in China's attempts to improve its bilateral relations with India in recent times. After working to curtail India's influence in various ways, China would not like to see India coming close to the US in order to contain China. In this geopolitical chessboard, both the US and China are using India towards their own strategic ends. India must resist the tendency of reacting to the actions of other. India's attempt to come up a coherent strategy towards China based on identified strategic objectives is of paramount importance. Prime Minister Manmohan Singh declared that it wants to have friendly relations with China, a reasonable foreign policy objective. However, without a clear articulation of India's national security objectives, pursuit of friendly relations with China should not become an end in itself. It should be a means towards achieving India's larger strategic objective of emerging as a major regional and global player.

India's China policy is also symptomatic of a larger misunderstanding in the Indian and political establishment with regard to a nation's foreign policy. For the left-liberal strand in the Indian polity, foreign policy is merely an extension of domestic policy. As such since India is a secular, democratic, and peace-loving nation, India's pursuit of its relations with other states should merely be a reflection of these virtues. This has given rise to much of the moral rhetoric in foreign affairs. On the other hand, the Indian right, because of its preoccupation with establishing a "Hindu" nation and minority bashing, have extended its narrow sectarian view to foreign policy. The consequence has been its obsession with Pakistan as evil incarnate in its foreign policy agenda and its inclination to view the world in black and white, friends and enemies, evil and noble. Shaped by these forces, Indian foreign policy has merely been one of responding to events around it rather than anticipating them and evolving long-term strategies to deal with them. India's China policy is a casualty of this reactionary approach.

India needs to develop its economic and military might without being apologetic. It needs to clearly articulate its national interests and engage China on a host of issues, from the border problem to the alleged dumping of cheap Chinese goods in the Indian market. India needs to recognize that appeasing China is neither desirable nor necessary even as a direct confrontation with China is not something India can afford, at least in the near future. It must also be recognized that while for India, managing its relations with China is at the top of its foreign policy agenda, China does not view India as a significant global player and is largely indifferent to India's growing profile. India is a rising power in Asia and there is nothing wrong in demanding its rightful place in the inter-state hierarchy. Simply put India and China are two major powers in Asia with global aspirations and some significant conflicting interests. As a result, some amount of friction in their bilateral relationship is inevitable. The geopolitical reality of Asia makes sure that it will be extremely difficult, if not impossible, for *Hindi-Chini* to be *bhai-bhai* (brothers) in the foreseeable future. This reality should be accepted by the Indian policy makers, rather than wished away. India should make a serious attempt to manage this friction by expanding the zone of cooperation with China even as it tries to steadfastly pursue its national interests. India should display the confidence to craft a foreign policy that best serves its national security interests without always looking over the shoulders to make sure that China is not displeased. Again, India can learn a lot by examining how China has managed its relationship with the US in the last few years. While India certainly needs to engage China in an effort at reconciling security and political perspectives, it is naïve to assert, as many do, that India should first be sensitive to China's concerns, real or imaginary, before defining its foreign policy goals and strategic agenda. Does China consult India in its pursuit of its own strategic objectives? It does not and neither should India expect it to. In a similar vein, India should define its foreign policy agenda in view of its own national security imperatives.

But for this to happen, the government of India will have to formulate a clear China policy and, more importantly, a broader national security strategy. Ad-hocism just won't do. This should be the top foreign policy priority of the Indian government if it wants India to emerge as a global power of any reckoning. India should heed to Sun Tzu's advice and recognize that a merely tactical foreign policy approach without the backing of a sound strategy will only lead to nowhere.

SINO-INDIAN CONVERGENCE: BILATERAL AND GLOBAL

Bilateral relations between India and the People's Republic of China (PRC) have indeed come a long way after they touched their nadir in the immediate aftermath of India's nuclear tests in May 1998. China had been singled out as the "number one" security threat for India by India's Defence Minister just before the nuclear tests. After the tests, the Indian Prime Minister wrote to the US President justifying Indian nuclear tests as a response to the threat posed by China. Unsurprisingly, China reacted strongly and diplomatic relations between the two countries plummeted to an all time low.

However, some six years later, the relations between the two countries seem to be on an upswing. The visit of the Indian External Affairs Minister to China in 1999 marked the resumption of high-level dialogue and the two sides declared that they were not threats to each other. A bilateral security dialogue was also initiated that has helped the two countries in openly expressing and sharing their security concerns with each other. India and China also decided to expedite the process of demarcation of the Line of Actual Control (LAC) and the Joint Working Group (JWG) on the boundary question, set up in 1988, has been meeting regularly. As a first step in this direction, the two countries exchanged border maps on the least controversial middle sector of the LAC.

The Indian Prime Minister visited China in June 2003, the first such visit in a decade. The joint declaration signed during the visit stated that China was not a threat to India. The two states appointed special representatives in order to impart momentum to border negotiations that have lasted twenty two years, with the Prime Minister's principal secretary becoming India's political-level negotiator, replacing the India-China JWG. India and China also decided to hold their first joint naval exercise later in the year and discussions on joint air exercise continue. India also acknowledged China's sovereignty over Tibet and pledged not to allow "anti-China" political activities in India . On its part, China has acknowledged India's 1975 annexation of the former monarchy of Sikkim by agreeing to open a trading post along the border with the former kingdom and later rectified official maps to include Sikkim as part of India.

India and China have found substantial convergence of interests at the international level. Both share similar concerns about the growing international dominance of the US , the threat of terrorism disguised as religious and ethnic movements and the need to accord primacy to economic development. India and China have both expressed concern about the US ' use of military power around the world and publicly opposed the war in Iraq . This was merely a continuation of the desire of both states to oppose the US hyperpuissance ever since the end of the Cold War.

Like other major powers in the international system, India and China favor a multi-polar world order where US unipolarity remains constrained by the other "poles" in the system. China and India zealously guard their national sovereignty and have been wary of US attempts to interfere in what they see as domestic affairs of other stares, be it Serbia , Kosovo or Iraq . Both took strong exception to the US air strikes on Iraq in 1998, the US-led air campaign against Yugoslavia in 1999, and more recently the US campaign against Saddam Hussein arguing that these violated the national sovereignty and undermined the authority of the United Nations system.

Both nations also favor more democratic international economic regimes. They have strongly resisted efforts by the US and other developed nations to link global trade to labor and environmental standards, realizing clearly that this would put them at a huge disadvantage vis-à-vis the developed world, thereby hampering their drive towards economic development, a top priority. Both have committed themselves to crafting joint Sino-Indian positions in the World Trade Organization (WTO) and global trade negotiations in the hope that this might provide them greater negotiating leverage over the developed states. They would like to see further liberalization of agricultural trade in the developed countries, tightening of the rules on anti-dumping measures and ensuring that non-trade related issues such as labor and environment are not allowed to come to the WTO. In recent years, India and China have attempted to build their bilateral relationship on the basis of their larger worldview of international politics. As they have found a distinct convergence of their interests on world stage, they have used it to strengthen their bilateral relations. They have established and maintained regular reciprocal high-level visits between political leaders. There has been a sincere attempt to improve trade relations and to compartmentalize intractable issues that make it difficult for their bilateral relationship to move forward.

India and China have strengthened their bilateral relationship in areas as distinct as cultural and educational exchanges, military exchanges, and science and technology cooperation.

Bilateral trade has recorded rapid growth from a trade volume of US $265 million in 1991 to US $3596 million in 2001. In 2001, bilateral trade saw an increase of 23.4 percent over 2000. It is expected to rise to $10 billion this year. The two nations are even evaluating the possibility of signing a comprehensive economic cooperation agreement and a free trade agreement by the end of this year, thereby building on strong complementarities between the two.

Both states are also taking steps to upgrade their military-related cooperation, leading to greater understanding on the bilateral military front, something that would have been unthinkable just a few years ago. As a first step in this direction, the Chinese and Indian navies carried out joint search and rescue operations off the Shanghai coast in November 2003. Both states are also seeking to cooperate on the nuclear front with China planning to import heavy water from India to be utilized in the pressurized heavy water reactors near Shanghai.

Many observers have also pointed out a subtle shift in Beijing's stance on Pakistan vis-à-vis India . China's "neutral" position during the Kargil conflict and the intense Indo-Pak crisis following the terrorist attack on the India's Parliament is seen by many as a reflection of China's sincerity in its attempts to improve ties. In keeping with China's attempts to project itself as a responsible regional player, China is seen by some as supporting peace and anti-terrorist efforts in South Asia by cooperating with the US and India. China is also seen as playing a central role in encouraging Pakistan to negotiate with India by using its leverage over Pakistan.

After assuming office Prime Minister Manmohan Singh's government made it clear that it favoured closer ties with China and would continue to work towards improving bilateral relations with China . In his first address to the nation, the Prime Minister, Manmohan Singh, also emphasized the carrying forward of the process of further development and diversification of Sino-Indian relations. The late J.N. Dixit, National Security Advisor in the current government, wrote that "the Congress will continue the process of normalizing, strengthening and expanding India's relations with China, which is the most important factor affecting Asian security and stability". One of the first foreign visits of the new Indian foreign minister, Natwar Singh, was to China to attend the Asia Cooperation Dialogue in Qingdao, in East China's Shandong province and apparently had "substantive discussions" with his Chinese counterpart.

All this reflects on India continuing to build its relations with China on the convergence of interests that the two nations have achieved in recent years. Aside from the positive developments, one should not ignore the enormous obstacles that confront this bilateral relationship. There has been a dominant tendency in the Indian foreign policy establishment to focus on the strengths of its bilateral relations with China while pretending that problems confronting the relationship would somehow take care of themselves. The challenges in the Sino-Indian relationship are by no means insignificant nor will China take care of Indian interests. It is for India to recognize them for what they are and evolve a coherent strategy to tackle them.

Divergences and Challenges

The number one priority for China's leadership today is economic growth and social stability. China recently underwent one of the most peaceful and orderly political transformations in its recent history, even though its exact ramifications remain far from clear. Hu Jintao became Communist Party chief in 2002 and President of China in 2003 replacing Jiang Zemin. He also finally ceded the effective control of the armed forces to Hu Jintao in September 2004. Hu Jintao is now formally in command of the vast party, government, and military bureaucracies that rule China . This shift, although important for the smooth working of the Chinese government, is unlikely to produce any radical change in China's foreign policy. China's focus is going to be on maintaining its high rate of economic growth in the coming years. It should be remembered that Hu Jintao is a product of the "evolutionary policies" of Deng Xiao Peng that emphasize economic growth and orderly governance. President Hu Jintao has made it amply clear that Western-style multiparty democracy is something that would not serve the Chinese people well, terming it a "blind alley" for China . Therefore, one can expect China to continue on its current economic trajectory and shaping its foreign policy accordingly.

China has enjoyed average annual rates of real income growth of around 10 percent in the last two decades of the twentieth century, something unprecedented historically. China accounts for about 5 percent of world trade and foreign direct investment (FDI) to China is predicted to reach an annual utilized rate of 100 billion in 2005. After its accession to the WTO, China's already-high global economic profile is set to rise manifold. China will continue to focus on maintaining its high rates of economic growth in the coming years, even as some of the economic challenges China faces will become more acute. The burgeoning income disparities, restructuring of its states owned enterprises and the problem of non-performing loans in its banks are just a few of the economic problems China's economy is likely to face in the coming years. So far China has managed remarkably even though the future remains uncertain.

Broadly speaking, Indians either view China's economic growth as a façade or envy it. While India has achieved some remarkable growth rates in the last few years enjoying average annual rates of real income growth of six percent in the last two decades of the twentieth century, it still lags behind China

. India accounts for less than one percent of world trade in goods and services. Currently, China outperforms India in terms of levels of growth, education, health, and living standards of its population, and global integration of its economy. China outpaces India , in sectors where the two compete for third country markets. Sino-Indian competition for these markets is bound to further intensify in the coming years.

Though some argue that the long term economic prospects of India are much better than China's, China remains the undisputed economic powerhouse of the moment driving the Asian and global economy with India somewhere far behind. The fact of the matter is so long as India does not place its own economic house in order; it will remain a second-rate power even in Asia . And China will remain the Asian power that the world will look up to when trying to manage problems in Asia .

What should be equally, if not more, significant for India is the fact that it is China's economic transformation that has given it the capability to become a military power with China spending as much as $65 billion a year on its military. China's military may or may not be able to challenge US supremacy in the next few years but it will surely become the most dominant force in Asia. According to authoritative sources, China is set to overtake Japan in the next decade to become Asia's major regional military power. The US involvement in the global war on terror has put the "containment" of China on the backburner and China has seized on this opportunity to strengthen its armed forces further.

China imbibed the lessons of US military undertakings such as the 1991 Gulf War, war in Afghanistan and the recent operation Iraqi Freedom. These have spurred China's pursuit of the latest Revolution in Military affairs (RMA) manifested in the buying, adopting of latest technologies and weapons systems (particularly from Russia) along with concomitant changes in doctrine and organizational structures. The People's Liberation Army (PLA) has been shedding its manpower since late 1990s to save funds so as to be able to focus on high tech.

Despite a western embargo on China preventing transfer of military technologies, China has been able to deftly use US corporations to garner and apply dual-use technologies. China is simultaneously pursuing a qualitative and quantitative transformation of its nuclear infrastructure. China plans to deploy new road-mobile, solid-fueled, long-range missiles over the next several years possibly to counter US ballistic missile defence.

Overtime, China's enhanced military prowess will lead it to assert its interests more forcefully, thereby, adversely affecting Indian interests. As China becomes more reliant on imported oil for its rapidly growing industrial economy, China will develop and exercise military power projection capabilities to protect the shipping that transports oil from the Persian Gulf to China . The capability to project power would require access to advanced naval bases along the sea lines of communication and forces capable of gaining and sustaining naval and air superiority.

China's assistance to Myanmar in constructing and improving port facilities on two islands in the Bay of Bengal and the Andaman Sea is the first step to securing military base privileges in the Indian Ocean . This can be used as a listening post to gather intelligence on Indian naval operations and a potential forward base for future Chinese naval operations in the Indian Ocean . India's traditional geographic advantages in the Indian Ocean are also increasingly at risk with deepening Chinese involvement in Myanmar . China's increasing naval presence in the Indian Ocean is of tremendous strategic consequence for India . There are also suggestions that the balance of air power in the China-India theater has shifted in China's favor with it acquiring an inventory of about 1500 modern combat aircraft for deployment in the theatre.

China remains the only major power in the world that refuses to discuss nuclear issues with India for fear that this might imply a de facto recognition of India's status as a nuclear power. It continues to insist on the sanctity of the UN resolution 1172 which calls for India (and Pakistan) to give up its nuclear weapons program and join the Nuclear Non-Proliferation Treaty (NPT) as a non-nuclear weapon state. This was reflected in China's lack of response to the Indian Foreign Minister's proposal of a common nuclear doctrine for China , India , and Pakistan . China would not like to get into any sort of nuclear dialogue with India that might give the impression of China recognizing India as a nuclear power. Moreover, while both India and China have a "no first use" nuclear doctrine, China's doctrine is not applicable to India as it is not a party to the NPT.

China has done its best to maintain a rough balance of power in Indian Subcontinent by preventing India from gaining an upper hand over Pakistan . It has consistently assisted Pakistan's nuclear weapons and ballistic missile programs to counterbalance India's development of new weapons systems. India's preoccupation with Pakistan reduces India to the level of a regional power while China can claim the status of an Asian and world power. China signed a charter to step up bilateral defence cooperation with Pakistan "to help maintain peace and stability in South Asia " even as it professes to improve its relations with India . Moreover, even as India and China share similar concerns regarding Islamic terrorism in Kashmir and Xinjiang respectively, China has been rather unwilling to make a common cause with India against Pakistan . China's use of India's neighbours to curtail Indian influence has not been restricted to Pakistan . China has actively sought to contain India all around its periphery by engaging Nepal , Bangladesh and Myanmar .

Despite resolving most of its border disputes with other countries, China is reluctant to move ahead with India on border issues. India's discussion of border issues with China is seen as a concession. India remains satisfied with the "positive" and "satisfactory" Joint Working Group negotiations on the boundary issue. Despite the need for an expeditious demarcation of the Line of Actual Control, the talks seem to be continuing endlessly and the momentum of the talks itself seems to have flagged.

The momentum of the issue of Tibet seems to have been lost. Tibet has become a platform for the projection of Chinese military power. India's tacit support to Dalai Lama's government-in-exile has failed to have much of an impact either on China or on the international community. Today even Dalai Lama seems ready to talk to the Chinese as he realizes that in a few years Tibet might get overwhelmed with the Han population and Tibetans themselves might become a minority. The proposed opening up of the Nathula trade route that connects Tibet and Sikkim has been much trumpeted by the Indian government as a major achievement of Indian diplomacy. However, this step is fraught with dangers as there is no certainty that internal security threat posed by Chinese infiltration would not get worse with the opening of Nathula. This has probably led to some rethinking in India on this issue.

There were disturbing reports during the Indian Prime Minister's visit to China , that Chinese troops had intruded into the Indian territory along a stretch of the unfenced border with Arunachal Pradesh. China refuses to recognize Arunachal Pradesh as part of the Indian territory , laying claim to 90, 000 sq. km. of its land. If recent reports are to be believed after a two-decade gap, China has resumed the supply of weapons to various insurgent groups fighting in northeastern India . China seems to be getting successful in hemming India in from both, the eastern and the western flanks.

China and India : Different Approaches, Different Outcomes

What the above discussion of the divergence and convergence between Sino-Indian interests reveals is the success of China in attaining its foreign policy objectives and the failure of India to preserve its vital interests vis-à-vis China . This cannot simply be attributed to China's economic and military strength. While China is definitely the bigger player in the region and the world at large but its success vis-à-vis India owes as much to its power as to the way that power has been cultivated and used. While realizing fully well that it would take China decades to seriously compete with the US , it has focused strategic energy on Asia . Its foreign policy is aimed at enhancing its economic and military prowess to achieve hegemony in Asia . China's recent emphasis on projecting itself as peaceful power is merely aimed at allaying the concerns of neighbours lest they try to counterbalance it. China's readiness to negotiate with other regional states and to be an economically "responsible" nation is also a signal to other states that there are greater benefits in bandwagoning to China's growing regional weight rather than opposing its rise in any manner.

However, while declaring that it will be focusing on internal socio-economic development for the next decade or so, China has actively pursued policies of preventing the rise of other regional powers. In case of India , this manifests itself in its cultivation of Pakistan as a close ally. From supplying it nuclear and missile technologies to building its military infrastructure, China has done all it can to build Pakistan as a counterweight to India . This policy has largely succeeded as India no longer enjoys its earlier conventional superiority vis-à-vis Pakistan possession of nuclear weapons by both nations ensures that any step that India takes to strengthen its nuclear weapons profile is viewed by the international community as highly destabilizing in the context of the "nuclear flashpoint" that South Asia has become for the world at large. China has thereby been successful in emerging as a "responsible" global player, despite its abysmal nuclear and missile proliferation record while the international community rails at India for making the world much more dangerous.

China's attempts to increase its influence in Nepal, Bangladesh, and Myanmar, its persistent refusal to recognize parts of India such as Arunachal Pradesh, its lack of support for India's membership to the United Nations Security Council and other regional and global organizations, all point towards China's attempts at preventing the rise of India as a regional and global player of major import. It is this strategy that China has consistently and successfully pursued without any apologies. In fact, this strategy has been so successful that today China no longer believes that India can be a serious rival for Asian hegemony and some have pointed out, India is off of China's diplomatic radar. In contrast to China's well-laid out policy vis-à-vis India , India has from time to time oscillated from one extreme to another. George Tanham has famously pointed out that India has shown little ability to think strategically on national security. In the case of India's China policy, it needs to be realized that there is nothing really sinister about China's attempts to expand its own influence and curtail India's. China is a rising power in Asia and the world and as such will do its utmost to prevent the rise of other power centers around its periphery like India that might in the future prevent it from taking its rightful place as a global player. This is not much different than the stated US policy of preventing the rise of other powers that might threaten its position as a global hegemon. Just as the US is working towards achieving its strategic objective, China is pursuing its own strategic agenda.

There is also nothing extraordinarily benign in China's attempts to improve its bilateral relations with India in recent times. After working to curtail India's influence in various ways, China would not like to see India coming close to the US in order to contain China . In this geopolitical chessboard, both the US and China are using India towards their own strategic ends. India must resist the tendency of reacting to the actions of other. India's attempt to come up a coherent strategy towards China based on identified strategic objectives is of paramount importance. Prime Minister Manmohan Singh declared that it wants to have friendly relations with China , a reasonable foreign policy objective. However, without a clear articulation of India's national security objectives, pursuit of friendly relations with China should not become an end in itself. It should be a means towards achieving India's larger strategic objective of emerging as a major regional and global player. India's China policy is also symptomatic of a larger misunderstanding in the Indian and political establishment with regard to a nation's foreign policy. For the left-liberal strand in the Indian polity, foreign policy is merely an extension of domestic policy. As such since India is a secular, democratic, and peace-loving nation, India's pursuit of its relations with other states should merely be a reflection of these virtues. This has given rise to much of the moral rhetoric in foreign affairs. On the other hand, the Indian right, because of its preoccupation with establishing a "Hindu" nation and minority bashing, have extended its narrow sectarian view to foreign policy. The consequence has been its obsession with Pakistan as evil incarnate in its foreign policy agenda and its inclination to view the world in black and white, friends and enemies, evil and noble. Shaped by these forces, Indian foreign policy has merely been one of responding to events around it rather than anticipating them and evolving long-term strategies to deal with them. India's China policy is a casualty of this reactionary approach.

India needs to develop its economic and military might without being apologetic. It needs to clearly articulate its national interests and engage China on a host of issues, from the border problem to the alleged dumping of cheap Chinese goods in the Indian market. India needs to recognize that appeasing China is neither desirable nor necessary even as a direct confrontation with China is not something India can afford, at least in the near future. It must also be recognized that while for India, managing its relations with China is at the top of its foreign policy agenda, China does not view India as a significant global player and is largely indifferent to India's growing profile.

India is a rising power in Asia and there is nothing wrong in demanding its rightful place in the inter-state hierarchy. Simply put India and China are two major powers in Asia with global aspirations and some significant conflicting interests. As a result, some amount of friction in their bilateral relationship is inevitable. The geopolitical reality of Asia makes sure that it will be extremely difficult, if not impossible, for Hindi-Chini to be bhai-bhai (brothers) in the foreseeable future. This reality should be accepted by the Indian policy makers, rather than wished away. India should make a serious attempt to manage this friction by expanding the zone of cooperation with China even as it tries to steadfastly pursue its national interests. India should display the confidence to craft a foreign policy that best serves its national security interests without always looking over the shoulders to make sure that China is not displeased. Again, India can learn a lot by examining how China has managed its relationship with the US in the last few years.

While India certainly needs to engage China in an effort at reconciling security and political perspectives, it is naïve to assert, as many do, that India should first be sensitive to China's concerns, real or imaginary, before defining its foreign policy goals and strategic agenda. Does China consult India in its pursuit of its own strategic objectives? It does not and neither should India expect it to. In a similar vein, India should define its foreign policy agenda in view of its own national security imperatives.

But for this to happen, the government of India will have to formulate a clear China policy and, more importantly, a broader national security strategy. Ad-hocism just won't do. This should be the top foreign policy priority of the Indian government if it wants India to emerge as a global power of any reckoning. India should heed to Sun Tzu's advice and recognize that a merely tactical foreign policy approach without the backing of a sound strategy will only lead to nowhere.

PRIME MINISTER MODI'S VISIT TO CHINA

Beijing pays especially close attention to border issues and bilateral ties, both of which it regards as sensitive. The Chinese realise that settlement of the border issue is central to any improvement in India-China relations, but have kept it unsettled over the decades to pressure India. China has simultaneously sought to weaken India's stand in the border negotiations by promoting doubts regarding the actual alignment and even legitimacy of the McMahon Line.

The Chinese are meticulous record keepers and the Chinese Communist Party (CCP)'s increasingly powerful Propaganda Department keeps tight control to ensure a narrative approved by the Party. It controls appointments and removals of senior editorial personnel in the state-owned audiovisual and print media nationwide. It additionally approves and closely supervises content by issuing instructions thrice a day detailing which topics should be covered, ignored or downplayed, and the prominence that each should be given. China's communist regime is adept at harmonising records with the Party's approved narrative and the predictably selective reporting by China's official media, including Xinhua, of important bilateral events and discussions is, therefore, important. Dr. SidharthIn the context of Prime Minister Modi's visit (May 14-16, 2015) to China, there have been an unusual number of comments and articles by China's normally reticent officials and media, including on the disputed India-China border. Bilateral relations and border issues are subjects that are usually off-limits for the Chinese media where only authorised officials are permitted to voice "views".

On April 18, 2015, China's authoritative official news agency 'Xinhua', reported the arrival in India on a 4-day (April 15-18, 2015) visit of a CCP delegation led by Politburo Member and Party Secretary of Shaanxi, Zhao Zhengyong. Zhao Zhengyong was quoted as saying that India and China were both "implementing the outcomes of Xi Jinping's visit to India, the momentum in development of China-India relations is good, and that there is positive progress in inter-party exchanges and regional cooperation". He said "China expects that Indian PM Modi's visit to China will give a new impetus to China-India relations". Hinting at the inequality in the two economies, Xinhua observed that the "Indian side admired the leadership of the CCP and China's economic and social achievements, and said that India is willing to learn from China's successful experiences and further deepen China-India pragmatic cooperation. Both sides hope that the Indian PM Modi's visit to China is an opportunity for both the countries and it will take bilateral relations to a new height".

A week later, the Chinese-language Meijiang Network, an economic news service established in December 2004 and owned by the State Financial Daily Press and Publication Administration, commented on the upcoming visit. It quoted

China's Ambassador to India as remarking that in case ongoing discussions concluded successfully then agreements totalling US$ 10 billion could be signed during Prime Minister Modi's visit. The chapter included explicit references to the New Silk Economic Road and, referring to Modi's itinerary, said his "first stop in China will be Xian, the historical city from where the Silk route begins". It sought to lure India into supporting the 'One Road, One Belt' by hinting at the potential for Chinese investments and pointing to the investments worth US$ 46 billion announced by Xi Jinping while on his recent state visit to Pakistan. It added that as "China-India are the two large developing countries in Asia, so trade and economic cooperation will be the main agenda of Modi's visit to China".

Wu Tiaoli, an Assistant Researcher at the Institute of Asia-Pacific and Global Strategy in the Chinese Academy of Social Sciences (CASS), described the Modi government's policy towards China as "reflecting a "double track policy". He said "India wants to expand economic, trade and investment cooperation with China and wants to decrease the balance of trade gap with China and, therefore, the deepening of China-India Trade will create new opportunities". Trying to put the gloss of economic development on China's relations with Pakistan, he reasoned that "construction of the China-Pakistan Economic Belt will eliminate the Indian doubts, moreover, it will help India to understand the project". He added that "China is also promoting the BCIM Economic corridor as part of the 21st Century Maritime Silk Route Project, which also requires India's support and participation". Wu Tiaoli assessed that as the world's two largest developing nations "China-India relations have gone beyond the bilateral context, and now have global and strategic significance". He described the bilateral trade volume of almost US$ 70 billion in 2014, as "modest".

The Deputy Director of the South Asia Research Institute of the Yunnan Academy of Social Sciences, Yang Siling, recalled Chinese President Xi Jinping's suggestion in New Delhi in September 2014, that India "converge" its 'Mausam Project' with the 'One Road, One Belt' and the observation of Chinese

Ambassador Le Yucheng that this would "make India a natural and significant cooperative partner of China". He conceded that "in comparison to China's enthusiastic attitude, India seems to be ambiguous about the initiatives of China's 'One Belt, One Road" and attributed this to its feeling "limited by the geopolitical competition".

Four questions relating to Prime Minister Modi's visit to China were raised in Chinese at the regular weekly briefing by China's Ministry of National Defence (MND) held on April 30, 2015. The fourth and last question sought clarification whether China's decision to invite India's Northern Army Commander indicated a change in its position on Kashmir. The MND spokesman's reply was categoric. Reiterating China's claim on J&K, the spokesman stated: "China has a consistent and clear stance on the issue of Kashmir. And on the specific arrangements of border defence exchanges, discussions between the two sides are still going on".

The reply to the second question was also interesting. Asserting that "the China-Indian boundary issue is a problem left over from history", the spokesperson added "joining hands to maintain peace and tranquility in areas along the China-Indian border is the important consensus reached by both sides. The Chinese defence troops have always been strictly abiding by the agreements reached by the two governments, and we hope the Indian side can meet China half way".

A Chinese-language Xinhua dispatch of May 7, 2015, which officially announced Modi's visit to China from May 14-16, went viral on China's social media. The dispatch listed Modi's itinerary and said "China has done its homework for the visit of powerful and popular Modi. Ten days before his visit, he opened Chinese Weibo to play the emotional card, and the blog posts are full of 'friendship', 'blessing' and other words. He is ready to embark on the road to the East. Modi expects a lot from China, and in the economic aspect his main focus is investment and the projects under negotiations, and political dialogue involving the Sino-Indian border dispute". Saying "It is foreseeable that Modi's pragmatic China policy will continue

—cooperation on economic and trade and balance in diplomacy" it pointedly asked whether "Modi can have both—the fish and bear's paw?"

Comments of the spokesperson of the Chinese Ministry of Foreign Affairs (MFA) at the regular briefing a day earlier (May 6) were carefully worded. Important was the Chinese Foreign Ministry spokesperson's statement that "The bilateral relationship boasts strategic significance and global influence. Over the past years, China and India have kept their relationship developing in a sound and steady manner and figured out a way to get along with each other that focuses on mutual benefit and cooperative development, accommodates each other's concerns and properly handles differences". The spokesperson added "President Xi Jinping paid a successful state visit to India last September when he mapped out the development of China-India strategic cooperative partnership for the next five to ten years together with Indian leaders". Stating that both sides are closely coordinating the visit and "It is believed that efforts by the two sides will ensure the success of Prime Minister Modi's visit and showcase the importance attached by the Chinese side to China-India relations and to the visit", the spokesperson said in conclusion that "We expect and believe that the visit will help enhance mutual understanding and mutual trust between the two countries, step up bilateral cooperation across the board and enable the bilateral relations to make bigger strides at a faster pace and in a more stable manner."

In the span of a week till May 15, 2015, the state-run 'Global Times', a subsidiary owned by the CCP's official newspaper People's Daily, published at least six articles on the visit. All underlined the mutual lack of trust and emphasised that China was far ahead of India in economic terms.

Particularly acerbic and critical was the article on May 11, 2015, by Hu Zhiyong, a research fellow with the Institute of International Relations at the Shanghai Academy of Social Sciences. Hu Zhiyong is reputedly close to the CCP leadership and articulates their views. Describing Modi as a "pragmatist, rather than a visionary," he said Modi had "been busy strengthening India's ties with neighboring countries to compete with China, while trying to take advantage of the tremendous opportunities for economic development created by China". It accused him of "also playing little tricks over border disputes and security issues, hoping to boost his domestic prestige while increasing his leverage in negotiations with China". Saying that "the ball is in India's court to deepen the bilateral relations" he added that "for China, developing friendly cooperation with surrounding countries has always been the foothold of its diplomacy" and that "close ties with India, China's largest neighbour in South Asia, is of great importance to China's perimeter security and stability". He added that improvement in Sino-Indian relations are "severely constrained" by the views of a number of Indian elites who "deem the rise of Beijing as a threat to New Delhi's development".

Asserting that the "two sides have never established real strategic trust" he listed steps that Modi should take, namely (i) "he should no longer visit the disputed border region in pursuit of his own political interests"; (ii) he should "not deliver any remarks that infringe on the consensus on bilateral ties"; and (iii) "the Indian government should completely stop supporting the Dalai Lama, and stop making the Tibetan issue a stumbling block to the Sino-Indian relationship".

Hu Zhiyong was equally uncompromising on issues of economy and trade, saying that "New Delhi is reluctant to admit the widening trade gap is its own fault, nor is it willing to examine its own economic structure and the quality of its exports to China", but instead repeatedly accuses or directs its anger at China. Scathing was the observation that "due to the Indian elites' blind arrogance and confidence in their democracy, and the inferiority of its ordinary people, very few Indians are able to treat Sino-Indian relations accurately, objectively and rationally". He accused some Indian media of "irresponsibly exaggerating the conflicts between the two sides, adding fuel to the hostility among the public". Hu Zhiyong concluded with the comment that "Modi should seize the chance of his China visit to enhance bilateral cooperation" and "political mutual trust between leaders".

Ding Gang, a Senior Editor of the CCP's authoritative mouthpiece People's Daily, apparently voiced the Party's views on May 13, 2015, in a column in the Global Times. He wrote that if India and China join hands they could change Asia's geopolitical and economic landscape, but "there seems always to be a lack of mutual trust between the dragon and the elephant". He added that "there is more competition than complementarity" between India and China leading directly "to a zero-sum game. In other words, one side moving up on the supply chain will likely squeeze the domain of the other".

Stating that there are many "unsustainable factors in the trade structure of China and India", he said if China invests more in India's infrastructure this may prove counter-productive as it could "cause more concerns for India about the flooding of Chinese commodities" and that involvement of Chinese enterprises could entangle them in "India's perplexing land system". He recommended that China "make well-planned and targeted industrial transfers in accordance with the development and investment ability of its enterprises and set up production bases in India to make use of its cheaper labour force and invest in training selected Indian workers through the Asian Infrastructure Investment Bank. He asked India to draw upon China's strength in technology and funding. He urged more access to local markets for Chinese telecommunication enterprises, saying China could do likewise for India's pharmaceutical companies and forecast that the two countries could "ultimately create a common market of 2.6 billion people".

Global Times on May 13, 2015, published an article by Swaran Singh, an Indian scholar in JNU, Delhi, which said that the PMO's last-minute decision to cancel BJP President Amit Shah's meeting with the Dalai Lama at Dharamsala on May 2, 2015, "showed the cost that the Modi government was willing to take to please Chinese leaders." Stating that the RSS has had a negative view on China since 1962, it referred to an article in the RSS' official paper Organiser, which said that "the well-calibrated symbolism of Modi and Chinese President Xi Jinping shows the duo has a better chance in achieving breakthroughs and bringing down negativity over political questions." The author said "the story compares Modi to the Buddha and the poet Tagore in having left a deep impression on China's popular consciousness". Stating that the "ruling establishment of India does not wish to leave any stone unturned to ensure the positive environment for the Xi-Modi summit, which is expected to usher in a subtle "reset" in China-India relations", it commented that "their summit should mark an important but first step in their long journey together into building, not just theirs, but Asia's future".

The article in the Global Times on May 14, 2015, by Liu Zongyi, an assistant research fellow of the Shanghai Institutes for International Studies (SIIS) and a visiting fellow of the Chongyang Institute for Financial Studies, Renmin University of China, was interesting. It blended veiled warnings with the potential promise of improved ties. Pertinent were the statements that "realizing regional security, including the stability in Afghanistan and the security in the Indian Ocean, requires concerted efforts from both China and India" and that "at present Washington is the major provider of security in the vast Indian Ocean, so if it exits, India will need the cooperation of other countries".

It candidly stated that "the boundary disputes are a conundrum in the bilateral relationship. If they can't be solved at an earlier date, the two sides should more closely stick to the code of conduct they reached before." It recalled the proposal by Xi Jinping made last September that "China and India should work together to establish a closer partnership of development rather than becoming rivals in competition" and said "Modi is considered as a state leader with strategic insights. He may become a Nixon-style statesman because of his pragmatism and capacity to resolve major contradictions between China and India and to tackle the common challenges of development". Acknowledging that "there is indeed competition and a lack of mutual strategic trust between the two rapidly emerging Asian powers" it said "over the past year, India, under the Modi administration, has become a star on the world stage." It cautioned, however, that "Modi's victory in the country's general elections last May has injected enormous confidence into India's economic development" but "had also offered hope to the US, Japan and other nations attempting to take advantage of New Delhi to contain China". It took note of India's ambiguous attitude towards China's 'One Belt, One Road', the 21st Century Maritime Silk Road initiatives, and the Asian Infrastructure Investment Bank (AIIB). In conclusion, the article observed that "India longs for economic integration in Asia. However, it is reluctant to see China acting as the single leader in the region but expects to share the role".

A Xinhua editorial of May 14, 2015, was more balanced. It described the "exchange of visits by the leaders from the world's two largest emerging economies" as signaling "warming relations between the two oriental giants". The report played up the fact that Xi Jinping had travelled outside Beijing to receive Modi and said "Sino-Indian ties could be among the most important bilateral relationships". It said "if the "Chinese Dragon" and the "Indian Elephant" co-exist harmoniously and realize peaceful, cooperative development, it will bring benefit to not only their combined 2.5 billion people, but also those living beyond their borders." Emphasising that "China is an infrastructure powerhouse, while India has infrastructure deficits" it said "China can help India upgrade its railway stations and overhaul its high-speed rail networks" thereby giving both economies a big boost. It noted that India has created world-class software and competitive pharmaceutical industries.

Another Global Times editorial on May 15, 2015, captioned 'Sino-Indian ties can conquer West's doubts' focused on the so-called attempts by the West to sow discord between India and China. It said "The dragon-elephant pas de deux has made headlines once again, but suspicions from the Western world soon poured in, saying the surface friendliness cannot cover the fact that Sino-Indian relations have irreconcilable maladies.

No matter how much cooperation they can establish, border disputes will offset all progress".

Asserting "it is obvious that the Western elite doesn't want to see India and China drawing closer to each other", the editorial said "it will be a long-term test for China and India to get rid of distractions imposed by the West and stick to a path which can benefit the national interest of both countries". Admitting that "the bilateral relationship is still vulnerable to many sensitive issues", it said "although no bullets have been fired along the border for decades, tensions still remain". The editorial conceded that "lack of mutual trust still disturbs both sides" and "media reports raise concerns about each other from time to time", but stressed that "China and India should think out of the box where delusions of persecution prevail" otherwise cooperation will not be possible when "only distrust and hostility are rife". It underlined this theme saying that it "is hard for China and India to develop a strategic partnership, but it will be dreadful for both sides to vie with each other" and that mutual fundamental interests demand that "no side should look at the other with contempt or arrogance, and their problems should be addressed between the two with no need to introduce a third party".

China's authoritative official news agency Xinhua on May 15, 2015, reported on the meeting between India's Prime Minister Modi and Chinese Premier Li Keqiang.

Stating that the two met in the Great Hall of the People on May 15 morning, Xinhua quoted Li Keqiang as saying, based on the statement issued by the Chinese Ministry of Foreign Affairs (MFA), that "Last year, the Chairman Xi Jinping successfully visited India. Yesterday, Chairman Xi Jinping carried out a fruitful meeting with you at Xian. My first state visit as the Chinese Premier was India. China and India are not rivals and should become an important partner". Stating that "Both sides need to expand their relation from Asia to the world, and promote strategic mutual trust, economic cooperation.... and promote the common development of China and India" it said "Li Keqiang pointed out that China is willing to join hands with India to build a closer partnership for development". Li Keqiang was reported as saying that the leaders of both countries should "make full use of wisdom to deal with sensitive issues such as borders, maintaining momentum in the negotiations to establish cooperation framework mechanism to ensure peace and tranquility in the border area, while focusing on promoting the bilateral strategic cooperation and common development, and promote the formation of a true "Asian Century". To complement their economic advantages and in a veiled reference to the 'One Road, One Belt', he said they should be "docking development strategies" and "pushing ahead BCIM Economic Corridor" etc. He pointed out that China is willing to participate in India's Industrial Corridor. The Xinhua report included no reference to Prime Minister Modi's comments on the need for China to reconsider its approach on the border and other issues which would otherwise restrict development of bilateral ties.

The focus of China's official media in the days around Prime Minister Modi's visit to China was clearly on the promotion of bilateral economic ties. There was a definite effort to push China's major economic initiative of 'One Road, One Belt' together with calls for enhanced access for Chinese companies. While authoritative articles and comments by senior CCP officials in the months leading up to the visit had emphasised China's unchanged stance on the issue of the border, in the days proximate to the visit the border issue found very brief mention. Where it did, like in the Chinese Defence Ministry briefing, India was urged to meet China at least halfway. Hu Zhiyong's article in Global Times on May 11, 2015, was rather blunt in listing the steps that India needs to take to improve bilateral ties. All articles underscored the distrust in the relationship. Pertinently, Xinhua and China's official media blanked out Modi's remarks urging China to "reconsider its approach" on the border and other outstanding issues, made during meetings with Chinese President Xi Jinping, Premier Li Keqiang and in his address to students in Tsinghua University in Beijing.

BEIJING IS OPTIMISTIC ABOUT CHINA-INDIA TIES UNDER NEW INDIAN PM NARENDRA MODI

Three days after Narendra Modi was inaugurated as India's new prime minister, his Chinese counterpart, Li Keqiang, called him up to discuss the future of China-India ties. According to *Xinhua,* Li told Modi that China is "willing to enhance mutual trust" with India and regards India's continued development as an opportunity for China. Li had previously issued a statement congratulating Modi on his inauguration and expressing a willingness to work together.

According to *Xinhua,* Modi said that "developing relations with China was one of the important tasks of India's diplomacy." He affirmed that the new BJP-led government attaches "great importance to India-China relations." *India Today* also reported that Modi had invited Chinese President Xi Jinping to visit India later this year. It would be Xi's first visit to India since assuming office in March 2013. *The Hindu* first reported that such a visit was in the works back in March, with Xi's presence in India designed to signal support for the newly-elected regime. Chinese Foreign Minister Wang Yi is scheduled to visit India in early June, where he might lay the groundwork for an eventual visit by Xi.

In fact, Beijing seems quite comfortable working with Modi. During his time as Chief Minister of Gujarat, Modi visited China four times, where he actively courted Chinese investment as part of his plan for boosting Gujarat's economy. India's *Economic Times* notes that the majority of China's $900 million in investments in India are centred in Gujarat. Given this background, and Modi's clear focus on jump-starting India's economy, China has largely dismissed concerns that Modi will take a hardline stance against China.

China is certainly interested in pursuing a closer economic relationship with India. In his conversation with Modi, Li expressed an interest in continuing to develop the Bangladesh-China-India-Myanmar (BCIM) economic corridor, one of many westward-looking economic plans promoted by Beijing. China also envisions India as a part of the new "Maritime Silk Road," an ambitious oceanic trade route linking China and Europe via Southeast Asia, India, and Africa. On both land and sea, India is an important part of China's vision for economic integration with western Asia and beyond. Beijing is optimistic that its vision will mesh well with Modi's economic goals for India.

However, to fully leverage their economic visions, China and India will have to manage their ongoing border disputes. And there are some suggestions that on this issue Modi will live up to his hardline reputation. An analysis from Sandipan Deb at *Livemint* suggests that Modi's decision to appoint a former army chief as the head of India's northeast was aimed directly at China. "The People's Liberation Army may now think twice before sending in troops miles inside" disputed regions, Deb writes. Given his right-wing base, Modi will face pressure to respond more forcefully to Chinese provocations in the disputed regions.

Still, China seems confident (at least for now) that its importance to India will provide an irresistible impetus toward cooperation. A Chinese-language *Xinhua* article jumped on Indian media suggestions that Modi must accept China's superior position in Asia, not only economically but militarily. Modi has no choice but to implement economic cooperation with Beijing. At the same time, Modi must change the existing China policy to take into account the existing power gap between India and its northern neighbour. In other words, *Xinhua* expects Modi to accommodate China not out of choice or inclination, but out of necessity.

If China and India can avoid challenging the status quo in disputed border areas, there's good reason to be optimistic about their cooperation. Modi's emphasis on the economy will create an incentive to work with Asia's largest economy, while China's "march west" and its desire for security in its western regions should provide a similar impetus to cooperate with Modi. As an added bonus, if the two sides can temporarily shelve the border disputes, Modi can claim credit for discouraging Chinese aggression, bolstering support with his base — making a "Nixon moment" even more possible.

Yet if the ongoing Sino-Vietnam dispute has taught us anything, it's that nationalism can trump more rational economic concerns, particularly where questions of sovereignty are involved. The sort of confidence expressed in *Xinhua* — the idea that Modi and India will have no choice but to accept China's superiority — could backfire spectacularly if Beijing uses this as the rationale for pushing hard on border issues.

THE MODI-XI SUMMIT AND CHINA-INDIA RELATIONS

Chinese President Xi Jinping will travel to India for a three-day visit to meet with Indian Prime Minister Narendra Modi and others there in government and business. The bilateral environment for this trip is better than last year when Chinese Prime Minister Li Keqiang went to India a few weeks after a border standoff and former Prime Minister Manmohan Singh traveled to Beijing in his last few months in office. Mr. Xi's visit is part of what have been three-plus months of intense Indian activity in the foreign policy realm since Mr. Modi took office in May. It comes a couple of weeks after the Indian prime minister's visit to Japan and the Australian prime minister's trip to India, just after the Indian president visited Vietnam, and less than two weeks before Mr. Modi meets with U.S. President Barack Obama in Washington. The Chinese president's visit, in particular, involves a country that poses both an opportunity and a challenge for the Modi government. As a result of this, and the fact that the state of China-India relations can potentially affect the situation in Asia and beyond, this visit is being watched closely. This piece looks at where the China-India relationship stands, the backdrop of the Xi visit, what the two sides will be looking for and trying to signal, the trip agenda, as well as what all this means for the United States.

Recently, the Indian foreign minister frankly noted that India's relations with China were currently "good," but involved both "competition and cooperation." Arguably, there is also a potential for conflict. The cooperative elements of the relationship include a burgeoning economic relationship, greater dialogue on issues like Afghanistan and counterterrorism, as well as cooperation in multilateral forums, including BRICS (Brazil, Russia, India, China and South Africa) and on multilateral issues such as climate change.

The competitive and conflictual elements that will hang over Mr. Xi's visit include the long-standing boundary dispute between the two countries, China's concerns about the presence of the Dalai Lama and other Tibetan leaders in India, as well as India's concerns about Chinese dam construction on its side of the Brahmaputra river and cyber-espionage and cyber-security threats. Each country also has broader concerns about the other's relationships with third countries. In China's case, India's developing relationships with countries in the Asia-Pacific, especially Japan and the U.S., and perhaps Australia and Vietnam. In India's case, particularly China's relationship with Pakistan, but also its overtures to India's smaller neighbours and Beijing's increasing interest in playing a role in the Indian Ocean region.

In addition, the very issue that was supposed to bind the two countries—economic ties—has been a source of trouble. Bilateral trade has actually fallen over the last few years from $74 billion in 2011 to about $65 billion in 2013. From India's perspective, what's also been problematic is its growing trade deficit with China ($31 billion in 2013). Furthermore, bilateral investment has remained limited, with both sides complaining about market access in the other country.

The Backdrop: A New Government in Delhi; A Beijing Looking for Partners

None of these problems is new, but what is new is the government in Delhi. The majority government in India—the first of its kind in two and a half decades—is led by someone who is no stranger to China. Mr. Modi traveled there when he was chief minister of the state of Gujarat in order to seek investments and markets for his state and its companies. In the past, he has expressed concern about China on the security front. However, he has also stated his admiration for its economic achievements and a desire to do business with that country, especially in order to deliver on his campaign promises of growth and development. Mr. Xi's visit thus offers an opportunity to attract Chinese investment, as well as elevate India's role on the world stage. Furthermore, there will be an underlying hope that the visit (and other recent ones) will encourage competitive courting by the U.S.

Chinese officials, in turn, welcomed Mr. Modi's election, emphasizing that they were ready to work with someone they see as a business-minded leader. The first senior official to visit India from the P-5 was indeed the Chinese foreign minister, sent as Mr. Xi's special envoy. For Mr. Xi, his own visit offers an opportunity to establish a relationship with the new Indian government and especially Mr. Modi. A stable relationship with India could ease pressure on one of China's borders. Furthermore, a good relationship could limit how far Delhi takes things with Tokyo and Washington. Mr. Xi's task, at least on this visit, has been made easier by the fact that he postponed his visit to Pakistan. But he will be cognizant of the fact that he is not the only one wooing India right now, and not the only country that India, on its part, is wooing. Moreover, in the outgoing Indian visits to Japan and Vietnam, China was a publicly unspoken theme and it'll likely be so when Mr. Modi visits the U.S. later this month.

Mr. Xi's Visit

These and other issues provide the backdrop to Mr. Xi's visit and in some cases will be agenda items. Economic issues will be a key focus of the visit. The Chinese government is aware that an imbalanced economic relationship poses a problem for broader ties and is not sustainable, not least because Mr. Modi stressed this point when he met Mr. Xi on the sidelines of the BRICS summit in Brazil. It is also an issue the Indian commerce minister discussed with her Chinese counterparts recently in Beijing. Chinese officials have noted that in order to help address this imbalance, Mr. Xi will take with him investment commitments of over $100 billion over five years. They have suggested that these will especially be targeted towards the infrastructure and manufacturing sectors, which are focus areas for Mr. Modi, and will likely involve the establishment of industrial parks, including one in Mr. Modi's home state. Offers of more Chinese financing for Indian companies are also likely to be on the table. Mr. Xi is also likely to seek Indian participation in Chinese initiatives for regional connectivity, an offer that India will likely consider but not to the exclusion of other such initiatives.

The economic component of the relationship is likely to be one of the main points of focus during Mr. Xi's first stop in Ahmedabad in Gujarat. This leg of the visit will also give Chinese officials a chance to highlight that the bilateral relationship does not just involve the central governments in both countries, but also states and businesses. Overall, the economic dimension is also providing Mr. Xi's government a way to try to one-up Japan, with the Chinese consul general explicitly comparing China's potential economic offers to the recent Japanese commitment of $35 billion over seven years.

Some believe that this moment also offers an opportunity for the two countries to move ahead on border talks, especially transitioning from managing the dispute to trying to solve it. Indeed, a former Indian foreign secretary has urged the Indian government to press this issue at what he sees is an advantageous time when China is courting India. During Mr. Xi's visit, we might see the announcement of the next step on this front.

In addition, there will likely be discussion of a number of global and regional issues, not least the situation in Afghanistan, as well as the Middle East.

This visit, however, is not just about substance, but also about style. Just as Mr. Li did last year, Mr. Xi has been trying to use this visit to (a) signal that China considers India to be important and (b) add a personal dimension to the relationship. An underlying irritant for many in India has been the sense that Beijing has, at best, treated India as irrelevant or peripheral and, at worst, been trying to contain India or prevent India's rise—not least through China's support of Pakistan, as well as its reluctance to endorse a permanent seat for India on the U.N. Security Council and past objections to Indian membership in the Nuclear Suppliers Group (NSG). In the lead up to the visit, Chinese policymakers have tried to mitigate some of these concerns, indicating support for India's membership in the Shanghai Cooperation Organization and inviting Mr. Modi to the Asia-Pacific Economic Cooperation meeting in Beijing. One thing to watch during Mr. Xi's visit is whether China will take further steps on this front—even if just rhetorical.

On his part, Mr. Modi is going out of his way for Mr. Xi in some respects, sending his national security advisor as his special envoy to Beijing to, among other things, stress the importance the government is placing on the visit. More significantly, he is making a "special gesture," possibly against the advice of a number of his diplomats, since it is a departure from Indian protocol, to greet Mr. Xi in Ahmedabad.

While the Chinese president perhaps can't compete with the personal relationship that Japanese Prime Minister Shinzo Abe has established with Mr. Modi over the last many years, Mr. Xi has tried to inject a personal dimension, saying that when he first met Mr. Modi he "felt like meeting an old friend." He is also travelling first to the prime minister's home state, and will visit the Sabarmati Ashram that is linked to Mahatma Gandhi and India's struggle for independence.

The Chinese president has tried to emphasize the commonalities not just between the two countries, but particularly between the tasks that lie ahead for Mr. Modi and him. There are indeed commonalities between Mr. Modi and Mr. Xi, two Asian leaders that have tried to emphasize that they will take "strong economy, strong security" approaches. Yet the contrast in terms of how the two leaders came to be in power couldn't be more different: one was elected democratically; the other was selected by a chosen few. As Dhruva Jaishankar of the German Marshall Fund has noted, the disparity in their backgrounds is also striking: one, a former tea seller; the other, a prince-ling.

Challenges and Questions

For this visit and beyond, challenges and questions lie ahead for the China-India relationship.

There are open questions with regard to China, including: How much can and will Mr. Xi do to assuage Indian concerns, particularly on the border and Pakistan? How will China react if the Modi government follows through with its plans for military modernization, border infrastructure upgradation and the development of India's northeast? What will Beijing do with regard to Tibet, particularly in the event of a transition in Tibetan leadership?

There are also a number of questions with regard to the Indian government:

Can Mr. Modi deliver domestically? A common challenge to all India's key relationships is that they are both motivated by and dependent on domestic transformation in India, especially on the economic side. Chinese capital, companies and attention will come to India if Mr. Modi's government is seen as delivering on his promises of growth, governance and getting things done. If there is a sense that he can't deliver, they might lose interest.

What happens if and when there's a crisis or if China crosses an Indian red line? We haven't seen major Sino-Indian tension or setbacks since Mr. Modi took over, but we have seen in his government's approach to Pakistan that its reaching out is contingent on a sense that the other country is acting in good faith. But the relationships with China and Pakistan aren't equivalent, and many will watch to see how Mr. Modi will respond if and when there's a sense that China hasn't acted in good faith.

Mr. Modi's predecessors have found that even minor crises can derail the bilateral relationship or at least result in a two-steps-forward-one-step-back dynamic. This is partly because the Indian media and public are not inclined to give Beijing the benefit of the doubt. There is still a lack of trust in the relationship, especially in India where narratives related to the 1962 Sino-Indian war continue to resonate. There remain questions in India about Chinese intentions, evidenced from the fact that in the press conference to preview Mr. Xi's visit, the Indian foreign ministry spokesperson found himself fielding skeptical questions about allegations of Chinese border transgressions. This lack of trust is compounded by a lack of (or limited) knowledge of the other on both sides.

Can Mr. Modi's government walk the China-India tightrope effectively, with the fine balance necessary to reconcile competing interests? The Indian diplomatic corps is no stranger to this challenge and we've already seen the new Indian government try to grapple with it. For example, the foreign minister stating that China "should understand and appreciate our sensitivities regarding Arunachal" while the foreign ministry has avoided answering the question of whether Indian minister of state for home affairs Kiren Rijiju (who is from the state of Arunachal Pradesh, which China claims) will attend the dinner for Mr. Xi. Or, the government making clear that the Dalai Lama and Tibetans will continue to be welcome in India while they will likely try to limit Tibetan protests—or at least their visibility—during the Chinese president's visit.

Mr. Modi has a base, a media and, arguably, a population that tends to be skeptical, if not suspicious, of China. It won't be lost on Mr. Modi that he's taking a risk; that some will question the nature of his welcome for the Chinese president, that some will draw comparisons with former Indian Prime Minister Nehru's embrace of the Chinese leadership before Sino-Indian relations turned sour. But Mr. Modi is likely calculating that the opportunity is worth it and that his "strong" credentials will dampen criticism.

The tag line that the Indian government is propagating is that its foreign policy will have a strong face, a sensitive face and a proactive face. And while the "sensitive" face will perhaps be more visible during Mr. Xi's visit, the Modi government has also been finding ways to convey that they will neither be push-overs nor hesitate to express Indian concerns, and will speak from a position of strength. Hence, early on, the invitation to Tibetan leader Lobsang Sangay to attend the government's swearing in. Last week, the Indian foreign minster asserted that her Chinese counterpart has been told, "If we believe in one China policy, you should also believe in one India policy." In Japan, we've seen Mr. Modi criticizethose who encroach on others' lands and seas, and state his preference for countries that emphasize a development-focused rather than an expansionist mindset. While the Indian foreign minister refused to confirm or deny that these were references to China, they only reiterated a sentiment Mr. Modi had explicitly expressed about China in Arunachal Pradesh during the election campaign. The just-concluded Indian presidential visit to Vietnam has, in turn, resulted in a joint communique that expresses support for "freedom of navigation in the East Sea/South China Sea," with India welcoming the chance to host the Vietnamese prime minister in October and the offer of additional oil and gas blocks for exploration by an Indian state-owned company.

The "strong face" is also being signaled through statements and suggestions that India is politically stronger and will be economically so as well. Furthermore, there is an attempt to convey this by taking on any suggestion that China is India's superior in civilizational terms—witness Mr. Modi's statements and tweets on how Buddhism traveled from India to China, a connection that China used to try to downplay. Finally, the government will try to signal this strength through the continued pursuit of a diversification strategy, highlighting that India has options by engaging with a number of countries, including Australia, Japan, Russia, Vietnam and the U.S.

Where Does the U.S. Fit In?

The India-U.S. relationship is partly driven and shaped by the two countries' perceptions of and relationships with China. Delhi and Washington, therefore, watch closely how the other is interacting with Beijing.

It's a complex, dynamic triangle. On the one hand, the U.S. would like to see a stable China-India relationship, especially given other tensions in Asia and the world. Furthermore, it won't necessarily mind if Chinese investment in India leads to a better Indian economy and, particularly, infrastructure that can redound to the benefit of American business as well. On the other hand, the U.S. would not like to see China and India grow too close, China dominate the Indian economy or for the two countries to form a tag team—with Russia possibly in tow as well—in multilateral fora.

Similarly, on the one hand, Indian concerns about a potential G-2 persist—the idea that China and the U.S., which are economically interdependent, will act together in a fashion that will be to India's detriment. A different manifestation of this concern is the assessment that the U.S. is not a reliable partner vis-à-vis China because it will choose China when push comes to shove. On the other hand, Indian officials don't want to see Sino-U.S. tensions that might destabilize the entire region, jeopardizing Indian domestic goals.

In addition, the Indian leadership recognizes that American concerns about Chinese intentions and the nature of the Chinese government are partly what make India important to key constituencies in the U.S.—something Delhi finds useful—but it also doesn't want to be asked to choose between China and the United States. Defense Secretary Hagel indeed recently acknowledged this Indian concern in Delhi.

Another dimension for India is that its officials realize that what is partly driving China's diplomatic and economic interest in India is its relationship with countries like Japan and the U.S. Thus, India will continue to reach out to these countries bilaterally and even in a trilateral context. Furthermore, even if not explicitly, the U.S. is also considered to be part of India's strategic insurance policy. The U.S. can help manage China's rise and assure the kind of Asia that India would like to see. The Indian government does not share what some have outlined as Mr. Xi's vision of Asia, with China the dominant country and with the U.S. playing a minimal role. The fact that India would like to see a different kind of Asia is reflected in the Tokyo declaration that notes that the responsibility that India and

Japan share to shape "the character of this region." It is also evident in the repeated statements from Indian officials that they would like to see a continued, effective U.S. role in the Asia-Pacific.

While they have various concerns about each other, however, it's also worth keeping in mind that China, India and the U.S. also share some common concerns—including those related to Afghanistan (and even Pakistan), the Middle East and climate change—and this offers the prospect of cooperation, or at least, consultation in the future.

7

Modi's Foreign Policy of Nepal

INDIA-NEPAL RELATIONS

India-Nepal relationship is shaped by the centuries old social-cultural, historical and geographic linkages. Extensive people-to-people contacts permeate all aspects of the lives of the people of India and Nepal and transcend borders and governments. Welfare of the people of the two countries is interlinked and developments in one country invariably have an impact on the other. Few other sovereign states in the world can take pride in a relationship as wide-ranging and multi-faceted as that shared between India and Nepal.

Beginning with the 12-Point Understanding reached between the Seven Party Alliance (SPA) and the Maoists in Delhi in November 2005. Government of India welcomed the roadmap laid down by the historic Comprehensive Peace Agreement of November 2006 towards political stabilization in Nepal through peaceful reconciliation and inclusive democratic processes, India has consistently responded with a sense of urgency to the needs of the people and Government of Nepal in ensuring the success of the peace process and institutionalization of multi-party democracy through the framing of a new Constitution by a duly elected Constituent Assembly. India was the first country to welcome the restoration of democracy in Nepal. India has also provided material assistance to strengthen the government machinery in Nepal and for successful CA elections. Overall, over Rs.170 crores of assistance in the form of supply and equipment has been extended as part of India's support to the peace process in Nepal in response to requests from the Government of Nepal.

The visit of Prime Minister Hon'ble Mr. G.P. Koirala to India one month after the restoration of multi-party democracy in Nepal saw India extend a comprehensive package of assistance to help Nepal tide over immediate financial needs and support peace, democracy and stability. A comprehensive economic package worth Rs.1000 crores was announced during the visit. A soft credit line of USD 100 million for infrastructure development projects was extended, and outstanding dues on defence purchases worth NRs. 1.6 billion waived. Government of India also agreed to doubling the number of GOI scholarships for Nepalese students and to supply of 25,000 metric tons of fertilizers to Nepal at subsidized prices.

Prime Minister Hon'ble Pushpa Kamal Dahal 'Prachanda' paid an official visit to India from 14-17 September 2008, and met President, Vice President, Prime Minister, and External Affairs Minister as well as Chairperson of UPA and the Leader of Opposition. A Joint Press Statement was issued at the conclusion of the visit, reiterating the special features of the bilateral relationship and committing both sides to work towards further improving relations. India agreed to implement the Naumure hydro-electric project on Rapti river besides the Rs. 20 crores assistance for Kosi breach relief. Credit of up to Rs 150 crores was also provided to GON to ensure uninterrupted supplies of petroleum products. We have also permitted export of 10,000 tonnes of wheat and 15,000 tonnes of rice to Nepal, along with lifting of ban on other food items. PM Prachanda visited India again from November 12-14, 2008 to attend the BIMSTEC Summit.

The Foreign Minister of Nepal Hon'ble Mrs. Sujata Koirala visited India from 5-10 August 2009 where she held fruitful discussions with their counterparts. Foreign Secretary of India visited Nepal on 14-15 September 2009 to exchange views on the future course of cooperation between the two countries. Prime Minister Hon'ble Mr. Madhav Kumar Nepal paid an official visit to India from August 18 – 22, 2009 at the invitation of the Prime Minister of India. The two leaders had also met earlier on the sidelines of the XVth NAM Summit in Sherm-el-Sheikh, Egypt.

The two Prime Ministers expressed their satisfaction on the age-old, close, cordial and multifaceted relations between Nepal and India and agreed to expand them further. India expressed full support for the ongoing peace process and the efforts to bring about economic transformation in Nepal. The two Governments decided to reinvigorate bilateral relations by ensuring effectiveness of all established institutional mechanisms.

The two sides also agreed to enhance bilateral trade on a sustainable basis. To facilitate Nepalese foreign trade, India agreed to utilization of Vishakhapatanam port for movement of transit traffic to and from Nepal. A MoU was signed for continuation of Indian grant assistant for "Goiter Control Programme" in Nepal.

Nepal assured India that it will not allow its territory to be used for any activity against India and India also gave the same assurance to Nepal. A number of projects with Government of India assistance with a total outlay of over Rs. 1600 Crores were agreed upon including, construction of National Police Academy in Nepal, construction of poly-technique at Hetauda, construction of two integrated check-posts, construction of 660 kilometres of roads in the Terai region, construction of two cross-border rail-lines and continuing provision of Indian faculty to B.P. Koirala Institute of Health Sciences, Dharan.

The two Governments also agreed to take up preventive measures and consultations to address the problem of inundation to border areas between Nepal and India. The Government of India also agreed, in principle, to double the number of scholarships offered to Nepalese students and to increase the number of slots offered for training of Nepalese Government officials.

The two sides also agreed to facilitate increased Indian public and private sector involvement to harness Nepalese hydro-power potential. It was also decided to cooperate bilaterally in areas such as culture, science and technology, tourism and sports and to facilitate contact and cooperation among the parliamentarians of the two countries.

The Minister of External Affairs of India (EAM), H.E. Mr. S.M. Krishna paid an official visit to Nepal from January 15 – 17, 2010 at the invitation of Hon'ble Deputy Prime Minister and Minister of Foreign Affairs of Nepal Ms. Sujata Koirala. During his visit, EAM called on Rt. Hon. Dr. Ram Baran Yadav, President of Nepal and Rt. Hon'ble Mr. Madhav Kumar Nepal, Prime Minister of Nepal. He conveyed to them the greetings of the Indian leadership and reiterated that India attaches the highest priority to its relations with Nepal.

EAM also called on Rt. Hon'ble Mr. Subas Chandra Nembang, Chairman of the Constituent Assembly and held an interactive discussion with Parliamentarians representing the different political parties in the Constituent Assembly.

He also met senior political leaders representing various political parties of Nepal. During his visit, EAM held official talks with the Deputy Prime Minister and Minister for Foreign Affairs of Nepal on all aspects of bilateral relations and issues of mutual interest. The two Ministers expressed their satisfaction regarding the age-old, multifaceted relations that exist between Nepal and India and agreed to expand these further.

They also reviewed the implementation of the decisions taken during the official visit of the Prime Minister of Nepal, Rt. Hon. Madhav Kumar Nepal to India from 18 – 22 August 2009. A total of four MoUs for various projects to be conducted with Government of India's assistance were signed that included (i) MoU for construction of Terai roads with an estimated cost of IRs. 805 Crores; (ii) MoU for construction of a Science Learning Centre at an estimated cost of IRs 16.6 Crores; (iii) MoU between Nepal Stock Exchange Limited (NEPSE) and Central Depository Services (India) Ltd. (CDSIL), India at an estimated cost of IRs.

9.2 Crores; and (iv) MoUs for electrification of five different VDCs in Nepal at a total cost of IRs. 6.3 Crores.

In keeping with the tradition of regular high-level exchange of visits between India and Nepal, President, Hon'ble Dr. Ram Baran Yadav, first President of Nepal, paid a state visit to India from 15-18 February 2010 at the invitation of our President. He was accompanied by Mr. Sharat Singh Bhandari, Minister for Tourism and Civil Aviation and a high-level official delegation. During the visit he met the President. The Vice President, the Prime Minister, Minister of Finance, External Affairs Minister, Minister for Home Affairs, the Chairperson of UPA and the Leader of Opposition and the Foreign Secretary called upon the visiting President. He also visited Haridwar and met a cross section of political leaders in India. During the visit of President of Nepal to India (15-18 February 2010) four MoUs/agreements were signed in the presence of the President of Nepal and our Prime Minister. These included (i) Air Services Agreement between India and Nepal; (ii) MoU for extension of railway lines to five cross border points along the India Nepal border; (iii) MoU on establishment of Nepal-Bharat Maitree Polytechnique at Hetauda and (iv) MoU on establishment of Nepal Bharat Maitri Sabhagraha in Birgunj. In response to Nepal's request for supply of food items, our Prime Minister announced that India will supply 50,000 metric tones of wheat, 25,000 metric tones of rice and 10,000 metric tones of pulses to Nepal. Our willingness to supply an additional 200 thousand metric tones of wheat, if required, was also conveyed. To facilitate economic and infrastructure development in Nepal, Prime Minister also announced the extension of a new concessional Line of Credit for US $ 250 million.

India remains steadfast in its commitment to extend assistance for Nepal's economic development and political stabilization. India's support continues to be in accordance with the wishes and priorities of the people and Government of Nepal. India Nepal Economic Cooperation stands to be further strengthened with the ushering in of a new era of hope and peace in Nepal.

NARENDRA MODI IN NEPAL

It takes centuries to build a national identity and less than few months to lose it completely. This is a lesson that the people of Nepal are to learn very soon. Nepal, because of its geo-political location, has been always a place of political and diplomatic maneuverings for the regional powers but never before was it done so openly and brazenly as it is being done now.

Under Narendra Modi India has become dangerously assertive in Nepal. Since he took over as the prime minister of India he had made it clear that India would actively involve itself in the affairs of South Asia.

The method would vary country-wise. In Nepal, he is trying to launch a powerful assault on the Nepali identity by evoking the Hindu identity. Interestingly, there is a complete lack of concern among the Nepali politicians and academia who, until recently, would jump the gun over anything they perceived as a threat to Nepal's sovereignty and nationality.

While he talks Gandhi and secularism to his Western audience, his regular conjuration of the Hindu identity in Nepal has become a matter of serious deliberation among the concerned Nepal watchers. Post 2002 Gujarat communal carnage, Mr Modi projected himself as the man of development in India and abroad, but for Nepali people, he has become a religious zealot, a crusader who felt it his duty to make them conscious of their religion.

Mr Modi has betrayed his obsession with Nepal quite often in the last few months. His fixation with Nepal is hardly a secret now. In his first visit to Bhutan he mistakenly referred the Bhutanese parliamentarians as the Nepali law makers. Later he praised Nepal in his maiden Independence Day speech to the nation.

In between these two references he toured Nepal and offered prayers in the Pashupatinath temple. The photograph where his forehead is smeared in the temple's holy ash created a sensation in the country. Even the hardcore nationalists saw it as a signal from India to have a good relationship. When he spoke in the Nepal's Constitution Assembly, the first head of any state to do it in recent memories, he repeatedly evoked shared Hindu identity by the people of the two countries.

Taking the step further, he planned a road trip to Nepal in November this year to attend the 18th SAARC Summit. Thankfully it didn't happen. Mr Modi's itinerary included Janakpur, a town considered to be the birth place of Ramayan's Sita, Muktinath and Lumbani. He had plans to address the people in all the three places.

Nepal and Identity

Birth of Nepal as a nation-state coincided with the expansion of the British Raj in India. In the south of Nepal, the two powers constantly disputed over trade and border issues in the last and the first decades of the 18th and 19th centuries. Finally, in 1814 the more than two-decade-long tension culminated in a fully fledged war. The Anglo Nepalese War of 1814-16 in which Nepal suffered a humiliating defeat sealed the fate of Nepal for more than a century and a half. That defeat also made Nepal extremely conscious of its existence. Over the years Nepal's foreign policy and relationship were moulded with a specific aim of protecting its existence. That was the reason, many believe, Nepal whole heartedly supported all British moves in Asia and the world.

During the first war of Independence in India in 1857, Nepal played a very crucial role in reestablishing English supremacy in the region. Then Prime Minister of Nepal Jung Bahadur Rana, who established the Rana autocracy or Ranacracy in Nepal, personally led the Gurkha army to crush the armed uprising in Lucknow and other parts of Northern India. Karl Marx called Jung Bahadur Rana 'the English dog-man'. Even after the rebellion was thoroughly crushed, the Rana regime continued to aid the British establishment in India. Thereafter, the Ranas would not allow any anti-British activities from Nepal. In the following years Nepal was the source of a large number of Gurkha recruits and slaves for the

English rulers. The successive Rana rulers continued to aid the British with Gurkha soldiers in the missions in Burma, Afghanistan, China, Malta, Cyprus, Malaya and Tibet. In the two world wars more than 2 lakh Gurkha soldiers fought along the British lines. During World War II there were 112000 Gurkha soldiers in the British Army, the highest ever.

Post British rule in Asia, precisely after India got freedom, when India's new rulers set the task of assimilating as many independent states as possible into India's fold, Nepal had to wake up to the new political reality. The hastily concluded Peace and Friendship Treat of 1950 with the new Indian government has signs of a desperate attempt by the then Nepali rulers to switch loyalty. Although the Rana rule ended soon after the treaty was signed, the treaty remained in effect. It still is. Since then this treaty is the core around which Nepali politics moves. The political trend in Nepal is that every political party would criticize the treaty when she is in opposition or leading an armed movement and go mum as soon as it would come to power or become part of the system.

The suspicion on India grew after Sikkim became the 22nd state of India in 1975. Many in Nepal saw it as a forceful annexation. This event added a new word in the Nepali political lexis, *Sikkimikaran* or Sikkimization. The merger made Nepali people more attached to their Nepali identity.

In the coming years, this attachment to identity first developed into cynicism and then transformed into socialism. The socialists in Nepal become the flag bearer of sovereignty and Nepali identity. This transformation happened due to the recognition and support Nepal got from the socialist China. China offered Nepal an olive branch to stand on its own, for itself against its mighty southern neighbor which, for many Nepalese, had followed the British legacy of expansionism and assertion.

Since 1950, there have been many attempts, deliberate or unintentional, to dilute the Nepali identity by the Hindu fundamentalists from the both sides of the border. Like today many Indian leaders had tried to influence Nepali masses by evoking common religious belief in the past too. However, Nepal for long remained unmoved from these assaults. In the last 60 years, Nepal has successful defied the Hindutva agenda of blending Nepali identity with the larger Hindu identity. Nepali people had always challenged the hegemonic rhetoric of its southern neighbor. Also, whenever they felt that the leaders or the kings couldn't be trusted in safeguarding the sovereignty of the country they had come out to protest. Often these protests have led to big political changes.

On the other hand, the kings too found it necessary for their own survival to keep the Nepali identity separate from the broader Hindu identity. Often they fuelled nationalistic sentiments to check growing Indian interventions in the country's sovereign affairs. The first king of Nepal Prithvi Narayan Shah warned his subjects from crossing the border and mixing with the Indian population. Later, the Rana rulers consciously chose not to be seen as an extension of India. However, from the second half of the 20th century, the idea of state-sponsored Nepali nationalism was challenged by the new and more inclusive form of nationalism i.e. socialist nationalism.

Nationalism(s) in Nepal

From 1950, there emerged contesting views of nationalism in Nepal. One view reflected the state sponsored top-down nationalism based on national pride centered on the Shah Monarchy and Hindu (not Hindutva) ideals while other view advocated bottom-up nationalism based on class unity of the marginalized and toiling masses. The former was intrinsically anti-woman, anti-dalit, anti-religious minorities and also against the people of Tarai (plains) known generally as the Madheshi. The latter view defined nationalism in Nepal's context as the unity of all the exploited people and demanded restructuring of Nepal based on the principles of socialism and democracy.

After a prolonged struggle the people of Nepal succeeded in uprooting the monarchy in 2008. The first Constituent Assembly saw the largest number of representation of hitherto suppressed minorities, nationalities, gender and castes.

It looked as if Nepal was on the threshold of resolving the contradictions it had been in since the emergence of modern Nepal. However the first Constitutional Assembly failed to write a constitution in the stipulated time and had to be dissolved. The second Constitutional Assembly, which came into existence in November last year, is not as representative as the first.

The number of women, dalits, Madheshis and other marginalized communities and minorities has come down to one third of the previous number. Nevertheless, the people still hoped for a better Constitution than they had previously.

However, things have been changing fast in Nepal since the Baratiya Janta Party came to power in India. This has also coincided with the weakening of the nationalist consciousness among the Nepali people. Nationalistic feeling subsided because people feel cheated by the nationalist leaders.

There is a feeling that the leaders cultivate nationalistic sentiments to further their self interests. It is not long ago when the Maoists were seen as the watchdog of national sovereignty. But they too proved to be the same old wine with a new label. It was during the premiership of the Maoist leader Dr Baburam Bhattarai that Nepal signed the worst bilateral trade agreement, the Bilateral INVESTMENT Promotion and Protection Agreement (BIPPA), with India.

Several studies have already proved that these agreements have always harmed the interests of the weaker economies. Besides, the Maoists have shown reluctance to speak on India's growing intervention in Nepal. In the name of pragmatism, they dared not offend India's goodwill.

Not long ago the Maoists would stop Indian motor vehicles from crossing to Nepal calling it the right of sovereign people. There were nationalists who burnt posters of Indian film stars and politicians they thought had hurt the Nepali sentiments. These leaders are now completely silent over the most ill-timed intervention by the head of India. The passivity is bound to cost Nepal very much.

The question of nationality is still relevant for the neo-colonized countries and nationalities. Although, it is considered an obsolete idea to emphasize on nationality and identity at the cost of the larger class question nevertheless the weakening of socialist movements across the world and rising assault of capitalist imperialism has made it inevitable to fall back to the Marxist line which, along with the class question, addresses the question of nationalism in the newly colonized or neo-colonized countries of the world. For these nationalities, as Lenin would see in various forms of struggles, the nationalist or identity struggle is a process of crystallizing the class struggle. In the last decades of the last century, the socialists in many countries of the world creatively blended the Marxist class line with the issue of nationalism and were not only able to win over the large masses of people but also sustain their power for a longer period.

The Maoists in Nepal must remember Lenin's warning when he said, "The bourgeoisie 'want' to curtail the class struggle, to distort and narrow the conception and blunt its sharp edge." Narendra Modi seems to be doing exactly this. He is trying to blunt the edges of the volatile class struggle in India and Nepal with a narrow nationalistic sentiment based on Hindu supremacy. The nationalists in Nepal, including the Maoists, must remember that nationalism is ultimately an idea. It cannot be saved, by stopping foreign goods and vehicles from crossing the border, shutting cinema halls playing foreign movies and other such rituals, useless the idea itself is saved.

PM MODI'S HIT PLAN FOR NEPAL

Assuring Nepal that India did not want to interfere in its internal affairs, Prime Minister Narendra Modi, the first Indian PM to visit the Himalayan nation in 17 years, on Sunday emphasised that their border should be a "bridge" and not a barrier even as he announced $ 1 billion Line Of Credit to the country.

As India makes efforts to deepen its diplomatic and economic engagement with its neighbours, Modi said he wanted to see

Nepal become a developed nation and was ready to work with that country in all its efforts and offered a "HIT" mantra—Highways, I-Ways and Transways for its development.

Allaying fears of Indian interference in Nepal's affairs, Modi said, "Nepal is a truly sovereign nation. We have always believed that it is not our job to interfere in what you do but to support you in the path you decide to take."

PRIME MINISTER NARENDRA MODI IN NEPAL FOR SAARC SUMMIT

Prime Minister Narendra Modi arrived in Kathmandu today with an aim to inject new momentum to regional bloc SAARC during its two-day summit beginning tomorrow as he said development of close relations with neighbours was a key priority for his government.

On his arrival in Kathmandu to attend his maiden SAARC Summit, Modi was accorded a warm welcome. He was given a guard of honour and a group of girls presented a cultural performance for him.

Modi will articulate India's position on various issues during the summit on November 26-7 and will hold bilateral talks with South Asian heads of state and government on its margins.

While Modi's official programme has no mention of his meeting with Pakistani counterpart Nawaz Sharif, he would be meeting Afghan President Ashraf Ghani, Bangladesh Prime Minister Sheikh Hasina, Sri Lankan President Mahinda Rajapaksa among others.

In his pre-departure statement, Modi said development of close relations with neighbours was a key priority for his government and he was also looking forward to holding talks with other South Asian heads of state and government on the margins of the summit. "Although this is my first SAARC Summit, during the last six months, I have interacted extensively with leaders of SAARC countries beginning with their auspicious presence at my swearing-in ceremony. Development of close relations with our neighbours is a key priority for my Government," Modi said. Noting that the summit's theme was "Deeper Regional Integration for Peace and Prosperity", he said India has always emphasised on the importance of greater regional integration at all levels for the socio-economic development of the South Asian region.

"We have undertaken several initiatives in this regard on bilateral, sub-regional and regional basis, and will continue to do more. We hope that the summit will lead to concrete outcomes, particularly in regard to various initiatives on enhancing connectivity that have been under discussion for a long time," he said.

"This will be my second visit to Nepal within four months, which reflects the importance we attach to our unique and special relations with Nepal. There has been significant progress in the implementation of the decisions taken during my visit to Nepal in August 2014. I look forward to reviewing the progress in our relations with Prime Minister Sushil Koirala and other Nepalese leaders," he added.

Prime Minister Modi's high-level delegation at the summit includes External Affairs Minister Sushma Swaraj, National Security Adviser Ajit Doval, Foreign Secretary Sujatha Singh and a number of senior officials of various ministries.

Modi, after becoming Prime Minister, has been pushing for a stronger SAARC and there has been a lot of enthusiasm among top diplomats of various countries about what he brings to the table to make the eight-nation grouping a regional powerhouse. The theme of the summit is "Deeper Regional Integration for Peace and Prosperity" and diplomats of a number of member countries said there have been expectations that the summit will make "breakthroughs" in some areas.

The leaders are also expected to deliberate on enhancing cooperation in the fields of education, healthcare, energy security and poverty alleviation. Diplomats said there will be a detailed discussion on removing hurdles for ensuring free flow of trade among the member countries. Acting Foreign Secretary of Nepal Shanker Das Bairagi said strong commitment and decisive actions are required to fully and effectively implement South Asian Free Trade Area (SAFTA) agreement.

The authorities have put in place an elaborate security cover deploying over 25,000 armed commandos across the capital which has been decked up to greet the leaders of the member countries.

Huge billboards and posters of SAARC leaders from Bangladesh, Bhutan, India, the Maldives, Nepal, Pakistan, Sri Lanka and Afghanistan, adorn the main streets.

As Foreign Secretaries of the member countries concluded two-day deliberations yesterday to finalise agenda of discussion for the summit, there have been apprehensions that India, Pakistan bilateral relations may overshadow the summit.

PM Narendra Modi winds up Nepal Visit with Slew of Sops

Prime Minister Narendra Modi on Monday wound up his "historic" visit to Nepal with a slew of sops focussing on the 4 Cs - cooperation, connectivity, culture and constitution - to enhance bilateral ties.

Modi, the first Indian prime minister to visit Nepal in 17 years, stressed the importance of the constitution writing to the Nepalese leadership including President Ram Baran Yadav and Prime Minister Sushil Koirala.

"You should not think about the party but the country.

Nepal needs a constitution at the earliest," Minister of external Affairs spokesman Syed Akbaruddin quoted Modi as telling them.

During the visit, Modi assured Nepal that India did not want to interfere in its internal affairs.

Seeking to allay fears here of Indian interference in Nepal's affairs, the Prime Minister said India has no intent to "dictate" anything to Nepal which should choose its own course in its endeavour to build a stable and prosperous democratic republic.

"Nepal is a truly sovereign nation. We have always believed that it is not our job to interfere in what you do but to support you in the path you decide to take," he said while addressing the Constituent Assembly yesterday.

The focus of Prime Minister Modi's visit to Nepal was on 4 Cs- cooperation, connectivity, culture, constitution, Akbaruddin said.

On cooperation, the spokesman said, India had yesterday announced USD 1 billion line of credit (LoC) to Nepal. He mentioned that the prime minister himself has said the USD 1 billion is in addition to any other existing LoC.

The Pancheswar Development Authority will be set up and a Detailed Project Report (DPR) will be finalised within a year.

The two sides also agreed to conclude a Power Trade Agreement (PTA) - a framework pact for the commerce and power sector within 45 days.

The two Prime Ministers directed the concerned authorities to conclude negotiations within 45 days on the Project Development Agreement (PDA) between the Investment Board of Nepal and GMR Group of India for the development of Upper Karnali hydropower project, he said.

The two prime ministers also directed the concerned authorities to conclude negotiations on the agreement on trade in power sector within 45 days. India will assist in construction of a multi lane motorable bridge on Mahakali river to facilitate shorter and easier route between western Nepal and Uttar Pradesh, Uttarakhand and New Delhi, the spokesman said.

The construction of the first phase of the link road between Nepal and Terai region of India, will be completed expeditiously. Delay in this project was one of the concerns articulated by Nepalese side including opposition parties, he said.

Akbaruddin said along with the first phase of this project India also agreed to commence work on second phase.

He said the prime minister donated 2,500 kgs of sandalwood to Pashupatinath temple. India also promised to provide assistance for restoration and renovation of the temple. For this 25 crores will be provided. ASI will begin work soon.

India also offered assistance for development of Janakpur, Baraha Chhetra and Lumbini, including linking Lumbini with the Buddhist circuit of India, based on specific proposals from government of Nepal, he said.

MODI SETS STAGE FOR BETTER INDO-NEPAL TIES

The commitments and candour in the expressions of Indian Prime Minister Narendra Modi during his meetings here have paved the way for the two countries to renew their bilateral relations with political leaders across the spectrum lauding his approach and statements. On Sunday evening, Modi addressed a section of Nepali politicians who regularly rake up anti-India sentiments and demand that the Nepal-India Friendship Treaty of 1950 be revisited, something that the Indian prime minister has promised to do.

"What kind of changes do you need in the 1950 treaty? I urge you all to come to a common ground and present a new proposal. But I also ask you not to do politics over it which would not benefit either side," Modi said in a banquet hosted by Prime Minister Sushil Koirala.

A section of Nepal's polity, particularly the Maoists, have been urging that the treaty be replaced, given the changed political context but have been failing to arrive at a concrete solution.

The recently-concluded third meeting of the Nepal-India Joint Commission agreed to work on a replacement and the ball is now in Nepal's court, say observers.

Though Modi's remarks have impressed Nepali leaders, it is very difficult for politicians in Nepal to arrive at a consensus given their fractured and almost divided ideology.

UCPN (Maoist) Chairman Pushpa Kamal Dahal aka Prachanda, who was seen thumping the desk repeatedly when Modi addressed the Nepali parliament on Sunday, was all praise for Modi. "Modiji open-heartedly supported the ongoing peace process in Nepal. As a signatory of the peace process, we are really happy over this comment." "The way Modi presented himself, the way he laid out the bilateral priorities, the time has now come to work together," said Nepali Congress Vice President Ram Chandra Poudel. Former prime minister Baburam Bhattarai, a key of Maoist ideology, said Modi's remarks were a "good gesture".

"PM Modi has won d heart&mind of Nepalese people with his magical address 2 d legislature-parliament of Nepal," Bhattarai tweeted.

Finance Minister Ram Sharan Mahat tweeted immediately after Modi's address to parliament: "Said many things in impressive manner making Nepali people proud. Also about our prospect if we work hard to make that reality."

MODI BREACHED DIPLOMATIC NORMS: NEPAL MEDIA

Prime Minister Narendra Modi's 'suggestion' to Nepal's political parties on how to write the new Constitution has been criticised by Nepal's leading newspapers and politicians.

On Thursday, the country's top Nepali dailies said Mr. Modi breached diplomatic norms and displayed the "old Indian habit of interfering in Nepal's internal matters".

During his remarks at the inauguration and hand over ceremony of Trauma Centre for Bir Hospital in Kathmandu on Tuesday, Mr. Modi, while pointing out the perils of delay in writing the new Constitution, urged political parties to write the statute by consensus. He went on to warn about the risks involved in deciding the statute through numerical strength in the Constituent Assembly (CA). The Opposition parties, which were defeated in November election for the Constituent Assembly, have been insisting on "consensus only" approach despite agreeing, in March this year, to go for voting if consensus failed.

"Indian PM breached diplomatic Lakshman rekha (norms)," the *Kantipur* wrote in its editorial. "He also has not taken into account provisions in our Interim Constitution by asking the parties not to decide on the Constitution on the basis of numerical strength." The Interim Constitution suggests writing the new statute through consensus but if that failed, process of voting needs to be adopted, a position taken by the ruling Nepali Congress and the CPN-UML.

Another daily, the *Nagarik*, also accused Mr. Modi of practising "new diplomacy" with his remarks. The newspaper noted that the Indian Prime Minister had demonstrated respect and goodwill during his August bilateral visit and desisted from displaying "big brother" attitude. "But he was apparently under intense pressure this time to correct that approach and hence resorted to the old policy."

Both the papers also objected to the Indian PM's warning about the risks of deciding then Constitution through majority. Another national daily, *Annapurna Post*, noted that the Prime Minister should have refrained from appearing to side with one political faction in Nepal.

Kantipur laid the blame on Nepali political leaders' failure and dependence on outside powers for this interference. However, *Kantipur*'s sister publication, *The Kathmandu Post*, took the suggestion positively in a brief mention in an editorial devoted to SAARC Summit. "It was well-intended advice," the newspaper wrote.

Mr. Modi had also suggested that the Constitution could be passed with agreed contents and that amendments could be made to the statute if required. The UCPN (Maoist) and Madhes-based parties are reluctant to take that approach. They have welcomed his suggestion on consensus approach since the ruling parties wield two-thirds majority in the Constituent Assembly.

"He spoke the right thing; we have been all along saying that Constitution should be written by consensus," Upendra Yadav, Chairman of Madhesi Janadhikar Forum Nepal told *The Hindu* on Tuesday.

While Krishna Bahadur Mahara of the UCPN (Maoist) welcomed the Modi remarks, his colleague, Narayan Kaji Shrestha termed it as an interference, an assessment that the

NC and the UML leaders share. "We are also in favour of writing the Constitution through consensus," Mr. Shrestha, UCPN (Maoist) vice chairman and former foreign minister said. "But the way Modiji tried to dictate his views, it was not proper. It smacked of interference."

The deadline for promulgating the new Constitution is January 22. However, the parties here have not been able to settle disputes regarding state restructuring, model of governance, electoral system and judiciary.

CHANGING PARADIGMS IN INDIA-NEPAL RELATIONS

Today Nepal stands at the crossroads amidst the swiftly changing political tracts and it becomes a scarce to found a closer understanding over the core issues among all the political parties. Such political opportunism truly missing the plight of democracy besides pulling down the national priorities in crucial matters; indeed it's an outcome of internal political strife instead from an imposed international pressure. Stability is very crucial for India in the case of Nepal where India hasn't any option except to see a sovereign Nepal; concerned authority in India's External Affairs Ministry has been consistently showing similar concern and landed all possible support to assist in Nepal's integration. Through an honest introspection it's easily revealed that India never resolute any action in past against the national interest of Nepal, further India never obstruct the formation of any democratic government even including the Maoist government and send their foreign secretary just three days before the government formation.

India-Nepal relations are so strong that it's very hard to shape in mere words because these two neighbouring nation has a history of deep ties and shared concern from ancient times. Quality of relationship between these two countries shouldn't be seen in terms of treaty; having faith in each other's role any dispute can be solved and consensus could be formed between these two friendly nations. Indeed there are no reasons among the peoples of the both side of border to involved in any sort of hate campaign against each other; any development in this regard would be ended with an impractical and unviable consequences. So, it must realized that that interest of India wouldn't affect the any move of peace process in Nepal; it's need of hour to end the causes of political insecurity among the diasporas on the both side of borders.

State of Nepal's internal security possessed as much concern as her own existential safety for India, so any anti Indian move will jeopardize the friendly terms and left alarming ramifications for both the country. India's concern over the presence of ISI's agents inside the territory of Nepal must be seen in genuine light by the Nepalese government since it could be highly disturbing in long term for Nepal's own sake as well. Indian government is very serious towards tackling the terrorist network with wrenched resoluteness and would keep affirming on Nepalese government to check their activities from their sovereign territory.

With more meticulous action some unfortunate developments may be easily avoided; that would required a consensus based approach in top notch Nepalese political circle and within their civil society towards the India's plight for security. India never felt any sort of discontents with the democratic proceedings in Nepal; of course Maoist should stay and play active role within their national political framework. Indian government would remains very keen for strengthening of democracy in Nepal and issues like human rights would be a key priority for them with putting finest efforts to see it in universal way beyond the geographical boundaries. In recent past Gorkha's role in Indian Arm Forces has gained some critical applauds from a reactionary section in Nepal which is quite unfortunate and is an effort to dampen the historic and marvelous symbolic ties between these two friendly nation.

The word consensus has been largely misused in Nepal consequently ultra nationalism in Nepal largely seen in the context of anti-Indian sentiment; a very lucid approach would be needed from Nepalese side over such relentless unfortunate developments. In international affairs domain Nepal needs to play more matured role and must develop a sense of its own best interest; mutual integrated relationship with India paves way for safe passages of trust between them which is quite symmetric to the actual requirements and should remain a foremost concern for both the countries to keep intact these flame of spirits; any constructive solution of joint interest would be emerged from mutual effort instead through isolatory stances.

In changing circumstances it's quite essential for both the countries to make immediate revisions in bilateral treaties and shaping them as per the suitability of present time. Infrastructures are major issues that needs to look on in such active manner since perennial floods is a major impediment for socio-economic structure of Terain region in Nepal and entire north Bihar. A radical shift in policy towards the existing infrastructure of water management is the first step that required to be taken by the governments of both countries. Water management possessed very crucial and strategic place in the sphere of India-Nepal relations as their catchments are very productive for the vast agricultural areas as well an alternative source of energy; projects like Pancheswar, Saptakosi, Naumure etc. needs rational handling as they are immensely crucial for the sake of both countries energy requirements. Border management is another issue that needs more regulated treatment though it should remain open as even before because prevalence of open border is the biggest asset of India-Nepal relation and it has potential to be framed as an ideal border of south Asia. Indeed open border plays utmost significance in the lives of population adjacent to border; since time immemorial they have been sharing the ties of Roti (Bread) and Beti (Matrimonial ties) which even creates complexities of identity.

In present state Nepal is coping with the difficulties of constitution making besides having to win the trust of peoples in democratic institution which shown severe fluctuation in immediate past. In this situation grooming of an idea of ethnic federalism and other major issues wouldn't be less than a fatal as handling of such major issues depends upon the state of stability which is completely out of seen in present circumstances. Terain's plight and refugee's problems are some other rudimentary issues that need proper concern and action from the governments of both the side as law and order situation is a matter that requires the co-operation of other side due to geographical nature and open borders. In decade long civil war like situation, the Terai region faced adverse setbacks and witnessed the losses of human lives, infrastructure, ecology, law and order etc. Even in last few months toll of losses in Terai is quite frightening, almost 1200 peoples has been killed and more than 3600 were abducted; situation is still very grim inside the Terai region and peoples have some distraught feeling as they used to feel during the bloody strife phase. Glorifications of Terain Armed groups are caused by the political affiliations and patronage that's making situation worse in any effort to contain and disband their growing role; catchments areas of North Bihar or Mithilanchal region becomes a hideout place for these groups in the absence of a specified and clear set of mechanism on joint level; a strategic move in this regard is immediately required.

Till today Nepal is missing the actual taste of democracy and whatever has been represented on the name of democracy that never touched the ground of actual aspiration of its citizen. Maoists short stint in government couldn't materialized their own professed goals instead they turn up to attack on religious identities, authoritarianism, non-pluralism, against right of property besides showing very immature stand on Nepalese Armed Force chief Rukmangad Kotwal; such bad conflict management with Arm force deciphered the feeble understanding of realpolitik in Maoist camp.

Before that incident Nepali Army has history of passive presence and following the civil supremacy which was very conducive with the expectation of Nepalese intelligentsias. But now stands humiliated, Nepalese Army becomes more powerful and strategic which may played crucial roles in further phage of development. India too witnessed some implications after this incident as the role of India felt prominent by a section of reactionaries in Nepalese politics; former Prime Minister Prachanda's remarks as "Promped by Prabhu" to present Prime Minister Madhav Kumar Nepal was clearly referred towards the India which was completely unjustifiable. India maintains silence over such rambling propositions even the Indian side never downbeat with the growing Chinese influence in Maoists rule and regarded it just as lacking immune system. India has utmost concern with Nepalese state of affairs in similar manner; Nepal too has immense benefits from a stronger India, so despite some ups and down in events it would be compatible to remains in same strong bond of sharing forever' Brotherhood always remains a great idea as in such set of relationship every member has some specific roles to play irrespective of identities like big brother and small brother; being sanguine for same must in case of India-Nepal relations.

INDIA, NEPAL INK THREE AGREEMENTS AFTER PM MODI'S GRAND WELCOME

India and Nepal opened talks in Kathmandu on Sunday, hours after Prime Minister Narendra Modi arrived to a rousing welcome on a two-day visit tipped to deepen relations between the two close neighbours.

Modi and his Nepalese counterpart Sushil Koirala met for one-on-one discussions which a cabinet source said would cover a range of issues including bilateral and regional matters.

After their 30-minute meet, delegation level talks between the two countries began.

The two prime ministers signed three agreements, including a NRs 69 million grant to Nepal to supply iodated salt to curb iodine deficiency diseases.

Under the first agreement, India will provide a grant assistance worth NRs 69 million to supply iodated salt to curb goitre and other disease s related with iodine deficiency.

The second agreement was regarding the amendment of Articles 17 and 18 of the Pancheswor Multiple Project, the Himalayan Times reported.

The third agreement is about cooperation between Nepal Television and Doordarshan, the state-owned television stations of both the countries, it said.

Earlier, Prime Minister Narendra Modi landed at Tribhuvan International Airport in Kathmandu on a 'historic' visit – the first bilateral trip to the Himalayan nation by an Indian head of government in over 17 years.

In a departure from protocol, Modi was welcomed at the airport by his Nepali counterpart Sushil Koirala. In 2006, then Prime Minister Manmohan Singh had also accorded a similar welcome to Nepal Prime Minister GP Koirala when the later visited New Delhi.

Soon after arrival, the prime minister was accorded a guard of honour by the Nepali Army followed by a 19 gun salute.

After the brief ceremony Modi departed to Hotel Hyatt Residency, where he will be staying during his trip.

The Prime Minister is accompanied by a high level delegation including national security advisor Ajit Doval, foreign secretary Sujatha Singh and other senior bureaucrats.

"I look forward to working with the leadership of Nepal to forge a new relationship for the new century between our two rapidly transforming countries," Modi said in a statement released on the eve of his visit.

The visit sees resumption of political dialogue at the highest level between the two neighbours and is expected to bridge the trust deficit that stemmed in the past 10 years due to so-called neglect of Nepal by the two UPA regimes.

"I hope my visit will open a new chapter in India-Nepal relations, characterised by more frequent political engagement and closer cooperation across the full spectrum of our extraordinarily broad based relations," he added.

Nepal and India are expected to sign three memorandums of understanding (MoUs) during the trip. A power trade agreement and a power development agreement for the 900 MW Upper Karnali hydro-power project which were on the table aren't likely to get inked.

"We are committed to continuing our support to Nepal in its development efforts," the statement further added.

On Saturday afternoon Modi will have a meeting with his counterpart Koirala at Singha Darbar, the official seat of Nepal government. Bilateral talks between both sides will take place after that.

Modi will address to Nepal's parliament around 4.25 pm – making him the first head of government from a foreign nation to address the Himalayan nation's parliament since parliamentary democracy was restored in the country in 1990.

On Sunday morning, he will perform special prayers at Pashupatinath Temple. This will be followed by a meeting with President Ram Baran Yadav, who will host a lunch for Modi at Shital Niwas, the president's official residence.

INDIA FOR HIGHEST-LEVEL ENGAGEMENT WITH NEPAL

External Affairs Minister Sushma Swaraj on Saturday met Nepal's key leaders, conveyed India's goodwill for the neighbour and pledged engagement at the highest level, officials said.

"The message is that the new government in India is ready to impart renewed momentum to the multifaceted relations between the two countries," External Affairs Ministry spokesperson Syed Akbaruddin told a press conference at the venue of the meeting of the Nepal-India Joint Commission (JC), where officials were negotiating on a range of bilateral issues.

Ms. Swaraj arrived here on Friday for a three-day visit, leading a high-level delegation for the JC meeting, which is being held after 23 years. The JC — co-chaired by Foreign Ministers of the two countries — is the highest-level bilateral mechanism and was supposed to meet every two years.

The fact that Prime Minister Narendra Modi is visiting Nepal in August before attending the SAARC Summit in Kathmandu later this year demonstrates the priority that India places on its relations with Nepal, the spokesperson said.

Responding to the widespread perception of India's "interference" in Nepal's affairs, the MEA official said it was for the people of Nepal to work out solutions that worked best for them. He said India was ready to work with Nepal to develop its hydropower potential. "Trade in power is a win-win situation for both countries," he said. "We stand ready to cooperate at a pace that Nepal is comfortable with." For Nepal, the added benefit was to reduce the huge trade deficit with India. In her meetings with Nepal's leaders, including President Ram Baran Yadav, Ms. Swaraj conveyed India's desire for a timely and inclusive Constitution that was "acceptable to all."

Ms. Swaraj expressed India's "support, goodwill and cooperation" to Nepal on a range of issues, including the new Constitution, said Nepal Prime Minister's Foreign Policy Adviser Dinesh Bhattarai. During her meeting with Prime Minister Sushil Koirala, Ms. Swaraj said the two countries were poised for a new beginning.

She also met leaders of the main opposition, UCPN (Maoist), who have taken the upcoming Modi visit "very positively."

"We raised three issues with Ms. Swaraj — India's goodwill to complete Nepal's peace process, engagement at the political level, and the need for India to announce a mega project for Nepal," UCPN (Maoist) leader and former Foreign Minister Narayan Kaji Shrestah told *The Hindu*. She met leaders of RPP and several Madhes-based parties in two days.

PM NARENDRA MODI SIGNS 10 AGREEMENTS WITH NEPAL, INAUGURATES BUS SERVICE

Flagging off the Delhi-Kathmandu bus service, Prime Minister Narendra Modi signed more than 10 agreements with Nepal on Tuesday, showing that India is prepared to go the extra mile for its neighbours. But if Saarc fails to move to the next level, the responsibility will not be India's. "We are moving with our neighbours on connectivity, power etc," said MEA spokesperson Syed Akbaruddin. "The Prime Minister presided over a large number of agreements with Nepal, and we have concluded similar agreements with other neighbours. Our commitment to regional integration is for all to see." India wants similar agreements through Saarc, but problems with Pakistan may put paid to the efforts. On touching down in Nepal on Tuesday, the PM also made it clear that India expected Nepal to draft an inclusive Constitution. "I request all political stakeholders to draft the Constitution by early next year as committed through consensus, which will reflect aspirations of all communities, including Madhesis, Pahadis and Maoists... failing to do so can cause difficulties to Nepal and your difficulty despite our expertise to help you in this field is a matter of sadness," Modi said.

A number of strategic issues, including defence and security, were discussed during the talks between Modi and Koirala over nearly 40 minutes. Talking about bilateral ties, Modi said, "When we trust each other, we can move forward very quickly."

"Projects that have been in limbo for 25 years are moving forward. I feel very satisfied," he said after inaugurating a trauma centre built by India at Kathmandu's Bir Hospital.

The new India-Nepal motor vehicle agreement envisages regular bus services between the two countries, including allowing private vehicles to cross the border, facilitating hassle-free movement of people and promote tourism. But it's not clear whether a similar Saarc agreement would be cleared.

Initially, bus services will work on three routes: Kathmandu-New Delhi, Kathmandu-Varanasi and Pokhara-New Delhi.

The two countries finalized the $1 billion line of credit announced during the PM's visit to Kathmandu in August. This will be utilized for hydropower, irrigation and infrastructural development projects. Officials said the LoC will be at a concessional rate of interest of 1% and will, in case of civil works, allow JVs and reduced Indian content requirement of 50%.

India will also help to build a police training academy in Nepal to train over 400 police officers annually. Currently, India trains 350 Nepali police officers every year.

The two countries signed agreements on traditional medicine, tourism and youth affairs for better coordination, even cooperation between stakeholders in both countries to exchange information, marketing of tourist destinations, which may be complementary. "Besides holiday, adventure and mountaineering tourism, immense scope exists in developing spiritual tourist circuits, such as the Buddhist Circuit (Lumbini-Bodh Gaya-Sarnath-Kushinagar)."

At present, India is the largest source of tourists in Nepal with 1,65,815 Indians visiting the country in 2012. Total tourist inflows into Nepal in 2012 was 803,092. After India, China came second with 71,861, followed by Sri Lanka (69,476), USA (48,985), UK (41,294) and Japan (28,642). A new pact was signed to set in place twinning arrangements between Kathmandu-Varanasi, Janakpur-Ayodhya and Lumbini-Bodh Gaya as sister cities.

Modi gifted a sapling from the Bodhi Tree at the Mahabodhi temple in Bodh Gaya to be planted near the Ashoka Pillar at the Maya Devi Temple complex at Lumbini.

Indians travelling to Nepal will now be able to use Indian currency notes of Rs 500 and 1000 denominations. At present, only Rs 100 denomination notes are allowed for Indian visitors, which hampers tourists and remittances alike.

8

Modi's Foreign Policy of Afghanistan

AFGHANISTAN RELATIONS

Bilateral relations between India and Afghanistan have been traditionally strong and friendly. While India was the only South Asian country to recognize the Soviet-backed Democratic Republic of Afghanistan in the 1980s, its relations were diminished during the Afghan civil wars and the rule of the Islamist Taliban in the 1990s. India aided the overthrow of the Taliban and became the largest regional provider of humanitarian and reconstruction aid. The new democratically-elected Afghan government strengthened its ties with India in wake of persisting tensions and problems with Pakistan, which was suspected of continuing to shelter and support the Taliban. India pursues a policy of close cooperation to bolster its standing as a regional power and contain its rival Pakistan, which it maintains is supporting Islamic militants in Kashmir and other parts of India. India is the largest regional investor in Afghanistan, having committed more than US$2.2 billion for reconstruction purposes.

POST-2014 AFGHANISTAN AND INDIA'S OPTIONS

The Afghan situation is unfolding rapidly. At the internal level, there is a clear lack of consensus on how to take the process of democracy forward. At the international level, there is a sense of fatigue, despite ongoing efforts to muster up financial support for sustaining the process of stabilisation of the Afghan state.

From the Bonn Conference in December 2011 till the Tokyo conference of July 2012, international meetings have been "an awkward mixture of hope, fantasy, and failure", according to an American observer.

At Tokyo, the international community did make a pledge of $16 billion for the next four years, which is much less than what the Afghan President had quoted at Bonn ($10 billion per year) and short of what the Afghan Central Bank estimated ($6-7 billion per year) as necessary for sustaining economic growth.

The adverse effects of decreasing international aid on critical areas—related to building democratic institutions, ensuring gender equality and strengthening of the media—have already decelerated the process of stabilisation in Afghanistan.

Moreover, the reconciliation efforts do not seem to be succeeding. There is no regional consensus on how to approach the post-withdrawal situation. Pakistan is looking for strategic depth; Iran wants to see the back of American forces from Afghan soil; China eyes Afghan resources without any definite commitment to invest in Afghan security and stability; Russia is ready to engage as a service provider if the funds can be arranged elsewhere. All in all, there is not enough international support for keeping the 'new Afghanistan' afloat. Therefore, the obvious alternative scenario is staring us in the face—incessant turmoil, political instability and possible civil war leading to chaos and disorder.

Against this backdrop, it is necessary to take stock of the evolving situation in Afghanistan and suggest policy options for India in the changing context.

Post 2014 Afghanistan: How Things May Evolve

Most foreign troops are scheduled to leave by 2014, although some will remain. They will be either in non-combat roles or at best in special action roles. The primary responsibility for security across the country will be that of the Afghan National Security Forces (ANSF).

The key question is: Will the Afghan forces be able to discharge their responsibility effectively? In similar circumstances, earlier in the 1990s, Najibullah's forces lasted for a few years but eventually fell.

However, Najibullah was isolated and did not have any external support. This time around the situation is different. The international community is prepared to help the Afghan forces by providing money, equipment and training.

But it is not known whether this help will be sustained over a longer period of time, say 10 years, or the Western interest will dry up after a point. The Afghan forces have a better chance of resisting a Taliban takeover for a longer time than Najibullah's forces. That is a positive sign. The most optimistic scenario of a stable Afghanistan democratising further and moving away from Talibanisation depends squarely on the capacity of the ANSF to provide security to the nascent constitutional government in Kabul.

There is also a possibility of the ANSF disintegrating along ethnic lines, in case the Taliban, a predominantly Pashtun-majority entity, successfully overruns Kabul after 2014. In view of the desertions from ANSF at the moment and incidents of ANSF recruits targeting their Western trainers, questions are also being raised about their motivation and interest to take on the Taliban in the post-withdrawal situation. Many may also melt into the Taliban ranks.

However, in case of such an eventuality, the non-Pashtun forces are likely to resist the Taliban onslaught. Since the Taliban are used as instruments of Pakistan's Afghan policy, and the return of Taliban to power may not be in Indian interests, India may have to look for the right options to leverage its position in Afghanistan and join efforts at all levels to prevent the possibility of Afghanistan emerging again as a hub of jihadi terror.

However, even if the ANSF were to stay together and puts up a brave front against the Taliban, buttressed by international efforts, the key challenge will still remain the Taliban safe havens in Pakistan.

The Afghan forces and the government will remain seriously handicapped if Pakistan does not take decisive action against the Taliban—the Quetta Shura and the Haqqani group—and myriad other groups seeking to take over Kabul by force.

Pakistan continues to be in denial mode despite proof of its provision of moral and material support to these forces. Pakistan continues to have a deep relationship with the Taliban and retains its leverages with them to use them as instruments against India; however its control over them is at best tenuous.

The Taliban are so far maintaining a facade of unity; however, there are several factions working at the ground level. The Haqqani faction seems to be divided too and the younger lot in the faction are averse to the idea of reconciliation. Some of them continue to have deep sympathies for, and might be working with, the al Qaeda. The Haqqanis are apparently opposed to the growing hold of the Hizb-e-Islami in President Karzai's administration. The Quetta Shura is busy retaining its grip over diverse sections claiming their affiliation to the Taliban.

There are many in the Taliban ranks who do not want reconciliation and are contemplating an armed takeover soon after troops withdrawal. Which vector will finally drive the Taliban policies remains to be seen. The possibility of different pro-Taliban factions confronting each other and also taking on Hizb-e-Islami, and Afghanistan relapsing into a long drawn-out civil war, cannot be ruled out.

The nature of domestic instability in Afghanistan will determine whether post-withdrawal the Afghan forces will be able to meet the challenges effectively.

It is still uncertain as to who will succeed President Krazai. There is speculation that Karzai may not leave at all, and may manipulate his continuation by some means. The fact remains that Karzai's popularity has ebbed and he has many political adversaries.

His relationship with the Western Governments is strained. The Western governments criticise him for nepotism, corruption, etc. One can expect political instability and jockeying for power in Afghanistan during 2013-2014. This may weaken the capacity of the government and exacerbate the security situation.

At present there are four different coalitions competing for influence and powerin Afghanistan today. They are:

i. The Ruling Coalition: (President Karzai, Hizb-e-Islami factions, Marshal Faheem, Karim Khalili, etc.)
ii. Change and Hope Coalition (Dr. Abdullah, Yonus Qanooni, Ahmad Behzad, Nur Muhammad Atta, etc.)
iii. National Front Coalition (Dostum, Ahmad Zia Massoud, Mohaqiq, Amrullah Saleh, etc.)
iv. Haq and Adalat (Truth and Justice) Coalition (Hanif Atmar, Azita Rahfat, etc.)

The two coalitions led by non-Pashtuns (Change and Hope & National Front) may come together to fight the others in the next elections. These two want a decentralised system in Kabul while the other two coalitions want a unitary, centralised state apparatus.

The broad realignment of political forces suggests that a Pashtun-non-Pashtun political divide may lead to ethnic polarisation and political instability, in case of integration of the Taliban into the Pashtun-heavy central government in Kabul. Already, there is a feeling among the Tajiks, Uzbeks and the Hazaras that Karzai has given a free rein to Pashtun nationalists who are impervious to the sensitivities of other ethnic groups.

Reconciliation with the Taliban is acceptable to the international community; but the process is turning out to be messy. The Taliban feel triumphant and are not in a mood to reconcile on the terms outlined by the Karzai government—adherence to the Constitution and renunciation of violence. The US and Pakistan have their own agendas, of which the

Afghan government is apprehensive and wary. Talks between the US and the Taliban have not succeeded because the US does not want to release some of the Taliban leaders as per their initial demands.

For its part, Pakistan wants to direct the course of negotiations through the Taliban representatives loyal to it. The process of reintegration which would have created the basis for wider reconciliation has petered out because of the lack of a clearly outlined plan of action and institutional support. The High Peace Council is ineffective and ongoing mediation by countries like Turkey and Germany has not made much progress.

The drugs issue remains unresolved. According to most estimates, the efforts to curtail the production of drugs and curb narco-trafficking have failed. Huge vested interests have developed in Tajikistan, Kyrgyzstan and Russia to facilitate drug trafficking from Afghanistan. Drugs will tear into the social, economic and political fabric of Afghanistan. Since the Taliban are dependent on drugs money at the moment, they are unlikely to accept any international efforts to stop drugs production in the short term.

There is a sense of fatigue among the wider population in the Pashtun majority areas in the south regarding the chronic state of uncertainty in Afghanistan. Nevertheless, the Taliban continue to recruit from among the younger population in these areas, even if their popular base seems to be shrinking.

This may be more due to lack of employment opportunities than because of ideological leanings. In certain places, like in Ghazni, local youth have gone to the extent of resisting the Taliban diktats to boycott schools and colleges. The vision of a new Afghanistan seems to be motivating people in the urban areas and this is slowly percolating to the peripheries as well.

In the post-2014 scenario, the role of regional countries will increase. The SCO, which has been on the sidelines until now, is gearing up to assume a bigger role in Afghanistan, thanks to new-found interest being shown by China.

Afghanistan has been admitted to the SCO as an observer member. China has signed a partnership agreement with Afghanistan and hopes to continue with its policy of resource mobilisation through investment in mining and communications. But the issue of security remains the paramount question. The SCO countries do not have the money to spend in Afghanistan but they can offer support for capacity-building.

There is a good chance that Afghanistan will increasingly integrate with Central Asia in the post-2014 phase. Afghanistan does have the potential to emerge as a transit hub between the Indian subcontinent and Central Asia. Apart from the Turkmenistan-Afghanistan-Pakistan-India (TAPI) gas pipeline, it can earn substantial revenue from overland trade. Given China's growing interest in building communication network in the region in general, and in Afghanistan in particular, as well as Pakistan's resistance to allow India transit through its territory, Afghanistan may become more integrated with Central Asia than South Asia.

There could be more cooperation between the CSTO and NATO in the post-2014 phase. The Russians and the Chinese both recognise that no matter how despicable the NATO presence may be, it does provide security to Afghanistan and should continue to do so in future. China has been depending heavily on the security offered by international forces for its investments in Afghanistan. Russia understands the adverse effects of a radical dispensation in Kabul and would support any future US-led efforts to provide security to a liberal and democratic government in Afghanistan. Thus, cooperation among rivals is a possibility.

Afghanistan has made some impressive achievements which cannot be denied. Girls are going to school, the security situation in northern and western parts is not bad and some developmental activity has taken place thanks to the aid and assistance from the international community. The Afghan security forces have also been able to put up a tough fight with the Taliban in several areas. If given solid and sustained support by the international community, they may be able to get the better of the Taliban. But the government has several institutional weaknesses that need to be addressed. That is where India can come in.

Options for India

India, by adopting a low-key role in the last few years, has set itself apart as a country which is genuinely interested in reconstruction and development. India's small-budget interventions in Pashtun areas have been well-received/ appreciated by the population in areas infested by the militants, which has even forced the Taliban to grudgingly acknowledge India's constructive role. Thus, India does have the acceptability to play a key role in Afghanistan in the next few years. The partnership agreement between the two countries allows India to strengthen linkages in the security sector too. The common Afghan, irrespective of her/his ethnicity, is keen that India continues to play a bigger role in stabilising Afghanistan. In contrast, Pakistan has lost credibility among the Afghans, who consider it as a country which does not have anything positive to offer, and can only export terrorism and destabilise the situation further.

There is a pessimistic view in certain circles in India that India will find it difficult to stay engaged given Pakistan's continuing nexus with the Taliban and its resolve to disallow space for India in Afghanistan after 2014. However, the situation in Afghanistan may not be all that bad at the moment. It has to be remembered that:

a. Pakistan is fast losing popular goodwill in Afghanistan;
b. it may not be possible for the Taliban to take over Kabul so easily given that support from Pakistan will be hard to come by because of both the gaze of the international community on Afghanistan and increasing preoccupation with the internal security situation; and
c. there is a recognition in Afghanistan cutting across all ethnicities and groups that the war ravaged country would need continued assistance from all possible sources and, among the regional countries, it could bank on

India as a reliable partner. Even the Taliban may not be too averse to receive continued Indian assistance. The perception that India is open to the idea of working with Pakistan in Afghanistan (even if it is impracticable) has enhanced India's image among ordinary Afghans.

Thus, if India retains the political will to remain engaged in Afghanistan, it can do so even as the latter becomes turbulent. India must be ready to provide the necessary resources to sustain its engagement. It needs to improve its delivery mechanisms and cut down on implementation delays. India must show greater receptivity to the needs of common Afghans and build contacts at multiple levels. India no longer has as much leverage with the erstwhile northern alliance members (Tajiks, Uzbeksas and Hazaras) like it had a decade earlier. These links will have to be reactivated. India must reach out to all shades of Afghans.

The India-Afghanistan relationship must go beyond aid and build a comprehensive economic relationship. An FTA with Afghanistan can be considered here. The recent investment summit on Afghanistan is a good beginning that must be sustained.

Afghanistan is in urgent need of measures to boost its revenue generating capacity. India can contribute in the field of revitalising agriculture, building infrastructure (railroads, highways, processing plants, etc.), which could spur long-term economic growth and create jobs, and building of institutions that will stabilise the process of democratisation.

But we cannot be wishful in our thinking. While Indian intervention in Afghanistan must be increased, this may not be easy. If the security situation worsens, we may have to be selective in our programmes. We must contribute to institution building. We should also have a regular political dialogue with the Afghan government to ensure that it adapts to the changing political scenario and adopts correct policies. India should take care that its role is not misconstrued as interference. We can increase the number of Indian developmental interventions in Afghanistan, offer more number of scholarships to Afghan students, relax visa procedures for Afghan businessmen, students and patients seeking medical attention in India, and encourage the private sector to invest in areas related to education, IT, healthcare systems, aviation, mining, media and communication.

India should also be part of multilateral efforts, particularly the SCO, CSTO, NATO etc. Since China is looking towards increasing its profile in Afghanistan, India should have a dialogue with China (and even with Iran and Russia) on the nature and scope of our future engagement with Afghanistan.

India must not get bogged down by Pakistan. India's policy in Afghanistan must be Afghan-centric and not be concerned about Pakistani efforts to gain strategic depth. In fact, by getting involved in Afghanistan, Pakistan is likely to endanger its own security and stability.

INDIA AND AFGHANISTAN RELATIONSHIP

India has traditionally enjoyed friendly relations with Afghanistan. President Hamid Karzai graduated from a university in India. Despite that, India supported the Soviet invasion and occupation of Afghanistan. Relations deteriorated after the Taliban took power in 1996.

India "unofficially" supported the Northern Alliance minority groups against the Pakistani-backed Taliban. During the course of the hijack of Indian Airlines Flight 814 in 1999, the Taliban requested recognition by India in exchange for help in negotiations. The request was not acted upon by the Indian government. After the fall of the Taliban in late 2001, India strengthened ties with the Islamic republic of Afghanistan by establishing consulates in most major Afghan cities. The Embassy of India is located in Kabul. India has participated in multiple socio-economic reconstruction efforts, including power, roads, agricultural and educational projects. Some of these include building dozens of dams and reservoirs, a number of hospitals or clinics, schools and government institutions. The long road from Bandar-Abbas in southern Iran to highway 1 in southern Afghanistan is carried out by state-owned Border Roads Organization (BRO), the mission statement of which states that the BRO is India's "most reputed, multifaceted, transnational, modern construction organization committed to meeting the strategic needs of the armed forces." The killing of a BRO employee by the neo-Taliban in 2005 prompted the Indian authorities to dispatch approximately 200 Indo-Tibetan Border Police commandos to in 2006 to provide security for Indians working in various construction projects in Afghanistan.

Political contacts between India and Afghanistan have increased in 2011, especially after the death of Osama bin Laden in Pakistan. During Indian Prime Minister Manmohan Singh's May 2011 visit to Kabul, it was announced that India's total aid to Afghanistan reached $2 billion after a package of $500 million was added. There are also military ties between Afghanistan and India, which is expected to increase after the October 2011 strategic pact that was signed by President Karzai and Manmohan Singh. India's the largest regional provider of humanitarian and reconstruction aid to Afghanistan.

History

Relations between the people of Afghanistan and India traces to the Indus Valley Civilisation. Following Alexander the Great's brief occupation, the successor state of the Seleucid Empire controlled the region known today as Afghanistan. In 305 BCE, they ceded much of it to the Indian Maurya Empire as part of an alliance treaty.

Alexander took these away from the *Persians* and established settlements of his own, but *Seleucus Nicator* gave them to *Sandrocottus* (*Chandragupta*), upon terms of intermarriage and of receiving in exchange 500 elephants. — Strabo, *64 BCE – 24 CE*

The Mauryans brought Buddhism from India and controlled the area south of theHindu Kush. Their decline began 60 years after Ashoka's rule ended, leading to theHellenistic reconquest of the region by the Greco-Bactrians. Much of it soon broke away from the Greco-Bactrians and became part of the Indo-

Greek Kingdom. The Indo-Greeks had been defeated and expelled by the Indo-Scythians in the late 2nd century BCE. Much of Afghanistan has been influenced by Buddhist, Hinduand Zoroastrian cultures until the arrival of Islam in the 7th century. But despite many Afghans accepting the message of Islam, the Muslims and Hindus lived side by side.

"Kábul has a *castle* celebrated for its strength, accessible only by one road. In it there are *Musulmáns*, and it has a town, in which are *infidels* from *Hind*." —Istahkrí, *921 CE*

Between the 10th century to the mid 18th century, northern India has been invaded by a number of invaders based in what today is Afghanistan. Amongst them were the Ghaznavids, Ghurids, Khiljis, Suris, and Durranis. During these eras, especially during the Mughal period (1526–1858), many Afghans began immigrating to India due to political unrest in their regions. Khan Abdul Ghaffar Khan and Khan Sahib were prominent leaders of the Indian independence movement and active supporters of the Indian National Congress. Although the NWFP became part of the Muslim state of Pakistan in 1947, active Pashtun support for the Indian freedom struggle led to great sympathy in India for the cause of Pashtun autonomy and freedom. The Indian government continued to support Pashtun leader Khan Abdul Ghaffar Khan in lobbying for greater Pashtun freedom in the NWFP. Indians are working in various construction projects, as part of India's rebuilding efforts in Afghanistan, although the Indian intelligence agency RAW is accused by countries such as Pakistan of working to malign Pakistan and train & support insurgents. These workers are estimated to be anywhere between 3,000 and 4,000. Indian nationals stationed in Afghanistan have often faced continuous security threats in the country, with kidnappings and many attacks (such as the February 2010 Kabul attack) deliberately carried out on them.

Soviet invasion to Taliban takeover

The Republic of India was the only South Asian nation to recognise the Soviet-backed Democratic Republic of Afghanistan and the Soviet Union's military presence in Afghan territories, and provided humanitarian aid to President Najibullah's Government in Afghanistan. Following the withdrawal of the Soviet armed forces from Afghanistan in 1989, India continued to support Najibullah's government with humanitarian aid. After its fall, India together with the international community supported the coalition government that took control, but relations and contacts ended with the outbreak of another civil war, which brought to power the Taliban, an Islamist militia supported by Pakistan. The Taliban regime was recognised only byPakistan, Saudi Arabia, and the United Arab Emirates (UAE). The destruction of the Bamiyan Buddha monuments by the Taliban led to outrage and angry protests by India, the birthplace of Buddhism. In 1999, the hijacked Indian Airlines Flight 814 landed and stayed in Kandahar in Afghanistan and the Taliban were suspected of supporting them. India became one of the key supporters of the anti-Taliban Northern Alliance.

Post 9/11

During the U.S.-led invasion of Afghanistan in 2001, India offered intelligence and other forms of support for the Coalition forces. After the overthrow of the Taliban, India established diplomatic relations with the newly established democratic government, provided aid and participated in the reconstruction efforts. India has provided US$650–750 million in humanitarian and economic aid, making it the largest regional provider of aid for Afghanistan.

India's support and collaboration extends to rebuilding of air links, power plants and investing in health and education sectors as well as helping to train Afghan civil servants, diplomats and police. India also seeks the development of supply lines of electricity, oil and natural gas. Also to give Afghan Students scholarships. The Indian Army's Border Roads Organisation constructed a major road in 2009 in the remote Afghan province of Nimroz, connecting Delaram to Zaranj. This has proved a viable alternative route for the duty-free movement of goods through theChabahar port in Iran to Afghanistan. Key to India's strategy in Afghanistan is to build up transportation links that bypass Pakistan, helping reduce the Afghan economy's dependence on Pakistan.

In 2005, India proposed Afghanistan's membership in the South Asian Association for Regional Cooperation (SAARC). Both nations also developed strategic and military cooperation against Islamic militants. Owing to the killing of an Indian national by Taliban militants in November 2005, India deployed 200 soldiers of the Indo-Tibetan Border Police (ITBP) to provide security for Indian nationals and the projects supported by India. Afghanistan strengthened its ties with India in wake of persisting tensions and problems with Pakistan, which was suspected of continuing to shelter and support the Taliban. India pursues a policy of close collaboration with countries such as Afghanistan, Bhutan, and Iran in order to bolster its standing as a regional power and contain its rival Pakistan, which stands accused of aiding and abetting Islamic militants in Kashmir and other states of India.

Three memorandums of understanding (MOUs) for strengthening cooperation in the fields of rural development, education and standardisation between the Bureau of Indian Standards (BIS) and Afghan National Standardisation Authority were signed between Afghanistan and India during Hamid Karzai's visit to India in April 2006. An agreement providing $50 million to promote bilateral businesses between Afghanistan and India was signed during the visit of the Afghan Foreign Minister Dr. Spanta between 29 June – 1 July 2006. During the same year, India raised its aid package to Afghanistan by $150 million, to $750 million. In 2007, Afghanistan finally became the eighth member of SAARC.

In July 2008 the Indian embassy in Kabul was attacked by a suicide car bomb – the deadliest attack in Kabul since the fall of the Taliban in 2001. The bombing killed 58 people and wounded 141. Senior Indian Army officer Brigadier Ravi Datt Mehta was entering the embassy gates in a car along with V. Venkateswara Rao when the attack took place. Both were killed in the blast. The Afghan government's official position implies that Pakistan's ISI was involved in the attack. This position has found support in recent leaks of classified information by Wikileaks.

During the 15th SAARC summit in Colombo, India pledged another USD $450 million alongside a further US$750 million already pledged for ongoing and forthcoming projects. In August 2008, Afghan President Hamid Karzai visited New Delhi. This visit further strengthened bilateral relations, and Prime Minister Singh pledged further aid for Afghanistan.

On 18 October 2009, the Indian Embassy in Kabul was attacked again by a car bomb, little more than a year after the previous attack. The attack killed at least 17 people. Another attack conducted by the same Pakistan-based terrorist organisation took place at the Arya guest house where Indian doctors were staying, resulting in the death of 18 people. India's pledge to rebuild Afghanistan has reached a total of US$2 billion in May 2011 after Manmohan Singh arrived to Kabul for a two-day visit.

The September 2011 assassination of former Afghan president Burhanuddin Rabbani was condemned by India, which stated that, "Tragically, the forces of terror and hatred have silenced yet another powerful voice of reason and peace in Afghanistan. We unreservedly condemn this act of great brutality," and reiterated the steadfast support of the people and government of India in Afghanistan's "quest for peace and efforts to strengthen the roots of democracy". India promised to stand by the people of Afghanistan as they prepare to assume the responsibility for their governance and security after the withdrawal of international forces in 2014. In October 2011, Afghanistan signed its first strategic pact with India. The military assistance will include training of Afghan security personnel. During his visit to India, Karzai told the media that "This strategic partnership is not directed against any country. This strategic partnership is to support Afghanistan." He also stated that "Pakistan is our twin brother, India is a great friend. The agreement we signed with our friend will not affect our brother." He also added that "However, our engagement with Islamabad has unfortunately not yet yielded the result that we want." Both sides will launch Partnership Council, topmost body to implement the Strategic Partnership Pact in May,2012. On 22 May 2014 the Indian consulate in Herat was attacked by 3 militants equipped with AK-47s, RPGs, hand grenades and suicide vests. "Our premises have been repeatedly attacked by those who do not support India's development work in Afghanistan. The attack will not dilute India's development assistance and its contribution to rehabilitation and reconstruction of Afghanistan," India's ambassador to Kabul Amar Sinha said at the time.

Economy

India seeks to expand its economic presence in Afghanistan as the international coalition fighting the Taliban withdraws combat forces through 2014. Especially, it wants to improve transport connectivity and economic collaboration with countries in Central and South Asia. India has already invested US$10.8 billion in Afghanistan as of 2012. More such projects are likely to come up after Nato's withdrawal. This includes setting up Iron ore mines, a 6 MTPA steel plant (by SAIL—Steel Authority of India Limited), an 800 MW power plant, Hydro-electric power projects, transmission lines, roads etc., India and Iran are set to ink a transit agreement on transporting goods to landlocked Afghanistan. The Indian government is investing more than US$100 million in the expansion of the Chabahar port in south-eastern Iran which will serve as a hub for the transportation of transit goods. Besides as a goodwill gesture, India is also constructing a new Parliament complex for the Afghan government at a cost of INR 710 crores (USD 115 million). This building will be inaugurated in October 2015.

INDIA'S AFGHAN POLICY: NEED FOR ROBUST REGIONAL ENGAGEMENT - ANALYSIS

India's Afghan Policy has to a great extent been focussed on reciprocal engagement with Afghanistan portrayed by its upgraded part in reproduction and recovery endeavors and reliance on American military technique.

New Delhi has taken up a proactive part regarding anticipating its delicate force picture by contributing in the ranges of framework, wellbeing, instruction and limit building. India's enthusiasm for building transport halls and putting resources into vitality extends additionally goes for accessing the Central Asian vitality assets. Its backing in basic financial territories has earned cooperative attitude of Afghans. Numerous assessment surveys propose that India is one of the most loved nations for the Afghans.

In any case, India's improved delicate force picture does not expand its capacities to shape Afghan circumstance taking after the American withdrawal. India went into vital association concurrence with Afghanistan in 2011 and raised the likelihood that it may prepare, prepare and assemble the limit of the Afghan armed force keeping in mind the end goal to balance out Afghanistan.

As needs be, the past Afghan President Hamid Karzai sent a list of things to get of military prerequisites that Afghanistan needed to acquire from India and the proposition was cool carried by the then Indian authority all together not to threaten Pakistan and lose the force of continuous peace activities with it. The Indian government under Modi's initiative has communicated its ability to supply four Russian-made helicopters to the Afghan armed force yet that is insufficient to guarantee strength in Afghanistan with the lessening American military help. Without a military impression in Afghanistan and capacity to viably extend hard power past its fringes, India's Afghan approach is prone to endure unless repaid by vigorous provincial engagement.

As a general rule, India was not able extend its delicate force assets to the bigger locale in so far as it neglected to develop and draw in different nations encompassing Afghanistan around regular perspectives and methods for battling fear based oppression and guaranteeing a steady and serene Afghanistan. India's over-reliance on American military methodology is to a great extent in charge of its pickle. India neglected to watch how the Central Asian system of the US as far back as the

Soviet breaking down did not co-select Indian interests. The US considered the Taliban a balancing out power in Afghanistan which could help it secure a pipeline bypassing Russia and Iran and along these lines could end their conceivable imposing business model over oil supplies. It is not implausible to trust that the Americans would not have gone up against the Taliban if the last had not moved in the opposite direction of the US circle of impact.

Shockingly, both the Ministry of External Affairs and the Ministry of Defense of India in their yearly report 1995-96 alluded no place to the American complicity in destabilizing Afghanistan and communicated worries over the Pakistani part in undermining peace in Afghanistan by propping up and helping the Taliban.

India rushed to bolster the US-drove War on Terror with the expectation that there would a hard and fast war against psychological warfare. Notwithstanding, contrasts surfaced soon as the Obama Administration contracted down the danger to Al Qaeda and communicated American backing for connecting with great Taliban in the compromise procedure. Additionally, the Af-Pak methodology of the Administration guaranteed huge American guide for Pakistan to battle fear mongering as well as to keep up its regional trustworthiness also.

The hidden shortcoming of India's Afghan approach started to unwind itself when it turned out to be clear that in spite of American reservations over Pakistan's part as a believable accomplice in battling psychological warfare, the last kept on accepting gigantic 'war help' from the US. The reason can be found in geopolitics in so far as Pakistan is viewed as instrumental in advancing the American interests in Afghanistan and Central Asia. The American task of 'More prominent Central Asia' places Afghanistan and Pakistan in the Central Asian geopolitics. While India is viewed as critical to contain China and is a piece of American Asia-Pacific system.

Over the years, India's dependence on the American war strategies in Afghanistan prevented it from seriously engaging itself with Iran and Russia on the Afghan issue although their partnership has been the key to India's successful role in Afghanistan and Central Asia. Iran and Russia share common stakes in the stability of Afghanistan and share concerns like the rise of Sunni fundamentalism and drug-trafficking. Central Asia is considered to be the strategic backyard of Russia.

Any Indian strategy to expand influence beyond Afghanistan into Central Asia has to depend on Russia. However, Indian leadership failed to convince the Russian leadership how critical their partnership is to secure a stable Afghanistan and realize their common objectives.

Second, New Delhi did not take serious steps to alleviate Moscow's concerns as regards its closeness to Washington. Moscow expressed its concerns about Washington getting an increasing share in defense acquisitions by New Delhi.

To India's further disadvantage, Russia moved closer to Pakistan and described the latter as its 'closest partner' taking additional care not to mention any linkage between Pakistan and terrorism. Moreover, Moscow promised Islamabad to supply advanced Sukhoi 35 fighters and MI 35 attack helicopters.

Similarly, it was through Iran that India secured connectivity to Afghanistan and with Iranian assistance developed Chabahar port and constructed 218 Km long Zaranj-Delaram road in the remote south-western Afghanistan to secure access to Central Asia. However, there was palpable American pressure behind India's vote against Iran's nuclear program and India backed three US – supported resolutions against Iran in the International Atomic Energy Agency and enforced UN Security Council sanctions against Tehran. As per the documents disclosed by Wikileaks, at a time when nuclear deal was being negotiated between India and the US, the latter had tried to pressure India over its ties with Iran and even objected to President Mahmoud Ahmadinejad's visit to Delhi, saying it would give "platform for an enemy of the US".

India's inability to push the Iran-Pakistan-India (IPI) pipeline project under American pressure affected Iran-India bilateral relationship. Over the years, Iran has inched closer towards Pakistan and there are bilateral discussions on trade, energy and security. Islamabad has kept itself away from Saudi-Iranian sectarian conflicts like in Yemen crisis to keep the momentum of relationship going.

Lack of efforts from the Indian side at engaging China on Afghan issues bilaterally or multilaterally on the ground that both share common concerns in the rise of Islamic radicalism given Islamic insurgency in Kashmir and Xinjiang respectively despite territorial disputes and prevailing trust-deficit on both sides could only push China towards the easiest option of seeking Pakistani assistance to address its concerns and enhance its influence in Afghanistan. It is irony that while India and China bilaterally engage each other and discuss various bilateral issues regardless of the outcomes, there is hardly any engagement on the broader regional issues or at the multilateral forums.

Indian withdrawal from IPI pipeline has induced Pakistan to go for Iran-Pakistan pipeline with Chinese assistance. This pipeline is an integral part of the China-Pakistan-Economic-Corridor project and China's ambitious Silk Road Economic Belt initiative.

China has incorporated a growing interest in enhancing connectivity with Iran through land and sea using Pakistan as a bridge. Iran, on the other hand, seeks greater economic integration with Pakistan and China as Pakistan is emerging as a market for Iranian energy resources while China is already the largest importer of Iranian oil.

Russia has also seen advantages in the Chinese initiative of 'one belt one road' working as a complementary to its own plan for a 'Eurasia Union'. Both Iran and Russia have become silent partners to Chinese-Pakistani initiatives on hosting peace talks between the Afghan government and the Taliban. Pakistan's centrality to the Chinese project and to the Iranian and Russian outreach to China in geopolitical terms despite the question whether it can be a credible partner in implementing the project given its dubious records of assisting radical Islamic groups fostering instability points to India's failure in formulating a coherent and consistent policy towards the regional powers. The Iranian nuclear deal with P5+1 opening the door for lifting of western sanctions has released fresh energy into Indo-Iranian relationship. India is keen to start an undersea pipeline project that would supply Iranian gas to India bypassing Pakistan. It assumes importance given uncertainties of other pipeline projects like TAPI. Similarly, Indian Prime Minister Narendra Modi during his visit to Turkmenistan proposed a land-sea route through Iran for the supply of Turkmen gas to India. India has also efforts to secure the Iran-Oman-India pipeline.

On 23rd December 2015, Modi left for Russia on a two-day visit and after reaching there Modi said to a Russian news agency that Russia will remain India's "principal partner" in defense sector. India and Russia are expected to sign a number of pacts related to defense and nuclear energy. Russia is likely to be the leading partner in joint research, development and production of advanced defense systems under Modi's Make in India initiative.

All these steps towards courting Iran and Russia can be viewed as important correctives for India's past mistakes. However, it is to be seen how seriously and consistently India engages these countries and actualizes these projects preventing the relations from cooling off again. India's engagement with these countries in these important areas will also have a definitive impact on the level of their cooperation on Afghan issues as they have similar concerns. It will also take much steam out of the Chinese-Pakistani diplomatic maneuverings in Afghanistan. India needs to simultaneously engage China on Afghan issues as there is a convergence of interests in several areas of like economic, technical and cultural which would not only help stabilize Afghanistan but would benefit each of them.

India must have begun to realize that over-reliance on extra-territorial great powers cannot address its security concerns in the region as their role in the region is contingent upon their geopolitical interests and convenience of actualizing them. India's foreign policy focus on great powers and bilateralism needs to give way to engagement of regional powers and multilateralism. India's engagement with other regional powers must be based on the ground that a secured Afghanistan is in the interest of all and competing strategy for securing spheres of influence would lead to a power vacuum eventually to be filled up by non-state actors as dangerous as ISIS.

AFGHANISTAN IMPORTANT TO INDIA

For a long time, strategic analysts in India had been criticizing the foreign policy establishment of India (including the Prime Minister's Office, the Ministry of External Affairs and other related departments) for not paying sufficient attention to the region. New Delhi has tried to address this imbalance during the last decade, enhancing its ties and presence in its immediate and extended neighborhood. From Nepal to Sri Lanka, and from Afghanistan to Myanmar, there has been an added emphasis in dealing with the region.

Afghanistan and Myanmar received the attention of Indian policymakers in particular. There was a push not only in terms of attention and bilateral relations with these two countries, but also an increased presence and support to their governments. Aid to the two countries increased disproportionately. Myanmar is seen as a link in India's larger strategy in Southeast Asia, and Afghanistan is important for its plans in Central Asia.

During the 1980s and 1990s, because of local and regional developments, India had lost contact with the governments and people in these two countries. Now, New Delhi is trying to re-establish the old ties.

Although India's investment in and aid to Afghanistan may appear less significant compared with the US and the EU, for India it is substantial. From building infrastructural networks to schools and hospitals, New Delhi has invested substantially in helping the government in Kabul and its people. The first major challenge for India in the post-2014 Afghanistan would be to protect this investment. Secondly, like all other countries in the region and the rest of international community, India would like to see a stable and democratic government in Afghanistan. New Delhi has established substantial linkages with the Karzai government including a strategic partnership. It would like to strengthen this relationship further and not want any future governments to rupture or sever these ties, as had happened during the mid and late 1990s, when India lost all contacts with Afghanistan. When an Indian passenger flight was hijacked from Kathmandu to Kandahar, it did not even have basic official communications with the government in Kabul. In future, India would like to avoid such a situation.

Today, despite all criticisms and cynicisms, Afghanistan is certainly better than it was during the late 1990s. Substantial investments have been made in every sector – from building local capacity, security forces to even a political understanding between various sub-nations within Afghanistan.

India would prefer that this process continues and the positive developments in the last 10 years do not get reversed because of violence.

A section in India is also apprehensive of Afghanistan becoming a center of radical ideology and violence again. Such a development would also affect Pakistan, and would inevitably reach India and spread further to other countries – Bangladesh, Sri Lanka and even Myanmar.

Such a development would not only undermine the stability of the Af-Pak region, but also the entire Central Asia-South Asia-Southeast Asia belt.

In particular, New Delhi would prefer the Afghan security forces remain stable and do not crumble because of any future onslaughts from insurgent groups. While India would be willing to assist the Afghan security forces in their training and it even supplies some anti-insurgency equipment, New Delhi is unlikely to send its troops into Afghanistan, even if there is a specific request from Kabul.

India also sees Afghanistan as an essential component of the TAPI (Turkmenistan-Afghanistan-Pakistan-India) pipeline. To address its energy needs to sustain its economic growth, pipelines from Iran and Central Asia would be extremely important. The general fear in India is that an unstable Afghanistan would hurt the construction of this pipeline and the subsequent flow of gas.

Finally, a section in India is extremely apprehensive of Pakistan attempting to scuttle India's presence and influence in Afghanistan. Every country in the region and elsewhere, depending on their interest and investment, would like to exert an element of presence and influence in Afghanistan, including Pakistan, because of its geographical proximity. While New Delhi should appreciate this, what it is afraid of is Islamabad and Rawalpindi playing a negative role in Afghanistan to undermine India's investments.

While no country including India would like to deny Pakistan's proximity and cultural linkages with Afghanistan, none, including New Delhi, would be comfortable with Islamabad abusing its leverage to install a puppet regime in Kabul, or undermine an existing framework, as had happened during the 1990s. In fact, a section even within Pakistan would be against such an approach. But the greatest question is what strategies to adopt if Pakistan decides to pursue a negative agenda in Afghanistan?

While Pakistan would like the rest of international community to understand its own fears and concerns in Afghanistan, the opposite is also equally true.

Since there is a widespread understanding at the regional level on the importance of a stable Afghanistan, can Kabul become a bridge bringing the countries of the region together?

The TAPI pipeline is likely to be a major connector, linking Central Asia with South Asia, especially Afghanistan, Pakistan and India.

The Asian Development Bank has agreed to be the advisor for the project recently and the countries have agreed on the transit fees.

The US on the other hand, is engaged in a dialogue process with Iran and there is a nuclear deal in the process. As a result, the Iran-Pakistan-India (IPI) pipeline is likely to face less opposition from the US. Both these pipelines are likely to change the energy future of Central and South Asia.

Afghanistan is also extremely interested in becoming the transit country for not only gas, but also an electricity grid. The CASA 1000 is a parallel initiative, linking Central Asia and South Asia, especially Afghanistan and Pakistan, with the electricity grid in Uzbekistan, Tajikistan and Turkmenistan.

Afghanistan and Pakistan are likely to become a major transit routes for pipelines and electricity grids. For India, there are threats and opportunities in Afghanistan. A stable Afghanistan is in everyone's interests and the regional security is intrinsically enmeshed with it.

AFGHANISTAN & INDIA: CRAFTING STABILITY IN THE REGION

Post 9/11 concern has been raised over where India stands on a number of issues, which includes it's approach to the relationship it shares with Afghanistan on all levels: economically, politically and socially. Security and stability in Afghanistan is of importance to India.

There has been claims of cultural co-operation in between India and Afghanistan, predominantly in the form of the entertainment sector in India, colloquially termed as "Bollywood", complimented by a positive perception of the country in general amongst Afghans, highlighted by various polls conducted over the years in the West.

This generally-speaking amicable relationship the two large countries share, has given rise to fear and resentment amongst many of the smaller countries outlining India's borders. Although, Afghanistan isn't susceptible to this partly owing to lack of border issues with such countries, it's important to point out that the subject of "Taliban" forces in the country has caused friction for it, when it comes to the relationship it has with many countries, including India and the United States of America.

India heavily scrutinizes the Taliban, despite the many allegations, news of which has reached the West, that portions of the terrorist activities carried out regionally there are part of the wider network that connects the Taliban and the Pakistan's military and Inter-Services (ISI).

Initially, it was perceived by the United States, Pakistan and the Afghan government that post-Taliban engagement with Afghanistan for India was somehow related to a strategy to weaken Pakistan.

However, in recent years perspective in foreign policy for India has shifted from an entirely anti-Pakistan rhetoric to a pro-Afghanistan one, where the government has unanimously declared a desire for more stability in the Middle Eastern country.

There has been far too much pro-Pakistan talks taking centrehold in the West, so much so that pressure from Pakistan has led to India being excluded from the January 2010 "International Conference on Afghanistan" held in Istanbul, which was a pretty bad joke given the fact that just within the span of 18 months, President Barack Obama announced that Western troops would pull out of Afghanistan, handing over power and responsibility to Afghan forces by 2014, crossing out the previous prevalent idea that it would take decades for NATO and its allies to keep its troops and craft stability in Afghanistan.

These policy changes have reflected amongst many in India that their engagement with Afghanistan, both in the community and the government level, can be deemed as correct, despite the exodus, so-to-speak, from international conferences.

In India, the 1990s saw a policy of support towards India's neighbours, followed by an election and a policy towards global domination, followed by another election and a Congress win, which saw more dominance towards regional improvement, which the former party in power, the Bharatiya Janata Party (BJP), had largely neglected. The Congress government has worked towards a pro-Afghanistan stance for India, emphasizing that stability there means stability at home in India. India has announced a commitment towards training Afghan security forces, although any involvement for India in Afghanistan is always looked at in USA, with a lot of skepticism.

India, for its part remains unsure of the West's commitment towards Afghanistan, due to the rapid change of involvement there.

India is very keen on investment in Afghanistan. The "New Silk Road" tale as declared by India at the 2012 "Heart of Asia" conference in Kabul, has led India to declare that it intends to support Afghanistan and integrate it into the regional economy, spurning out commercial and trade developments for the country, and the whole region in general. It intends to craft out Afghanistan as a sort-of a bridge that can smooth out trade and commercial ventures between South Asia, Central Asia, the Middle East and Eurasia.

Afghanistan is a land rich in mineral sources, with the country's government putting it close to a wealth value to an approximate $3 trillion. India has bilateral trade agreements with Afghanistan already, mostly in the form of assistance in categories such as food aid in the form of wheat, etc. and support for infrastructure projects, like the construction of the 'Salma Dam Power Project' and contribution towards the building of the Parliament.

India needs to move forward from the shadow of "upsetting" Pakistan, and think about what it can positively do for Afghanistan after its landmark election this year, which saw throngs come out and vote, despite the threat of escalating violence; the elections are heading for a second round after no party gained the required 50percent vote to govern Afghnistan.

Signs of investment by Indian companies in Afghanistan does show good work in promoting stability and it's attitude towards commitment in the region. Afghanistan for its part has chosen to remain largely silent on the subject, even though thousands of students from Afghanistan study in India, many on Indian scholarships, provided by the Indian Council for

Cultural Relations. Although, it is commendable that India's perspective on Afghanistan is largely a historical one, where the future seems positive instead of the very bleak one Western powers have been projecting for decades, India needs to do more to gravitate towards crafting stability in Afghanistan.

INDIA'S GROWING ROLE IN AFGHANISTAN

Head administrator Narendra Modi is liable to go to the initiation of Afghanistan's new Rs 710-crore Parliament assembling, financed and developed by India. The parliament building-part of a $2 billion (Rs 12,800 crore) help bundle is typical of India's backing for strife-torn Afghanistan, as it battles to move into a steady vote based system.

The development of the parliament building, began in 2009 by India's Central Public Works Department, has missed its due date by three years. Once finished, the building-assaulted by fear based oppressors on 22 June, 2015-will have the capacity to withstand dread assaults and quakes up to 8 on the Richter scale.

India has given about Rs 2,000 crore ($300 million) in help to Afghanistan in the course of recent years, in the wake of consenting to a Strategic Partnership Arrangement in 2011. The measure of help has expanded about 80% from Rs 327 crore in 2011-12 to Rs 585 crore in 2013-14, as indicated by information tabled in the Lok Sabha.

India's guide to Afghanistan is assorted, connects with Iran too India has additionally subsidized the development of different ventures, including a Rs 1,500-crore dam in the Herat territory in western Afghanistan.

The dam will generate 42 mega watts (MW) for Afghanistan, a country that has one of the lowest electricity produced-per-capita's in the world. Power cuts in the capital Kabul last up to 15 hours, as this recent analysis noted.

India's Border Roads Organisation (BRO) is building a 218-km, Rs-600-crore road from Zaranj to Delaram in south-western Afghanistan.

This is a key link to Iran's Chahbahar Port via Afghanistan's garland highway, linking the Afghan cities of Herat, Kandahar, Kabul and Mazar-e-Sharif. It will also allow access to the landlocked Central Asian countries that border Afghanistan.

India signed an agreement with Iran to develop Chahbahar Port in May 2015. Afghanistan is crucial to India's energy security, as a pipeline from Turkmenistan to India, the TAPI project, will pass through the country (and Pakistan). Afghanistan also represents investment potential for Indian companies in several sectors.

The country is home to resource deposits worth one trillion dollars, according to the US Geological Survey. A consortium of six Indian companies led by public-sector Steel Authority of India (SAIL) won a 2011 bid to mine steel in the province of Bamiyan; it will invest around $10.8 billion (Rs 69,120 crore).

AFGHAN INVESTMENTS COME AT A PRICE

India's engagement with Afghanistan has made it a terrorist target. India's embassy in Kabul was been attacked in 2008 and 2009, as were the consulates in Herat (2014) and Jalalabad (2013). India has accused Pakistan of being behind these attacks. But India will press ahead because Afghanistan, apart from its strategic importance, holds business potential for Indian companies. "India's interest lies in an economically-sustainable, politically-stable and socially-inclusive Afghanistan, protected by a strengthened national security apparatus," said Monish Tourangbam, assistant professor at the Department of Geopolitics and International Relations, Manipal University.

Afghanistan's security situation has deteriorated. The number of conflict-related civilian casualties (deaths + injuries) has almost doubled from 5,968 in 2009 to 10,548 in 2014, according to data compiled by United Nations Assistance Mission in Afghanistan (UNAMA). This comes as a 13-year US-led intervention ends.

"The implementation of India's development assistance of $2 billion has taken place under the umbrella of the security provided by the International Security Assistance Force (ISAF) forces led by the United States," said Tourangbam.

After the withdrawal, the onus for ensuring Afghanistan's security will lie entirely on Afghanistan's National Security Forces (ANSF). The security forces are currently struggling to maintain a stalemate with insurgents after enduring a lethal Talibani spring offensive.

This year has already seen an increase of more than 50% in deaths of Afghan security forces as compared to the first six months of 2014, according to data accessed by The New York Times. India has trained personnel of the Afghan National Army (ANA) in Indian military institutions such as the Indian Military Academy. While India has provided military hardware such as trucks, jeeps and helicopters, it remains reluctant to provide "lethal" weapons such as tanks and artillery guns, fearing they could fall into the hands of the Taliban.

AFGHANISTAN 2015: INDIA SHOULD KEEP OFF THE STRATEGIC MUDDLE

Afghanistan in 2015 presents a complex vital jumble for which India is neither politically, deliberately, nor militarily prepared, to rival the developing key meeting of Russia-China-Pakistan interests in spite of intrinsic self-inconsistencies among the three, and the unfurling Afghan-ISIS encounter.

As a matter of fact, India has huge honest to goodness national security interests in the security and dependability of Afghanistan, other than authentic ties of shared vital unions on checkmating Pakistan's constant desire for political and military control of Afghanistan.

In 2015, the Afghanistan picture for India stands definitely changed with the command into force in Kabul of President Ashraf Ghani. Afghanistan's new President soon side-lined India in Afghanistan's security math for Pakistan and China, his first ports of approach getting to be President. His graciousness approach the Pakistan Army Chief amid his Islamabad visit was unbecoming of the Head of State of

Afghanistan. He lined this up with cancelation of arms deals contracts with India and sending Afghan military officers for preparing in Pakistan and further reporting coordination of Afghanistan's insight set-up with Pakistan Army's knowledge organization the ISI.

Require more be said in regards to which way the wind is streaming in Kabul to the extent India is concerned? Was India arranged to meet this projection by its political foundation and its insight offices? Then again was India's Afghanistan approach been a setback of the political force move in New Delhi?

The stark the truth is that in 2015 India was not set up as far as approach definitions and choices on the looming vital vacuum unfurling in Afghanistan with the slowing down of the US military nearness in Afghanistan of about fourteen years with dicey additions and an indeterminate future.

India is not politically, deliberately and militarily prepared to recover the unfurling circumstance in Afghanistan once more into its support. Essentially put in 2015,.Pakistan has outflanked India in Afghanistan by actuating China, and China thusly prompting Russia , to fill the vital vacuum in Afghanistan with the United States not slanted to manage the Afghan cross any more.

Actually for quite a while there were voices inside the American vital group that China ought to be required in Afghanistan's security to settle Afghanistan. It is not clear in the matter of what influences China has over Afghanistan to balance out it other than the intermediary utilization of the Pakistan Army. Alternately is it that we can expect direct Chinese Army association in Afghanistan?

Politically in 2015, India can hardly outbid the convergent strategic interests of the Russia-Pakistan-China Troika on Afghanistan for the time being, especially when US strategic permissiveness hovers in the background for the same. Why has the United States once again abandoned Afghanistan? Why did the United States leave Afghanistan to Russia and China to step in? Did the United States confer with India on its unfolding intentions on Afghanistan? Has the United States been a party to side-line India's legitimate strategic interests in Afghanistan?

The answers to these questions should prompt the Indian policy establishment to revise its policy stances on Russia, China and the United States. Pakistan the king-pin of Afghanistan's strategic muddle needs a separate policy treatment. India's policies in the Indian Subcontinent should focus on side-lining of Pakistan in regional politics.

Strategically, other than drawing-in Iran for concerted policy initiatives on Afghanistan because of shared strategic interests on keeping Pakistan, out of Afghanistan, India has no other strategic option.

India lost the Iran-leverage by voting against Iran at the UN on the nuclear issue under US pressure by the previous Congress Government. Further with Iran's close ties to Russia and China, it is unlikely to go against the new Russia-China interest in Afghanistan for geopolitical compulsions.

In the absence of geographic contiguity with Afghanistan and India not having developed sizeable military intervention capabilities in the region, India is not militarily equipped to intervene in Afghanistan. This may have been possible as a serious and viable option if India –Iran Strategic Partnership forged in the last decade was not allowed to wither by the previous government.

There is yet another new and disturbing dimension being added to the Afghanistan muddle and that is the building violent rivalry between the Pakistan-sponsored Afghan Taliban and the growing encroachment of the Middle East terrorist grouping of the ISIS.

The ISIS is emerging as a potent force in Afghanistan's playground of Islamic Jihadi forces and outfits in Afghanistan's domestic domain. So much so that the Afghan Taliban was forced to declare that the ISIS should not intervene in Afghan affairs and let the Afghan Taliban spearhead the Islamist struggle in Afghanistan.

It will be an interesting scenario if the ISIS were able to eclipse the Afghan Taliban in the Afghan domestic power play of Islamist outfits. Let us not forget that in the Middle East it is reported that the ISIS draws support from Saudi Arabia and Turkey.

As far as the Afghan Talban is concerned it is Pakistan's protégé and prior to 2001, only China and the UAE maintained official contacts with the Afghan Taliban. Presently too China can be said to be the Afghan Taliban's patron and facilitating their talks with other Afghan groups.

It needs to be noted that neither Russia nor China have any significant stakes in Afghanistan's long term stability; their investments in Afghanistan would be limited to keeping away the spill-over of Islamists Jihadis into proximity of Russian peripheries and in case of China into Xinjiang where China is facing a virtual Islamic Jihad. With such limited aims one should not expect Russia or even China to emerge as long-terms determinants of Afghanistan's future.

Therefore in 2015 Afghanistan presents a dismal strategic muddle which defies any prospects of security and stability emerging despite the Russia-China-Pakistan Troika attempting to fill-in the strategic vacuum.

Afghanistan stands famously termed as the 'Graveyard of Imperial Pretensions'. Russia has earlier met this fate and the United States recently.

Let now China meet the same fate. Why should India bother? Future events may themselves fashion themselves out in a manner that the United States persuades India, without the Pakistan-Russia-China baggage, to join in a joint effort to facilitate emergence of a secure and stable Afghanistan.

In the following interregnum India must make serious assessment of its Afghanistan policy options and putting into place the wherewithal to implement those options.

India must also seriously ponder that in any future policy options on Afghanistan, there is not much scope of 'Soft Power' diplomacy. What will be required is to add the vitamin-supplement of "Hard Power" too to add muscle to Indian Afghan policies.

Concluding, the nett assessment is that India should keep out of Afghanistan's strategic muddle and let Russia once again and China more specifically in 2015 muddy its hands and reputation in untangling the Afghanistan muddle. Nor should India join any regional initiatives on Afghanistan sponsored by Russia and China, so that they could add more respectability by involving India.

Bibliography

Ajey Lele: *Strategic Technologies for the Military : Breaking New Frontiers*, Sage, Delhi, 2009.

Amitabh Sikdar: *India and China : Strategic Energy Management and Security*, Manas, Delhi, 2009.

Anil, K.C.: *Military and Democracy in South Asia : Challenges, Politics and Power*, Sumit Enterprises, Delhi, 2009.

Ashton, S.R.: *British Policy Towards the Indian States, 1905-1939*, London: Curzon, 1982.

Barbara, Adams : *Traditional Textiles of Bhutan*, White Orchid, Bangkok, 1984.

Baviera, A. S. P.: *China's Relations with Southeast Asia: Political Security and Economic Interests*, Philippine APEC Study Center Network, 1999.

Blanche, Christin : *The Dragon Kingdom: Images of Bhutan*, Boston: Shambhala, 1988.

Budge I: *The New Challenge of Direct Democracy*, Oxford, Polity Press, 1996.

Cheek, Timothy: *Mao Zedong and China's Revolutions: A Brief History with Documents*. Boston: Bedford/St. Martin's, 2002.

Digumarti Bhaskara Rao: *Military Conversion : Impact on Science and Technology*, Discovery, Delhi, 2003.

Dixit, A.K. : *Military Wars and Rescue Techniques*, Cyber Tech Pub, Delhi, 2010.

Evelyn Goh, *Meeting the China Challenge: The U.S. in Southeast Asian Regional Security Strategies*, DC: East-West Center, 2005.

Friedman, G.: *The Future of War of Cyber Crimes*, N.Y., Random House, 1996.

Gaur, Sanjay: *Narendra Modi : Change We can Believe In*, Yking Books, Delhi, 2014.

Giersch, H. : *Trade Policy and Demand Management*, Tübingen, J.S.B.Muhr, 1973.

Huntington, S.P.: *The China Defence Modernisation Military and the State*, N.Y., Vintage Books, 1964.

Ian Storey: *ASEAN and the South China Sea: Movement in Lieu of Progress*, Washington, D.C., Jamestown Foundation,2012.

Imtiaz, A.: *State and Foreign Policy: India's Role in South Asia*, New Delhi, Vikas, 1993.

Itoh, Mayumi: *Pioneers of Sino-Japanese Relations: Liao and Takasaki.* Palgrave-MacMillan. 2012.

Jha, Prem Shankar : *India and China : The Battle Between Soft and Hard Power*, Penguin Books India, Delhi, 2010.

Joon Ahn: *The Rise of China and the Future of East Asian Integration*, Asia-Pacific Review, London, Carfax Publishing Company, 2004.

Kapur, C.K. : *Chinese Military Modernisation*, Manas, Delhi, 2003.

Nag, Kingshuk: *The NaMo Story - A Political Life*. Roli Books. 2013.

Nayyar, K K : *National Security : Military Aspects*, Rupa, Delhi, 2003.

Nishioka Keiji : *Flowers of Bhutan*, Asahi Shimbum, Tokyo, 1984.

Pommaret Francoise : *Tibetian Mountain Fortress of the Gods*, Serindia, London, 1997.

Posen, B.R.: *The Sources of Military Doctrine*, Ithaca, 1984, Cornell Univ. Press.

Randeri, Kalindi: *Narendra Modi : The Architect of A Modern State*, Rupa, Delhi, 2009.

Rao Y Sudershan : *Buddhism and Modern Society*, Deep and Deep, Delhi, 2008.

Rosen, P.: *Societies and Military Power: India and its Armies*, Ithaca, Cornell University Press, 1996.

Saksena, N.S.: *India: Towards Anarchy, 1967-1992*, New Delhi, Abhinav, 1993.

Samuel P. Huntington: *The Soldier and the State : The Theory and Politics of Civil-Military Relations*, Natraj Pub, Delhi, 2005.

Sardesai, Rajdeep: *2014: The Election That Changed India*, Delhi, 2014.

Sarvepalli Gopal: *Jawaharlal Nehru: An Anthology*, Delhi, 1980.

Stuart R. Schram: *The Political Thought of Mao Tse-Tung*. New York: Praeger, 1969.

Theodore, William : T*he Buddhist Tradition in India, China and Japan*, New York: Vintage Books, 1972.

Index

E

F

G

H

I

J

K

L

S

T

W

❑❑❑